LEARNING TO THINK THINGS THROUGH

A GUIDE TO CRITICAL THINKING ACROSS THE CURRICULUM

Fourth Edition

Gerald M. Nosich
Buffalo State College

Boston   Columbus   Indianapolis   New York   San Francisco   Upper Saddle River
Amsterdam   Cape Town   Dubai   London   Madrid   Milan   Munich   Paris   Montréal   Toronto
Delhi   Mexico City   São Paulo   Sydney   Hong Kong   Seoul   Singapore   Taipei   Tokyo

Editor-in-Chief: Jodi McPherson
Acquisitions Editor: Jodi McPherson
Editorial Assistant: Clara Ciminelli
Vice President, Director of Marketing: Margaret Waples
Marketing Manager: Amy Judd
Operations Supervisor: Central Publishing
Operations Specialist: Laura Messerly
Production Management: Jerusha Govindakrishnan
Composition: PreMediaGlobal
Cover Designer: Suzanne Behnke
Cover Image: © white78/Fotolia

Credits and acknowledgments borrowed from other sources and reproduced, with permission, in this textbook appear on appropriate page within text.

Library of Congress Cataloging-in-Publication Data

Nosich, Gerald M.
    Learning to think things through: a guide to critical thinking across the
      curriculum / Gerald M. Nosich.—4th ed.
      p. cm.
    Includes bibliographical references and index.
    ISBN-13: 978-0-13-708514-9 (alk. paper)
    ISBN-10: 0-13-708514-1 (alk. paper)
  1. Critical thinking-Study and teaching. 2. Interdisciplinary approach in
    education. I. Title.
    LB1590.3.N67 2012
    370.15'2-dc22
        7 2020   2010050281

www.pearsonhighered.com   ISBN 10:   0-13-708514-1
                                         ISBN 13: 978-0-13-708514-9

To Matt
And to my I-Group: Mickey, Francis, Mari, Gus

Contents

What Is Critical Thinking?   I

CHAPTER 2

The Elements of Reasoning   47

CHAPTER 3

What Is Critical Thinking within a Field or Discipline?   86

CHAPTER 4

Standards of Critical Thinking   133

CHAPTER 5

Putting It All Together: Answering Critical-Thinking Questions   168

New to the Fourth Edition

One goal of this new edition is to expand the emphasis on the critical writing that is so important a part of learning to think critically in a discipline. A second goal is to make the book clearer, more sharply focused, and more up to date. A third goal (actually a goal since the first edition) has been to make the book short enough (a) to function as a guide for students who may well have extensive discipline-based materials to work through in addition, (b) to allow students, if possible, to read the whole book near the beginning of the semester (see pages xxvii–xxviii), and (c) simply not to look daunting. Accordingly, though new sections have been added to each chapter, this edition is shorter than the previous two.

- **Ideas for Writing.** In keeping with a greater emphasis on critical writing, there is a new section at the end of each chapter on "Ideas for Writing." This section suggests topics or questions from the chapter or the book as a whole for students to write about in a short assignment, a longer essay, or in their journal. The section also prompts students to come up with similar ideas for writing on their own.

- **Tell Your Story.** A section at the end of each chapter asks students to reflect on and write about their own personal history, their own story, with respect to critical-thinking or discipline-based concepts. For example, a topic in Chapter 1 is "Egocentrism as an Impediment to Critical Thinking," and a question in the "Tell Your Story" section asks: "Think of your life as a whole. How has your own native egocentrism changed in your life from childhood to the present?" Or in Chapter 2: "How have your *goals* and *purposes* changed over the course of your life?" Or in Chapter 3: "What is your attitude toward the discipline you are studying? How has your attitude toward it changed over the years, maybe even before you ever took a course in it? What are some factors that might help you personally to become more open to it?" (Note that writing about the "Tell Your Story" questions may not always involve *critical* thinking. Rather, the questions ask students to engage in *reflection* on their lives in a way that lays a foundation for further *critical* reflection, after they have learned to use the elements, the standards, and the discipline itself.)

■ I have gone over each sentence of the third edition to make the book more compact and more streamlined. I have made changes, including substantial cuts, to virtually every page. These changes not only made the book shorter, but allowed the addition of new sections as well.

■ I have made extensive revisions to Chapter 5. In addition to making explanations more focused throughout, I have (a) completely revamped the section on Thinking in Systems and (b) incorporated "thinking in the discipline" directly into "The Core Process of Critical Thinking" (see page 169). This latter change removes some of the separation between *critical thinking* and *critical thinking in a discipline*. It emphasizes the idea that, in any question where the disciplines are relevant (and that in the end includes most questions), I need to incorporate concepts from the discipline into my thinking.

■ The critical-thinking character traits are now introduced in a single, focused subsection, instead of being mentioned piece-meal, one or two at the end of each chapter. Logically, it is now part of the section "How Do You Fit into the Picture? Becoming a Critical Thinker."

■ Over 70 percent of the discipline-based textbooks used in examples and exercises have been updated, eliminated, or changed to texts published after 2006.

Another thread of the fourth edition further emphasizes the theme of "believing the results of one's reasoning"—internalizing ideas learned in class and importing them into one's ordinary life, making them part of one's reality. Helping students learn to do this (and even to do it habitually) is, for me, one of the great challenges of teaching. In several places in the fourth edition, a question is asked in ordinary, everyday language, for example:

> Suppose you are selling your car to a man who doesn't know much about cars, and he is willing to pay you much more than you know the car is worth. What should you do?

Then the question is asked again, this time specifically from the point of view of the discipline, for example in an ethics course:

> Address the following from either a rights perspective or a consequentialist perspective, or both: Suppose you are selling your car to a man who doesn't know much about cars, and he is willing to pay you much more than you know the car is worth. What should you do?

The point is that these are not two separate questions. They are, at the very least, closely related. In many cases they are really identical (or should be identical, if I take the discipline seriously). The intent here is to help break down the barrier between what is learned in school ("school stuff" page 117 and the reality of everyday life. (See the box on pages 120–121, exercises 3.10, 5.11, 5.12, as well as several sections and exercises retained from earlier editions.)

To the Instructor

This book is a guide for learning to think critically in a discipline, a subject matter, an area, or a field of study. I use these terms more or less interchangeably throughout the book. The book applies to disciplines taught at any level of generality, at any educational level. This includes courses in humanities, social and natural sciences, business, arts, nursing, professional areas, the freshman experience, and so on, as well as multidisciplinary courses.

I specifically mean to include courses that emphasize *doing* as well as *understanding*: Composition courses stand out in particular. (There are exercises suitable for student writing, and the text promotes full integration of the composition course with other courses students are taking, across the curriculum.) But the book applies to *any* discipline that emphasizes mindful *doing*: physical education, nursing, business, math, veterinary science, agriculture, foreign languages. (In fact, in the purest sense, all courses emphasize doing: learning physics is learning to *do* physics—learning physics is learning how to engage actively in the process of thinking one's way through the physical world.)

Although this book was not written to be the main text in a course specifically in critical thinking, I have used it that way in my own courses, and many teachers of critical thinking have used Richard Paul's model in their courses (see page xx). In my own critical-thinking courses, I have asked my students to use the model to analyze and evaluate newspaper editorials; to apply it to problems in their personal lives; to analyze their relationships with other people; to analyze, compare, and evaluate news sources and advertising; to evaluate their own study skills; to think through their own egocentric and sociocentric tendencies; to think through artworks and a wide variety of other topics. Several times the only other texts required in my course were ones from *other* courses the student was taking. There, the goal was to help the students learn to think through the disciplines or subject matter they were studying in those other courses. What permits this diversity is the great flexibility of Paul's model of critical thinking.

This book is a guide to critical thinking in the curriculum and intended to be inexpensive, so it can be used economically as an adjunct text in a course. I have tried to keep it short enough so students can be required to read it all the way through near the beginning of the semester. That way they can refer to it again and again, applying specific critical-thinking concepts to different parts of the subject matter as the course moves along, gradually coming to integrate those parts. *Learning to Think Things Through* works best, I believe, when used in a course in conjunction with subject-matter materials, including textbooks or readings brought in by the teacher or the students. "Readings" can include video or audio material of any sort, chapters, specific problems, case studies, primary sources, journal articles, or virtually any outside material. Many questions in this book direct students to apply critical-thinking concepts to the texts in the course.

Many teachers in a field or discipline want their students to learn to think critically about the subject matter they are studying and to learn to think about the world in terms of that subject matter. They want their students not to be passive recipients of information absorbed from the teacher or the text. Rather, teachers want their students to become active learners who pay attention to crucial elements of reasoning, such as assumptions, purposes, implications, and consequences, and who do this in a way that meets high intellectual standards. This book will help accomplish those goals.

Using *Learning to Think Things Through* in a Course

Teachers can use this book in a range of ways. I favor using the text as a highly integrated part of the course as a whole. The goal, again, is to keep students actively thinking their way through the course and the subject matter, rather than sinking back into being passive recipients.

As the teacher, I can have them identify key concepts of the discipline for each chapter, unit, lesson, lecture, and presentation. I ask them to construct applications of the concepts from their own experience, integrate the concepts, and draw up concept maps. Students can be given frequent practice at formulating key questions, finding relevant information and evaluating its significance, and searching for alternatives. I can have the students analyze readings or important course material right from the beginning of the course. The model of SEE-I (pages 30–33) is particularly valuable in helping students learn to clarify and deepen their understanding of *anything* in the course; it also helps students' note taking and review for exams; for the teacher, it provides a flexible way to assess students' understanding, both informally and on exams. (In my own courses, a substantial portion of my tests asks students to state, elaborate on (in their own words), give an original example and an illustration of the important concepts or ideas in the course. It has transformed my exams.)

In addition to giving students ongoing practice at thinking critically within the discipline, activities such as these furnish you with valuable insight into where exactly your students are in the course. These activities can be done in group work or individually, in class or as homework assignments, in written or oral form, with or without specific feedback from you. Activities such as these and many others are identified in *Learning to Think Things Through*, and exercises on such thinking activities appear at the end of each chapter.

This book can be used in courses in any number of other ways. You can have students work through the book on their own. Assigning exercises at the end of each chapter (some of which have suggested answers) can significantly help students in their critical thinking with minimal input from you.

Many teachers find it valuable to devote some class time to helping students learn how to assess their own work and the work of fellow students, giving one another critical feedback on the thinking. The elements (Chapter 2) and standards (Chapter 4) are an ideal vehicle for this. Devoting this class time, even though it might seem at first glance to cut down on the amount of time devoted to teaching the discipline, allows you to give frequent short written assignments throughout the semester (shown to be highly effective in helping students retain and internalize the discipline) and to make sure students receive at least some feedback on them. Having students assess one another's work does this without increasing the amount of valuable time you spend on reading and correcting student assignments. In my classes I often keep copies of student responses that apply a critical-thinking concept to a discipline. After getting permission from those students, I pass out their responses (anonymously) to students in subsequent classes. The brunt of learning is placed where it ought to be, as a responsibility of the students themselves. You are then freer to become the resource and the facilitator of learning.

The elements, standards, and subject-matter concepts make this task of self-assessment focused and beneficial both for the student being assessed and the student doing the assessing. Both are engaged in doing critical thinking about the subject matter. This book contains exercises specifically on such self-focused assessments, and many more can be readily constructed from the elements and standards.

Consider a simple example. One of the elements is *purpose*, and one of the standards is *clearness*. In my courses, I give frequent written assignments. For each of them, I ask students to write down at the top what, in their best judgment, is the purpose of the assignment. This exercise in and of itself helps students to focus their thinking (and to be aware that the assignments in fact *have* a purpose—sometimes a surprise). Then I ask students, in pairs or in groups of four, to assess how *clearly* each statement of purpose was written.

That gives students specific critical-thinking feedback on an important standard, and the clarity of their responses almost invariably improves. Similar feedback can be given from student to student about any of the elements and any of the standards.

One further note on using *Learning to Think Things Through*: the model presented here is highly integrated, and there is great benefit in having students read the entire book near the beginning of the course, rather than piecing it out as the course progresses. The flexibility and comprehensiveness of the model are not as available to students when they learn one part at a time and *then* try to get a sense of the whole. After getting a sense of the whole, students can then work on those aspects that give them difficulty.

The Model

This book, built on Richard Paul's model of critical thinking, is intended as a short, connected presentation, suitable for use in a subject-matter course. Essential parts of it are set forth in Paul and Elder's *Critical Thinking: Tools for Taking Charge of Your Learning and Your Life*[1] and in *Critical Thinking: Tools for Taking Charge of Your Professional and Personal Life*.[2] The model is the one Paul, Linda Elder, I, and a number of other workshop facilitators at the Foundation for Critical Thinking, have used in workshops and academies over the years.

The model has quantitative empirical backing. Jennifer Reed, in her doctoral dissertation, tested Paul's model in history classes at the community college level. It fared well not just compared to a didactic course in history, but also compared to an alternative model of critical thinking where the key concepts were taught implicitly rather than explicitly (with no significant differences in knowledge of history content).[3]

Two parts of this model form the core of this book:

1. **Elements of reasoning.** These are the central concepts of reasoning itself. Paul often describes them as the "parts" of thinking. When I reason through something, I may be trying to do any number of things: I may be trying to see the *implications* of holding a certain *point of view*, for example, or I may be trying to come to some *conclusion*, based on certain *assumptions* I start out with. I may be deciding that I need more *information* to decide this *question at issue*. I may simply wonder what my *purpose* is in a certain venture and what my *alternatives* are. The elements of reasoning extract the common concepts from this virtually unlimited set of reasoning activities. Thus, to learn to reason is to come to mastery of concepts like implications, points of view, conclusions, assumptions, information, question

at issue, and purpose. Concepts such as these are elements of reasoning. Chapter 2 is devoted to the elements.

2. **Standards of critical thinking.** It can be seriously misleading to say critical thinking is learning how to think. Critical thinking is learning how to think *well*. It is thinking that meets high standards of quality. Again, I can think through something well in many ways. I can figure out that one conclusion is more *accurate* than another. I can see implications more *clearly* than I saw them before. I can focus on the most *important* aspects of a problem. I can realize I have thought through an issue *sufficiently*, and now it is time to act. The standards are an attempt to formulate the heart of what constitutes the quality component in critical thinking. Like the elements, the standards are a set of concepts. I think through an issue *well* when I think it through accurately and clearly, when I focus on what is most important to deciding the issue, and when I think it through sufficiently. To learn to reason well is to come to mastery both of the elements and of standards such as accuracy, clearness, importance, and sufficiency. Concepts such as these are standards of critical thinking. Chapter 4 is devoted to the standards.

The general injunction, then, in Paul's model, is this:

Take any problem, in any area, and think it through using the elements of reasoning and in accord with the standards of critical thinking.

Developing a greater ability to think in terms of the elements and standards promotes a flexibility that is ideally useful, and maximally transferable, in teaching for critical thinking in a subject-matter course anywhere in the curriculum.

In *Learning to Think Things Through*, both elements and standards are applied to thinking within the discipline. Part of this, in any field, is learning to think the way someone in that discipline thinks. That means being able to think in terms of specific systems taught in the discipline (Chapter 5). More than that, it means being able to think in terms of those fundamental and powerful concepts and central questions that lie at the heart of the discipline, and to view the world at large from the point of view of the discipline. These are described in Chapter 3.

My presentation of Paul's model differs from his in a few respects. I have added *context* and *alternatives* to his eight elements, and I have given only the briefest introduction to intellectual traits, such as intellectual courage and intellectual humility.

Putting It All Together

A general picture is presented in Chapter 5. It is a picture of the core process of critical thinking, of answering critical-thinking questions in the subject matter. It is tagged by the acronym **QEDS**. You begin by looking critically at the **q**uestion being asked (Q). You think it through using the **e**lements (E) and the central concepts and questions of the **d**iscipline (D). You assess and revise your thinking using the **s**tandards (S).

This core process, common to all areas of thinking, is what makes critical thinking transferable. By internalizing it in your course, students can learn to think more effectively in other courses, in the interconnections between disciplines, and in their lives as related to the disciplines.

Critical Writing Across the Curriculum

An emphasis on critical writing runs through the book. It is addressed in the text, in insert boxes in chapters, in any number of exercises (of course, you can easily change pure writing assignments to group discussion questions), in new sections added to the fourth edition, and in a model for "Using the Core Process to Write a Paper."

A Note on the Exercises

A number of key guiding concepts run all the way through *Learning to Think Things Through*, and students can be assigned to apply them to the discipline again and again, in many different ways. There are exercises on each of them:

- individual elements, or the elements assembled into a circle
- the standards individually, or as a standards check
- evaluating around the circle
- SEE-I (state, elaborate, exemplify, illustrate)
- fundamental and powerful concepts
- the central question
- the point of view of the discipline
- impediments to critical thinking
- thinking in systems
- critical writing
- raising good questions
- reasoning things out
- believing the results
- intellectual traits of a critical thinker

You can also, independently of the exercises, give students assignments that require them to apply these guiding concepts to *anything* in the course: to their writing, reading, experiences, theories, research, and so forth. These can be assigned at any point in the course, even before students have read about them in *Learning to Think Things Through*, or long after they have finished reading it. (I myself would like to see questions based in these key guiding concepts as the central part of a capstone course, requiring students to bring together insights from courses across their whole educational experience.)

The exercises in each chapter have a section called "Daily Practice: At incorporating critical thinking into your life and your learning" (see the instructions on pages 44–45). I've tried in these sections to address what I think is a difficult problem in student learning: to help students start to do the subtly hard work of generalizing these concepts and organizing their understanding of the world in terms of them, and to do this in an ongoing way that doesn't stop as soon as they leave the classroom.

Teachers of physics see forces and energy at work everywhere. Teachers of sociology see social forces at work everywhere. Both kinds of force are obvious, unavoidable. But I believe we sometimes underestimate how radically different that is from students' experience. This is not really a remark only about students. I believe it is a remark about almost all of us. Teachers of physics are not in the habit of seeing social forces at work all around them. Teachers of sociology are generally not explicitly noticing the physical forces that are omnipresent.

This is subtle because many students can often do this kind of generalizing if the instructor *prompts* them the right way: "Find three examples of social forces in your life." But that doesn't mean they will do the generalizing themselves unprompted. Many of the fundamental and powerful concepts in courses—and this includes critical-thinking concepts—are alien to students' experience in this sense: students have years of seeing families just as families, as if that category was sufficient in itself. If I'm teaching the social structure of the family, my hope is that they will start to see families in terms of social forces—and that they will do so on their own, in an ongoing way, unprompted by me except at the beginning. There is a sense in which, as a teacher, what I am aiming for is nothing less than a transformation, at least a small one, in the way they view their own experience. I want them to see the world in terms of critical thinking and the discipline. Thus, the "Daily Practice" sections are an attempt to ask students to spend some time each day doing whatever they ordinarily do—but to conceptualize it in terms of one of the guiding concepts just listed: to filter the world through the elements, standards, and concepts of the discipline.

In addition to those specific sections, some other exercises work the same way. They can be assigned to students more than once during the course, thus fostering intellectual perseverance and allowing them to rethink earlier conclusions they came to, so their responses can change and deepen. These exercises can be applied at any time in the course (even as a pre-test before the appropriate reading has been done), to virtually any topic, in the discipline or to students' lives outside school:

- Exercises 1.1, 1.7, 1.10, 1.14, 1.18, 1.19
- 2.1–2.3; each of the exercises on individual elements: 2.4–2.13; 2.16, 2.17, 2.18
- 3.7, 3.9, 3.11, 3.15, 3.17, 3.21
- 4.2, 4.3, 4.5, 4.7, 4.9, 4.11–4.14, 4.16
- 5.1 a b c d; 5.13, 5.16, 5.18

How to Contact Me. If you have questions about *Learning to Think Things Through*, or if you are just willing to share how you use it in your classes, I would appreciate hearing from you.

Dr. Gerald Nosich
Department of Philosophy
Buffalo State College
1300 Elmwood Avenue
Buffalo, NY 14222
E-mail: gnosich@uno.edu

Acknowledgments

It is a pleasure to express my gratitude to Richard Paul and Linda Elder. I told Richard I would "try on" his model for a year (1991–92). At the end of the year, I found it had transformed not just the way I taught critical thinking but the way I thought about my life as well. My debt to Richard and Linda goes well beyond this book. Every time we meet I look forward to the vivid, focused intellectual conversations the three of us have. They have been my close friends for many years.

I am greatly indebted to any number of thinkers I have worked with and been close to: A. J. A. Binker, Mike Donn, Bill Dorman, John Christman, Bob Ennis, Edward Johnson, Ralph Johnson, Ann Kerwin, Marybeth Oliver, Marlys Witte; to those who also gave me their time and critical-thinking examples during the writing of this manuscript: Anne Buchanan, Francis Coolidge, Randall Curren, John Draeger, Ines Eishen, Jerel Fontenot, George Hole, Jennifer Reed, Ian Wright; to Kerry Rubadue; to Jean Von Ah, who gave me help and encouragement at the beginning of this project; and to the students in my critical-thinking and BSC 101 classes.

I want to thank the reviewers of the first and second editions for their encouraging and invaluable commentary: Jean Chambers, SUNY–Oswego; Paul Grawe, Winona State University; Jim Pollard,

Spokane Falls Community College; Susan Quarrell, Lehman College; and Carolyn Vitek, St. Mary's University of Minnesota. I would also like to thank my editor at Prentice Hall, Sande Johnson.

Any inaccuracies or questionable assumptions in this book are my own.

For deep personal support, I want to thank not only Richard Paul and Linda Elder, but also Ralph Johnson, Matthew Nosich, Andy McCaffrey, Nicole Fargo, and the members of my I-Group, Spirit Group, and NOMC.

To the Student

The aim of this book is to help you improve your critical thinking about the subject matter of the courses you are taking. A secondary goal, a by-product of the first, is to help you improve your ability to think effectively in your life as a whole. The way you use this book is likely to be different from the way you use most books in courses.

First, this isn't a book you can just read through. You can't get stronger by *reading* about how to exercise. In the same way, you can't get better at critical thinking merely by reading about critical thinking—not even if you're very intelligent. You have to *do* it. You have to take problems or questions the text asks and actually think them out as you work your way through the book—at least some of them. In addition, it helps if you can get feedback on your thinking. You have to do this again and again.

What this book teaches is not a body of information. If the book is successful for you, you will learn to *do* something that requires more than just learning information, and more than just learning skills. It is not just about *how* to think critically—it is about *actually thinking* critically.

Learning to do something cannot be accomplished just by reading about it. You can't get thinner merely by reading about dieting; your basketball game won't improve merely by hearing about how to shoot free throws. Your writing won't improve merely by learning that you have to consider your audience—you actually have to *consider* your audience. To improve the way you do something takes both instruction (in this case, reading the book, receiving feedback) and practice (doing it).

Second, depending on what your instructor says, you may need to read the book all the way through right near the beginning of the course, including doing the thinking work. That's because the book gives a unified overall model for critical thinking, and you have to see how the parts all fit together. In the model presented in this book, you think in terms of the elements of reasoning (Chapter 2), the subject you are studying (Chapter 3), the standards of reasoning (Chapter 4), and putting it all together (Chapter 5). You need a grasp of the whole model to think your way through questions in the discipline. In the end, the book promotes a different way of approaching the world—by thinking your way through it.

In some fields you proceed step by step, learning a skill well, and only then going on to the next skill (and hoping you don't forget the first one on the way). Critical thinking is different. A major goal of critical thinking is always to keep the whole in mind as you are working through the parts.

So, with this book, it is better to work all the way through to the end and get the big picture, even if there are some glaring gaps in your understanding. (That's probably the way you learned almost all complex skilled activities, particularly those that are important in your life: you don't learn to drive by first mastering the gas pedal and only later starting to work on how to use the brakes. The same is true of shopping for groceries, learning to dance, raising children, and understanding yourself and others: you engage in the process *as a whole*, gradually filling in gaps, sometimes making mistakes, improving, coming to insights within the process.)

Third, *Learning to Think Things Through* is not a book you can work through once and then be done with. Instead, you'll have to refer back to it whenever problems arise for you. After working all the way through it the first time, there *will* be glaring gaps in your understanding of various aspects of critical thinking. When you have trouble with assumptions, for example, you need to reread the section on assumptions in Chapter 2. But also look in the index under "assumptions" for other passages that may help. Do some of the exercises on assumptions, especially those that are starred (*) and have suggested answers in the back of the book. At the end of the course, some parts will still be unclear and confusing. Even so, you can still use the model as a whole. It will still be practical: in the course you are taking, in other courses, and in decisions you have to make in your own life.

Fourth, this is a guide to thinking critically within the discipline you are studying: composition, geology, educational psychology, business—any field or subject matter. Only a fraction, if any, of the examples in the text and exercises, however, will be from the discipline you are actually studying. It is still vitally important that you work your way through them. They have been selected so as to convey critical-thinking concepts across the curriculum, for all disciplines.

No technical knowledge is presumed in this book. Except for the discipline you are currently studying, you are not expected to know the specific field being discussed.

Critical thinking *transfers*. If you consciously learn critical-thinking techniques in one field, you may have those techniques available for another field. By the end you may find your learning in your other courses becomes faster, more in your control, more lasting, and more beneficial for your life outside school.

Finally, in the end you will have to be the judge of whether using the model here improves your thinking. Certainly it won't be all or nothing. Critical thinking is a matter of degree. At the end of the course you should find yourself more often checking for accuracy, identifying assumptions, drawing relevant conclusions, thinking questions out in terms of the fundamental and powerful concepts of the discipline you are studying.

One way to think about the process is to imagine yourself in the hands of a good coach, a critical-thinking coach. This book is the manual the coach is asking you to follow, and the coach will give you feedback along the way.

Who is the coach? Well, in a way, it is your instructor. On a much deeper level, though, it is the healthy, thinking organism within you. In the end, you are going to accept processes and thinking guidelines only if they work for you. You will have to see them pay off—in your studies, in your grasp of the subject matter, in your understanding of your relations with other people—before you incorporate them into your life. But you first have to give them a chance to see if they do pay off.

For Students!

Why is this course important?

This course will help you transition to college, introduce you to campus resources, and prepare you for success in all aspects of college, career, and life. You will:

- Develop Skills to Excel in Other Classes
- Apply Concepts from College to Your Career and Life
- Learn to Use Media Resources

How can you get the most out of the book and online resources required in this class?

Purchase your book and online resources before the First Day of Class. Register and log in to the online resources using your access code.

Develop Skills to Excel in Other Classes
- Helps you with your homework
- Prepares you for exams

Apply Concepts from College to Your Career and Life
- Provides learning techniques
- Helps you achieve your goals

Learn to Use Media Resources
- **www.mystudentsuccesslab.com** helps you build skills you need to succeed through peer-led videos, interactive exercises and projects, journaling and goal setting activities.
- Connect with real students, practice skill development, and personalize what is learned.

Want to get involved with Pearson like other students have?

Join www.PearsonStudents.com

It is a place where our student customers can incorporate their views and ideas into their learning experience. They come to find out about our programs such as the **Pearson Student Advisory Board**, **Pearson Campus Ambassador**, and the **Pearson Prize** (student scholarship!).

Here's how you can get involved:

- Tell your instructors, friends, and family members about **PearsonStudents**.
- To get daily updates on how students can boost their resumes, study tips, get involved with Pearson, and earn rewards:
  - Become a fan of **Pearson Students on Facebook**
  - Follow **@Pearson_Student on Twitter**
- Explore **Pearson Free Agent**. It allows you get involved in the publishing process, by giving student feedback.

See you on **PearsonStudents** where our student customers live. When students succeed, we succeed!

PEARSON
mystudentsuccesslab

Succeed in college and beyond!
Connect, practice, and personalize with MyStudentSuccessLab.

www.mystudentsuccesslab.com

MyStudentSuccessLab is an online solution designed to help students acquire the skills they need to succeed. They will have access to peer-led video presentations and develop core skills through interactive exercises and projects that provide academic, life, and career skills that will transfer to ANY course.

It can accompany any Student Success text, or be sold as a stand-alone course offering. To become successful learners, students must consistently apply techniques to daily activities.

How will MyStudentSuccessLab make a difference?

Is motivation a challenge, and if so, how do you deal with it?
Video Presentation – Experience peer led video 'by students, for students' of all ages and stages.

How would better class preparation improve the learning experience?
Practice activities – Practice skills for each topic - beginning, intermediate, and advanced - leveled by Bloom's taxonomy.

What could you gain by building critical thinking and problem-solving skills in this class?
Apply (final project) – Complete a final project using these skills to create 'personally relevant' resources.

MyStudentSuccessLab Feature set:

Topic Overview: Module objectives.
Video Presentation - Connect: Real student video interviews on key issues.
Practice: Three skill-building exercises per topic provide interactive experience and practice.
Apply - Personalize: Apply what is learned by creating a personally relevant project and journal.
Resources: Plagiarism Guide, Dictionary, Calculators, and Assessments (Career, Learning Styles, and Personality Styles).
Additional Assignments: Extra suggested activities to use with each topic.
Text-Specific Study Plan (available with select books): Chapter Objectives, Practice Tests, Enrichment activities, and Flashcards.

MyStudentSuccessLab Topic List -

1. Time Management/Planning
2. Values/Goal Setting
3. Learning How You Learn
4. Listening and Taking Class Notes
5. Reading and Annotating
6. Memory and Studying
7. Critical Thinking
8. Problem-Solving
9. Information Literacy
10. Communication
11. Test Prep and Test Taking
12. Stress Management
13. Financial Literacy
14. Majors and Careers

MyStudentSuccessLab Support:

- **Demos, Registration, Log-in** - www.mystudentsuccesslab.com under "Tours and Training" and "Support."
- **Email support** - Send an inquiry to MyStudentSuccessLab@pearson.com
- **Online Training** - Join one of our weekly WebEx training sessions.
- **Peer Training** - Faculty Advocate connection for qualified adoptions.
- **Technical support** - 24 hours a day, seven days a week, at http://247pearsoned.custhelp.com

Introducing
CourseSmart
The world's largest online marketplace for digital texts and course materials.

A Smarter Way for ...

Instructors

▶ **CourseSmart saves time.** Instructors can review and compare textbooks and course materials from multiple publishers at one easy-to-navigate, secure website.

▶ **CourseSmart is environmentally sound.** When instructors use CourseSmart, they help reduce the time, cost, and environmental impact of mailing print exam copies.

▶ **CourseSmart reduces student costs.** Instructors can offer students a lower-cost alternative to traditional print textbooks.

Students

▶ **CourseSmart is convenient.** Students have instant access to exactly the materials their instructor assigns.

▶ **CourseSmart offers choice.** With CourseSmart, students have a high-quality alternative to the print textbook.

▶ **CourseSmart saves money.** CourseSmart digital solutions can be purchased for up to 50% less than traditional print textbooks.

▶ **CourseSmart offers education value.** Students receive the same content offered in the print textbook enhanced by the search, note-taking, and printing tools of a web application.

Institutions & Partners

▶ **CourseSmart helps meet market demand.** Partners can use CourseSmart to meet the demand for digital materials in a way that grows share of student purchasers.

▶ **CourseSmart reaches new student populations.** Students who may have done without textbooks due to high cost and lack of digital options can now purchase high-quality, affordable educational materials online.

▶ **CourseSmart complements traditional brick and mortar offerings.** Partners earn a percentage of sales of materials purchased through CourseSmart.

CourseSmart Is the Smarter Way

To learn for yourself, visit www.coursesmart.com

This is an access-protected site and you will need a password provided to you by a representative from a publishing partner.

Chapter 1
What Is Critical Thinking?

Often, a good way to begin the process of thinking critically about a subject is to do some conscious thinking about it *before* you do any reading or hear any presentations in the subject. Thus, if you are going to study biology or sociology or writing, a good way to begin is by writing down some of the main ideas you already have about biology or sociology or writing itself *before* you do any reading or listen to lectures. This allows you to be an active listener rather than a passive recipient of information. It helps you to become aware of your assumptions about the subject so that you can assess them more accurately in light of what you will later read and hear.

Some Definitions of Critical Thinking

Here are three definitions of critical thinking by leading researchers. First, Robert Ennis's classic definition:[1]

> Critical thinking is reasonable, reflective thinking that is focused on deciding what to believe or do.

Even before you start reading this text, begin by examining your own concept of critical thinking. Respond to the following in a paragraph or two:

What is your concept of *critical thinking*? (You can respond by giving a description. An alternative way to address it, though, is to use examples: Describe a situation in which you thought through something critically; then describe a situation in which you did not think through something critically.)

Next, write a paragraph describing how, in your best judgment, critical thinking is necessary within the subject matter you are studying?

Next, Matthew Lipman's definition:[2]

Critical thinking is skillful, responsible thinking that is conducive to good judgment because it is sensitive to context, relies on criteria, and is self-correcting.

Finally, in informal presentations, Richard Paul uses this definition:

Critical thinking is thinking about your thinking, while you're thinking, in order to make your thinking better.

Each of these is an excellent definition of critical thinking. It pays to read them several times and to stop and reflect on every aspect of each definition. Why did the expert include this word rather than another? Just what are the experts trying to capture with the words they have chosen? What overlap is there in the definitions, and what main differences of emphasis are there?

It may seem hard to believe, but each of these definitions, brief as they are, is the product of a long period of intense pondering about how best to describe critical thinking. Each definition is an attempt to convey in words the essence of an activity, a "thing"—critical thinking. Before trying to define it, each expert had an intuitive grasp of what critical thinking is, based on years of working with it. This was what the experts tried to capture in the words they chose.

So in reading the experts' definitions and in the discussion ahead, one very important goal to keep in

Revise your concept of critical thinking over the semester. Reformulate it (maybe starting over entirely) so that it accords with your deepening grasp of what critical thinking is.

mind is for you to develop a solid intuitive grasp of just what critical thinking is and what it is not.

Some Prominent Features of Critical Thinking

Critical Thinking Is Reflective

Critical thinking is different from just thinking. It is metacognitive— it involves thinking about your thinking. If I enter a social studies course where one of the topics to be studied is conformity, it is likely that I already have views about conformity: what it is, how prevalent it is, what influences people to conform or not conform. I have these views even if I haven't formulated them explicitly for myself. Each view is an example of thinking, but not necessarily an example of critical thinking. Critical thinking starts once I reflect on my thinking: Why do I have these views about conformity? Since my views are really conclusions I have drawn, what evidence are they based on? How do other people look at conformity differently? What are their views based on? How can I tell which are more accurate, their views or mine?

Critical Thinking Involves Standards

Critical thinking involves having my thinking measure up to criteria. I can think about something accurately or inaccurately. I can use evidence that is relevant to an issue or irrelevant, or somewhere in between. When I reason out and try to understand the main ideas in a course I'm taking, I can do so on a superficial level or I can try to understand them deeply, trying to get at the heart of the matter.

Accuracy, relevance, and depth are examples of standards or criteria. The words "critical" and "criteria" come from the same root, meaning "judgment." For my thinking to be critical thinking, I have to make judgments that meet criteria of reasonableness.

Critical Thinking Is Authentic

Critical thinking, at its heart, is thinking about real problems. Although you can reason out puzzles and brainteasers, the essence of critical thinking comes into play only when you address real problems and questions rather than artificial ones. Critical thinking is far more about what you actually believe or do. It is about good judgment. Puzzles and narrow problems may help occasionally when you want to hone or practice special skills, but even those skills help only if you consciously transfer them to real-life settings. Honing your skills at guessing the endings of murder mysteries is not likely to be good preparation for becoming a criminal investigator. In murder mysteries, all the clues are provided, the murderer is one of the characters, and someone (the author) already knows the murderer's identity. None of that is so in a criminal investigation.

Real problems are often messy. They have loose ends. They are usually unclear: clarifying and refining them are part of thinking through them. They often have no single right answer. But there are wrong answers, even disastrous answers: there may not be any unique right person to take as your partner in life—but there are certainly people it would be disastrous to choose.

AUTHENTIC PROBLEMS

To get the feel of authentic problems (in contrast to "school problems"), think of good novels you have read, or plays or movies you have seen. (Exclude contrived movies where everything automatically works out according to a formula.) Now consider the problems that are facing some character. Those will likely be *authentic* problems. They are full of complications and other people's cross-purposes; actions don't work out exactly as planned; emotions and desires are heavily involved in the decisions people make.

Choose an example or two like that, and try to reason through decisions that the character could make.

Critical Thinking Involves Being Reasonable

There are no surefire rules of reasoning. There are no rules so foolproof that they guarantee your reasoning will be successful. There are guidelines; there are even "rules" sometimes, but these always need to be followed thoughtfully. You need to apply them with sensitivity to context, goals, and a whole host of realities. For thinking to be critical thinking, it must be reasonable thinking.

Compare critical thinking to driving a car. There are rules for good driving (e.g., merge when entering an interstate), but merely following the rules won't make you a good driver. To be a good driver you have to follow the rules *mindfully*. What does that mean? It means, for example, following the rules while being aware that the purpose of merging is to allow traffic to flow more smoothly and reduce collisions between fast- and slow-moving cars, that weather and traffic conditions affect how you should merge, and so on. Notice that this is an open-ended list of what a mindful driver is aware of while merging.

We often long for surefire, step-by-step procedures, and the more personally important or threatening a situation is, the more we want foolproof rules. But there are no rules that guarantee our thinking will be correct—and that is especially true in very important or threatening situations. We must use our reasoning to evaluate rules, rather than vice versa. The only way we can decide whether to follow certain rules is if we use our best reasoning to determine that those rules are reasonable, that they lead to reasonable results when followed. Critical thinking is "self-correcting" at least partly because it is the court of last resort. There is no level of greater certainty beneath it that we can use to evaluate our reasoning.

Three Parts of Critical Thinking

Full-fledged critical thinking involves three parts. First, **critical thinking involves asking questions**. It involves asking questions that need to be asked, asking good questions, questions that go to the heart of the matter. Critical thinking involves noticing that there are questions that need to be addressed.

Second, **critical thinking involves trying to answer those questions by reasoning them out**. Reasoning out answers to questions is different from other ways of answering questions. It is different from giving an answer that we have always taken for granted but never thought about. It is different from answering impressionistically ("That reminds me of ..."), or answering simply according to the way we were raised, or answering in accordance with our personality. It is also different from answering by saying the first thing that comes into our mind, and then using all our power of reasoning to defend that answer.

Third, **critical thinking involves believing the results of our reasoning**. Critical thinking is different from just engaging in a

> **CRITICAL WRITING**
>
> Write down three questions you have about critical thinking. Then, write down three questions you have about how you will be using critical thinking *in this course*.
>
> (If you can't think of any real questions, even after pushing, what conclusions do you draw from that?)

mental exercise. When we think through an issue critically, we internalize the results. We don't give merely verbal agreement: we actually believe the results because we have done our best to reason the issue out and we know that reasoning things out is the best way to get reliable answers. Furthermore, when we think critically through a decision about what to do in a situation, then what follows the reasoning is not just belief, but action: Unless something unforeseen occurs, we end up taking the action we concluded was most reasonable.

Asking the Questions

Critical thinking begins with asking questions. If a teacher assigns a homework problem to solve, a good question to ask is "How can I best solve this problem?" Often, though, students don't ask this question at all. Instead, they just jump in and try to solve the problem by any method that springs to mind. Thinking critically about solving a problem, on the other hand, begins with asking questions about the problem and about ways to address it:

- What is the purpose behind the problem?
- What is a good way to begin?
- Do I have all the information I need to start solving the problem?
- What are some alternative ways of solving the problem assigned?
- Can the problem be solved? Does it even make sense?

All of these questions are relevant when a problem is assigned. But when teachers assign problems, they have already done a fundamental part of the questioning. Posing a problem is asking a question. So, a major part of learning how to think critically is learning to ask the questions—to pose the problems—yourself. That means noticing that there are questions that need to be addressed; recognizing that there are problems. Often, this is the hardest part of critical thinking.

This is true not just in school, but in daily life as well. People often do not ask themselves, "How can I best get along with my parents (my partner, my co-workers, my friends) in this situation?" Instead, they continue relating to them in habitual and unexamined ways. If your goal is to improve some aspect of your daily life, begin by asking yourself some questions: What are some concrete things I can do to make better grades? To meet new people? To read more effectively? To make the subject matter of this course meaningful in my life?

To be effective, you need to really *ask* these questions. It's not enough just to say the words. In fact, when you look at the questions just posed, they can seem empty. But that's not because they are empty. Whether a question is empty or not depends a great deal on the spirit in which you ask it. If you ask it in an empty way, just going through the motions, then it's not a genuine question at all, not for you, and it will not be the beginning of thinking critically through that question.

Here are some questions that teachers list as ones that students do not ask, but should be asking, in their courses:

- How does what I learn in this course relate to my own experience?
- How can I use what I learn here in my own life?
- Can I think up my own examples?
- How does this subject matter relate to other courses I am taking?
- What is the evidence behind this?
- How do the topics in this course fit together?
- What is the purpose of the course?
- Why?

Identify some situations in your life that are problematic, ones that are not going as well as you think they should. Write them as questions. Be specific in how you describe them. Don't just say "How can I get along with my friends?" Focus it: "How can I best deal with Arthur when I feel him pressuring me to do X and I really don't think I should be doing X?"

Write a list of some further questions you should be asking about those situations?

Reflect on your educational experience a little. Which of the questions listed by teachers are ones you tend to ask yourself in courses you are taking? Which of them do you never (or almost never) ask?

Try keeping a journal of questions that arise during a course you are taking now. Questions maybe about the subject matter itself, about how it affects you (or *does not* affect you), about how you can use it, about implications of the course, about the way it is taught, about the assignments given, about assignments *not* given.

Reasoning It Out

Though asking questions is necessary to begin critical thinking, merely asking the questions is not enough; the questions need to be answered (or at least addressed). Often we raise questions only to worry about them, or to torment ourselves, or even to put off action, instead of trying to answer them by thinking them through.

For example, a significant number of students have difficulty in math-related fields. They sometimes ask the question, "Why am I so bad at math?" They then use this question to make negative judgments about themselves ("I'm just hopeless at math, and I always will be") or about the field ("I don't need to know math to be a nurse"), or they answer it with unhelpful generalities ("I'm no good at it because of the way I was taught"). Reasoning it out, however, requires approaching the question in a different way and with a different spirit. It is the spirit of *intellectual engagement*, of genuinely wanting to figure out a clear, accurate answer to a question that is important to you. It might begin with reformulating the question in a more neutral and helpful way: "What are the main causes of my problems with math, and what are some good ways to begin dealing with them?" You might then read a little about what causes problems in learning math and apply the information to your own case. You could talk to counselors about alternative approaches that have helped other students, take seriously what the counselors say, and note any resistance you feel to the new approaches. Reasoning it out may not "solve" the problem, but it does provide a significantly better way of addressing the problem than not reasoning it out at all.

On the other hand, there are many *uncritical* ways to try to answer questions, ones that do not involve much reasoning. You can:

- Ask someone (and simply accept the answers uncritically)
- Answer according to the way you have been raised (without examining whether it was a healthy way to be raised)
- Answer without looking for information, even if it's readily available
- Answer in accordance with your personality (without examining the extent to which your "personality" helps or hinders you in this kind of situation)
- Answer with what first comes into your head

It is easy to misunderstand questions about reasoning. Thus, you might interpret the second item listed as implying that critical thinking is opposed to the way you were raised, but that is not what it means. What critical thinking is opposed to is acting in the way you were raised, without examining it. For example, someone raised in a family where violence and abuse were taught, or where blind obedience to authority was taken for granted, should not simply follow those values.

The two greatest difficulties in reasoning are not what you might expect. It isn't that people aren't good at reasoning, or that they make mistakes. People are good at it in some areas and not so good in others; everyone makes mistakes; everyone can improve. But these are not the most crucial difficulties. They go deeper. The first is that, when presented with a problem, people often don't think to reason in the first place. It's just not the usual human reaction to a problem. This is partly because societies do not encourage reasoning as an approach to important questions. The second difficulty is that people often do not know the difference between reasoning through something and other ways of responding. As a result, people respond with what seems to be reasoning, but isn't.

For example, a discussion is not automatically an example of critical thinking. Often in discussions, each participant says what he or she believes, and that's the end of the matter. In a reasoned discussion, on the other hand, listening is as important as speaking. Participants try to understand the reasons behind other people's beliefs, and they try to identify both the strong and weak points of the views expressed. The whole spirit is different.

So, "reasoning things out" really means reasoning them out well. What does it mean, then, to reason through something well?

Reasoning itself is drawing conclusions on the basis of reasons. Good reasoning, therefore, is drawing conclusions on the basis of reasons and giving due weight to all relevant factors. Relevant factors include the *implications* of drawing those *conclusions*, the *assumptions* on which the reasoning is based, the *accuracy* of the reasons used, the *alternatives* available, and a number of other elements (Chapter 2) and standards (Chapter 4).

Though it's not difficult to define good reasoning in an open-ended way, the challenge is to spell

REASONING VERSUS NON-REASONING

What are some important differences between a debate and a reasoned debate? Between writing a reaction paper and a reasoned reaction paper? Between evaluating an essay and giving a reasoned evaluation of an essay?

it out in a way that is usable by you, one that lays a foundation so that your ability to reason well can improve and deepen during the rest of your life. A good deal of the rest of this book is devoted to that.

Believing the Results

Critical thinking, in the fullest sense, results in belief. It even results in action. Here is an example. A teacher lowers my course grade because I missed too many classes, and I feel unfairly treated. So I raise the question: "Was my teacher being fair in giving me this grade?" Next, I reason my way to an answer: I collect information (maybe I ask the teacher about it; I check what the syllabus said about missed classes; maybe I check to see if other students were treated the same way); I consider the teacher's point of view on the issue and her purpose in lowering my grade because of absences. After reasoning it through—reasoning it through well, I believe— I come to the conclusion that my teacher was fair in what she did. The next step seems so obvious as not to need stating: I believe the results of my reasoning; I believe that my teacher's actions were in fact fair.

However, taking this last step isn't always easy. Even after reasoning it out, I may still have feelings of being unfairly treated, and I may still suspect that I was treated unfairly.

What is going on in this example is an indication that I have not thought through the issue critically, at least not in a complete enough way. Maybe there are other questions I should be raising ("Could my feelings of being treated unfairly arise from other circumstances in my life?" "What concept of fairness am I using in my thinking?"). Maybe there are alternative explanations to consider; maybe I am making some unstated assumptions that are influencing my feelings. Or else, maybe I should just believe the results: the teacher was being fair and my original estimate of unfairness was really off the mark (and I need to remember that feelings of being unfairly treated, even if they are unjustified, often take time to go away).

Believing the results is a rough test or measure of the completeness of your critical thinking. If you have reasoned something out and come to a conclusion but find you still don't really believe it, that indicates the reasoning is probably not complete. Important factors probably are missing—factors that lead you to resist internalizing the results.

It is more controversial to link critical thinking to action. Suppose, for example, I continue to smoke or to eat too many saturated fats despite the fact that I've done a lot of reasoning about the importance of giving them up. Is that a flaw in my critical thinking? If I can state all the compelling reasons but still do not act on my reasoning, how good is my critical thinking? Experts disagree on the answer.

The suggestion here is that there is some flaw in the critical thinking. The flaw can lie in how I think about my own body, about my life, or about the relation between abstract statistics and my chances of survival. I might have an overriding background belief that those statistics don't apply to me, or that even though it's important for me to give up smoking, it's not important that I do it now. Sometimes you can even get the impression that certain people don't believe that they will ever die. There is a subtle relation between denial and lack of critical thinking, one that has not yet been fully explored.

It is difficult to identify examples of not believing the results of our own reasoning. That's because, paradoxical as it may sound, it's hard to become aware of what we actually believe and don't believe. There are four indicators of when we are not believing the results of our reasoning (but only the last one is even moderately easy to spot in ourselves):

1. I reason something out, but strong emotions arise within me against the result.
2. I find myself believing contradictory things.
3. I believe something very strongly, but I find I am unable to come up with any good reasons for the belief. In fact, I don't think I even need reasons. Thinking the opposite seems ridiculous.
4. I reason something out, but my actions do not follow my reasoning.

The following are examples of the first three indicators (but they may not be convincing to you, especially if you share the beliefs in question):

1. ■ Michael reasons out the issue of capital punishment as a deterrent. He gathers information and concludes that it does not significantly deter murder or other violent crimes. But after his investigation, he feels angry. He says, "Maybe that's true, but I'm still in favor of capital punishment because you have to do something to stop criminals."

   ■ Maria, taking a course in gender studies, reasons her way through the argument that there is no non-sexist reason why a woman should adopt her husband's name at marriage. Like Michael, Maria discovers that the more she follows the argument, the angrier she gets.

2. ■ Pete believes that all cultures and all cultural practices are equally valid. He believes that people do not have a right to say that a particular culture's practices are wrong. But he also believes that it's part of our Western culture to impose our ideas on others, and that it's wrong for us to do that.

   ■ Most of us believe that everyone should be treated equally, but that does not prevent us from thinking that we deserve special breaks.

3. ■ Some people think that eating dogs, cats, or seagulls is revolting, but that eating cows or chickens is quite reasonable. They believe this despite the fact that all their reasoning shows the cases are identical. They find themselves trying to make up reasons that they know don't work (such as "Dogs and cats are pets! That's why it is wrong to eat them").

    ■ In critical-thinking presentations, Vincent Ruggiero asks, "Why not turn cemeteries into parks where children can play?" (Can you give a good reason against it?) "We're running out of room: why not bury people in the median strips of highways?"

When you've thought through something critically and come to the conclusion that seems most reasonable to you, it should follow (a) that you believe it, and (b) that you start acting in accordance with that belief.

An appropriate exercise would be to ask you to identify situations where you do not believe the results of your reasoning, where each of the four causes applies to you. But that is extremely difficult. Can you identify any examples where indicators (1), (2), and (3) apply to you? If you can find even one, that's a major insight into yourself. (It sometimes helps to begin with other people, and then apply the results to yourself.)

With indicator (4), on the other hand, it should be easy to identify some examples of actions you continue to engage in even though your best reasoned thinking tells you that you should not.

What Critical Thinking Is *Not*

There are a number of widespread misconceptions about critical thinking. These can throw off your understanding of critical thinking and influence the way you develop in your thinking skills.

Critical Thinking and Negativity

Critical Thinking Is Not Negative

The word *critical* often has negative overtones. A "critical person" is one who does a lot of faultfinding. To "criticize" someone usually means to say something negative. A "critic" is often thought of as someone who is against something.

But the word *critical* in "critical thinking" has no negative connotations at all. It is related to the word *criteria*: it means thinking that meets high criteria of reasonableness. To learn to think critically is to learn to think things through, and to think them through well: accurately, clearly, sufficiently, reasonably. Some people have proposed the term *effective thinking* as a synonym for "critical thinking," and using that term can help in removing negative overtones.

> Using the word *critical* in the sense of *critical thinking,* what would you say are the main earmarks of critical reading? What is the difference between reading your text and reading it *critically*?
>
> How about critical listening? What is the difference between listening to a lecture in a course and listening to it *critically*?
>
> Can a person listen critically and not disagree at all?

The Importance of Negative Feedback

Another aspect of negativity must be considered. Sometimes sensitivity to negative feedback gets in the way of critical thinking. Suppose someone makes a judgment about your work—that it is inaccurate or unclear, or not relevant to the question asked. Maybe the person even personalizes it, criticizing you when he or she is actually talking about your work. The person might say that you are unclear or inaccurate. Maybe the person even says it harshly.

You need to sort out the judgments, separating out the harshness or the over-generalization on the speaker's part. You are left with feedback about your work on this occasion. Many people view such feedback as negative, but you don't have to view it that way. Instead, you can choose to view it as a source of valuable information. If you can distance yourself from the negativity, you can free yourself to look for the kernel of truth it may contain.

Because the judgment is not binding on you, you can choose what to learn from it. You may learn something about the other person ("My teacher values grammar very highly. Just how important is grammar?"); but you may also learn something about your work and the way you think ("Oh, I didn't even realize I was being unclear! Maybe I should elaborate more").

Critical Thinking and Emotions

Critical Thinking Is Not Emotionless Thinking

One of the most widespread myths about critical thinking, and one of the most harmful too, is that critical thinking is somehow opposed to emotions. According to this myth, the best way to think critically is to be devoid of emotions or, if emotions arise, to put them aside, don't let them influence your conclusions. The image in this myth is of someone coldly rational, someone who puts aside his or her feelings in order to be "logical."

This is one of the most misleading myths there is, and it is all the more damaging because there is a grain of truth in it. Some emotions do indeed get in the way of critical thinking: rage and panic, for example. It is extremely difficult for people to think clearly about a decision when they are enraged. But, by contrast, certain other emotion-laden states actually help with critical thinking: the love of truth is an example. So are the joy of discovery, anger at biased presentations of information, and fear of making an unreasonable decision in a crucial situation.

Consider as an example something that intrinsically involves a lot of emotion: love. Suppose you are the mother of a child. What will help you in being a good mother? A good mother is one who acts in accord with high standards of critical thinking: she has the best interests of her child at heart; she does not neglect her own well-being, but she nurtures and makes wise decisions in the best interests of her child, weighs relevant alternative courses of action, and understands the child's growing need for both autonomy and safety; she is creative about finding ways to help her child develop in a healthy way. Now, what is the role of love in this? It should be clear that love—far from being an impediment to clear thinking—is *essential* to being a good critically thinking mother. Love is a large part of what motivates the thinking, grounds it, helps her to assess choices that confront her as a parent. The emotions that go along with love are not in any way opposed to the thinking required to be a good parent.

The same can be said about romantic love. Sometimes it may seem that being in love is opposed to critical thinking, but often this stems from a superficial concept of love. For example, people who are in love often engage in wishful thinking. Suppose Ashley is in love with Lou and Lou is an alcoholic. A common scenario is that Ashley keeps thinking that Lou will be cured any day now, even though it may be clear to others that Lou is not on the road to recovery. But thinking, against all the evidence, that Lou's cure is just around the corner is not an example of love interfering with critical thinking. It's deeper than that.

To sort through this example requires thinking through the concept of love in a deeper way and distinguishing it from neediness and from a desire to mold the person according to an image. Part of loving someone, romantically or not, is seeing what that person is actually like, respecting his or her boundaries. To love someone, rather than just to love an image of that person, is to accept the person as he or she is. Loving the person is exactly what can help you see clearly who that person is and your relationship to him or her.

Emotions Give Us Data

There is another area in which emotions are essential to critical thinking. Emotions often give us data, and much of the time it's fool-hardy to ignore that data. For example, if two people are in love, it is *unreasonable* for them to ignore that fact when they make important decisions about, say, whether to go to schools that are far apart. Being in love is directly relevant to that decision. Ignoring important data is *not* thinking critically. (For the same reason, it would also be unreasonable to base the decision *only* on the fact that they are in love. There are other facts that are relevant as well.)

In a more general way, though, we receive important data from our emotions all the time. Suppose that while walking through a neighborhood at dusk, you become afraid that you are in danger. Sometimes people have a narrow view of rationality. If they cannot pinpoint what is dangerous about the situation, they draw the conclusion that their fears are unfounded. But under most circumstances, that's not reasonable at all. There is a good chance that you are picking up clues you are not aware of, triggering your fear. There

Describe some situations where, in your best judgment, your emotions led you astray in your reasoning. Then, describe some situations where, in your best judgment, your emotions made a positive contribution to your reasoning.

Try to discover patterns in your emotional reactions, so that you can assess when your emotions tend to be accurate responses to reality and when they tend not to be.

For example, think about the people you have been in love with in the past. Have they generally been caring, respectful people who, on the whole, treated you well? If so, that's a pretty good reason to rely on your feelings of love as an indicator of who is good for you: you're pretty good at picking good people. On the other hand, if they were abusive or manipulative, that's a good reason not to let your feelings of being in love with someone guide you too strongly in your choices.

is nothing unreasonable about heeding that data. On the contrary, what is unreasonable is to pretend that you are not afraid when you are. The reasonable thing to do is neither to ignore the data of your emotions, nor to give them too much weight.

Being Logical Is Linked to Having Feelings

If we think of desires as intertwined with emotion, then the tie between critical thinking and emotions is even stronger. That is because, in the end, it is not possible to engage in critical thinking without desires and their attendant emotions. Unless I have goals—desires, things I want, things I'm emotionally attached to—I have no reason to think critically, no reason to take action X rather than action Y.

In the movie *Star Trek* (2009), the character Mr Spock is based on a character in an old TV series. In the series, Mr. Spock often said that he puts aside whatever feelings he has in order to be what he called "logical." But he also saves the ship and the crew again and again. The problem with this scenario is that if he is not emotionally attached to the crew members, he has no reason to save them. Unless he *wants* them to live, it is not "logical" for him to save them. Spock's answer is that saving the *Enterprise* is the "right thing to do." But, unless he's emotionally attached to doing the right thing, he has no reason to do the right thing either. The question is always: Why should he try to achieve *any* purpose? It is "logical" for him to do something only if achieving his purpose is something that matters to him, matters to him in terms of his emotions and desires. Being logical requires having goals that are emotionally important.

The relation between emotions and critical thinking is a complicated one, without easy solutions. (For example, not all philosophers would agree that emotions and desires underlie rationality.) There is no doubt that emotions can cloud judgment, but they can also illuminate it. Fear can make you run from a decision that is in your best interests. But fear can also alert you to dangers in decisions, dangers that you're not consciously aware of. Anger is often a very sophisticated emotion, alerting us to subtle evidence of people's willingness to cross our boundaries. Whether to rely on emotions in any particular case, and how much to rely on them, is itself a matter for critical thinking.

Impediments to Critical Thinking

The way we think is an adaptation to the surroundings we have lived in. The patterns in our thinking are ways that we have developed to make sense of what goes on around us. These patterns can be effective, but they can also be dysfunctional. Most likely, for each of us, the patterns are variable: effective in some areas, wildly ineffective in others, and mixed most of the time.

Many aspects of the world we live in can be impediments to learning to think more critically.

Forming a Picture of the World on the Basis of News Media

Most of us form a picture of what the world is like based, directly or indirectly, on news media: TV news, blogs, newspapers, and so forth. Even if you don't watch the news much, you indirectly form a good deal of your picture of the world from it. You get a picture of what the world is like by talking to friends, by connecting through Facebook or Twitter, by listening to comedy shows or reality TV, or just through hearsay. But when we trace it back, all those people form their picture of the world ultimately from the news media. So, indirectly, you and I do too.

Here is a question I ask students in Louisiana. (You may not know much about Louisiana, but answer the question anyhow):

> Consider people who are convicted of murder in Louisiana, and sentenced to life imprisonment. How much time do such people, on the average, actually spend in prison? (Remember: the question is not how many years they are sentenced to; it is how many years they end up actually spending in prison.)

a. 0–5 years
b. 5–10 years
c. 10–20 years
d. 20–50 years
e. until they die.

Choose an answer before you read on.

I have asked thousands of students this question over the last few years or so; almost no one ever gets it right. Even with myself, it was hard to become convinced of the right answer. The first few times I heard it, I simply didn't believe it. (The answer is in the footnotes.[3])

Now, this is a purely factual question, not a critical-thinking one. But there is a critical-thinking question behind the mistaken answers. Where do we get our false impression? We get it, directly or indirectly, from the news media. But how? We do not get the wrong answer because the news tells us the wrong answer. News media are very careful to check the accuracy of factual statements they report.

Rather, the news media tell us *stories*. They report on someone getting released from prison early. Maybe over the course of time they report several such stories, including some where a criminal then commits a violent crime while on parole. Maybe we hear politicians or relatives of a victim talking about how life means only twenty years, and we believe them. (These people too get their impression from the news.) These stories are vivid. They are simplified and made dramatic. Often there is stirring footage. They register in our minds. Whether we are aware of it or not, we form a general picture that violent criminals (including murderers sentenced to life in Louisiana) are getting out of prison early all the time.

Any picture like that one, formed on the basis of news presentations, is likely to be seriously distorted. This is because the news media report not on what is usual or typical, but on what is *unusual*. That's why it is called news: it reports on what is out of the ordinary. That's also why it works so well as entertainment. In contrast, what is usual is for people to wake up in the morning, eat breakfast, go to work, eat lunch, come home at the end of the day, watch TV for a while, go to bed. That is not a news event. Rather, what the news reports on is Afghanistan (hardly a typical country), a tornado hitting a trailer park (not a common event), a postal employee going berserk (extremely unusual), or a highly controversial bill in Congress (not the hundreds of bills that are passed on a regular basis).

If you want an accurate picture of what the world is usually like, you need to look to reputable books, studies, or web sites that deal with the subject in depth. Textbooks are usually an excellent source. And, of course, you have to do some intensive critical thinking about the topic as well.

This doesn't imply that it's wrong to consult the news media regularly. On the contrary, the news—especially if it has more in-depth coverage—is an excellent way to keep up with the unusual, even earthshaking, events of our time.

Discuss how likely you are to get a false picture of the following topics from the news media:

- The danger of small airplanes
- The amount of crime in your area
- New findings in science
- The chances of winning the lottery

(continued)

(Continued)

Write down a few important topics of your own where your picture of the world is likely to be seriously distorted if you base your impression mainly on what is reported by news media. Where, specifically, would you look to get a more accurate impression?

In the Discipline. Are there topics related to the discipline you are studying that appear from time to time in the news? Is the picture you receive from the media likely to be distorted? In what ways? Again, where specifically would you look to get a more accurate picture?

Forming a Picture of the World on the Basis of Movies, TV, Advertising, Magazines

If forming a picture of the world on the basis of the news results in distortion, forming a picture on the basis of fictionalized or sensationalized material results in vastly more distortion. Sometimes the distortion is obvious, at least to reflective adults: people do not get thrown through plate-glass windows and emerge intact; there is no reason to believe that there are aliens among us; the clothes in the glossy picture will not make most of us look like the model in the picture; products often have unmentioned defects. Other examples are more subtle and affect our attitudes in deep and disturbing ways: trying your hardest, though it may give you personal satisfaction, will not usually result in beating the competition (especially since they may be trying their hardest too); most people's grades (or height or intelligence or abilities) cannot be above average; everyone cannot be glamorous, young, physically attractive, or strong; being a lone-wolf rebel who can't get along with superiors does not usually bring success.

List some of the subtle messages acquired from movies, TV, magazines, or advertising that tend to give people a false sense of what the world is like. How about school in particular? How is high school or college usually depicted? How is the subject matter of your classes presented in these sources? Are there stereotypes?

All-or-Nothing Thinking (Black-and-White Thinking), Us-versus-Them Thinking, Stereotyping

Each of these ways of thinking is deeply ingrained in us. Each stands in the way of critical thinking, and for similar reasons—they give us a way of simplifying our in fact, though, each of them vastly oversimplifies the complexity of reality, and each serves as an excuse for not thinking things through.

Effective thinking requires us to pay attention to the complexity of things. It requires us to develop a tolerance for ambiguity and an acceptance of less-than-certain answers. It requires a commitment to seeing both sides of an issue and to trying to find out the truth, rather than merely trying to bolster our side: our country, our race, our gender, our political views.

Describe a situation—either from your own life or from disciplines you have studied—where you engaged in all-or-nothing thinking.

Then describe a contrasting situation, one where you were tempted to engage in all-or-nothing thinking, but instead addressed the subtleties of the situation and therefore came up with a more careful answer.

Describe a similar pair of contrasting examples for us-versus-them thinking, then for stereotyping.

Fears

Although, as we have seen, all fears are not automatically an impediment to critical thinking, some fears do tend to become obstacles. That's especially true of:

- Fear of making mistakes
- Fear of trying something new, of sticking your neck out
- Fear of looking foolish

The full exercise of critical thinking requires that you develop intellectual courage. For example, making mistakes is an essential part of critical thinking. What important skill have you ever learned that did not involve making many mistakes? Most critical-thinking experts believe that you learn a great deal more from mistakes than from successes. In fact, though you may make fewer critical-thinking mistakes as your higher-order thinking skills develop, there will always be mistakes to be made and learned from.

The same will be true when you try new ways of thinking, when you risk looking foolish by exposing how you think about issues, and when you take the risk of giving original solutions to old problems.

Some Educational Practices Discourage Critical Thinking

Some prevalent educational practices discourage critical thinking, and internalizing them as a model of what education should be can seriously affect your critical thinking. These practices are based on assumptions like:

- The student's role is to be a passive recipient of knowledge.
- The student's role is to memorize and regurgitate information.
- The teacher's role is to dispense knowledge.
- Questions on exams should be taken only from what has been covered in class.
- Problems assigned to students should always be clearly formulated.
- There is an adequate answer to every question.
- Everything is just a matter of opinion.

How much of your past education has emphasized the teacher or student roles listed?

Formulate your idea of what education should be about, your philosophy of education.

Make some well-considered judgments about how the roles listed fit in with or oppose your idea of education.

Deeper, More Pervasive Impediments to Critical Thinking

In addition to the specific impediments listed previously, there are other, deeper and more pervasive obstacles to critical thinking. Four of them are briefly discussed below, but they are not separate from one another. All four are deeply interwoven. In addition, they are difficult impediments to come to terms with. Maybe it is fair to say that none of us ever completely overcomes them. We can, however, gain deeper insights into how they work, and that can help us overcome their influence.

Egocentrism

Each of us is at the center of our own experience. We live in the middle of our feelings, pains and pleasures, the things we want and the things we are afraid of, the experiences that have shaped our lives and our attitudes, whether we know it or not. Our experience is heavily influenced by how we think and, conversely, how we think is influenced by our experience.

In accord with this, people often have a way of thinking that always puts themselves first. When they are engaged in such egocentric thinking, they tend to make judgments about how things are, but they may base those judgments on wishful thinking or mere self-interest. This occurs in all of us, probably a good deal of the time. Sometimes it's so blatant that, when it is pointed out to us, we easily see it. Most of the time, though, it operates far beneath the surface. It is easy to delude myself into believing that I am working in the best interests of humanity as a whole when in fact I am working for my own interests and even against the interests of humanity. This is always easier to see in other people than it is in myself.

Egocentrism interferes with critical thinking on all levels, from the deepest to the most superficial. It stands in the way of the empathy that is such an important part of critical thinking. If I am in the health-care professions, for example, it's easy to stay bound up in my own desires and needs and not see things from the patient's point of view. Egocentrism stands in the way of fair-mindedness too, another essential critical-thinking trait. Part of thinking effectively is being able to understand points of view that are opposed to my own. Sometimes when I feel threatened, though, I can't even hear what the other

Write a brief response to the following questions (your response can be just a few lines, but it is important that it be written):

1. Advertising. In your judgment, how heavily are people influenced by advertising?

2. Conformity. In your judgment, to what extent do people conform to roles dictated by the society they live in?

3. Driving. In your judgment, are people generally good drivers?

Write your responses before you look at the answers (see Exercise 1.3 at the end of the chapter).

person is saying. For many people, when someone critiques their country or culture or religion or family, all they hear is the fact that they are being criticized. Anger rises, and often they can't even repeat the substance of the comments the person made. This interferes with their ability to give a fair evaluation of their country, culture, and so on. If I can't hear a critique, then I can't come to a balanced conclusion, and that deprives me of information I can use to assess the validity of my beliefs.

In course work, egocentrism can lead to my seeing education only in terms of grades, in effect causing me to miss out on all the other benefits to be derived from education. It can lead to plagiarism and cheating, or thinking that teachers are unfair even if they're not.

One of the most valuable things to be gained from critical thinking is an increased ability to see the egocentricity of our own thinking.

Developmental Patterns of Thinking

We acquire many of our patterns of thinking as we go through different stages of psychological and physical development. As children, we have a number of deeply felt needs: a need to feel safe, a need to be loved, a need for physical contact; we have a need to individuate ourselves from others as well as a contrary need to join completely with another person. Moreover, many of our standard ways of thinking were acquired during childhood, even during early childhood. After all, that's when we

Think about the need to feel safe. This is a need that develops in early childhood and never really goes away.

Begin by focusing on other people. Use obvious examples of persistent irrational behavior in people you know: maybe they are abrasive and drive friends away; maybe they identify with groups or with causes that don't seem to serve their interests; maybe they continue to hold beliefs when the vast preponderance of evidence goes against those beliefs. Now try out the hypothesis that this behavior is partly the result of looking for feelings of safety along paths established during childhood. (If I drive people away, for example, it can feel as though I don't have to take the risk of depending on them; identifying with groups can give me a feeling of belonging, of safety.)

A much harder exercise is to apply this not just to others, but also to yourself.

first learned how to conceptualize and deal with emotions, frustration, authority figures, strong desires, pain and hurt. Many of the strategies we devised back then still persist, beneath the surface, throughout our lives. Thus, when we feel threatened, we can easily revert back to a child's way of thinking. Problems that can be solved may seem overwhelming. (Think of how overwhelming problems can be to a child.) People can be going about their business with no reference to us at all, and we may feel victimized by it (e.g., waiters who don't see us at their table or drivers who go slow in the left lane). We might resort to manipulation or even physical bullying when we don't get our way.

So, another great benefit of learning to think critically is that you can start identifying the *assumptions* you used to make about life, and you can distinguish them from the more mature assumptions you can make now. You can separate your past from your present *purposes*. You can take seriously the much more extensive *information* you have now, the *context* in which you now live, the *alternatives* that are now available to you that were not available when you were younger. You can draw different *conclusions*. (The italicized terms are essential critical-thinking concepts, elements of reasoning; see Chapter 2.)

Previous Commitments, Previous Personal Experience

Suppose someone makes a point about a controversial issue, about politics maybe, or capital punishment, or the benefits of a trade agreement. The most usual way to evaluate the person's statement is first to see how much it agrees with my views, and then give reasons for or against it based on the amount of agreement.

This might be reasonable if my views were the product of extensive critical examination on my part. But often my views are ones I just happen to hold; they only seem to be the result of previous examination. There may be no reason to think that my previously held beliefs are more likely to be correct than the newer points I am evaluating for the first time.

We can also think in a biased way with respect to evidence. If I lean toward a certain belief, then just a small amount of evidence weighs heavily in its favor for me. If I believe in aliens visiting earth, or herbal remedies for cancer, or homeopathic cures, or predestination, then even the negative fact that such views have not been absolutely disproven counts heavily in their favor in my eyes.

On the other hand, if I oppose a belief, then a vague piece of evidence, or just the fact that it has not been absolutely proven, weighs heavily against it:

> "I don't believe in global warming. Nobody has *proved* the earth is getting warmer. Last winter it was very cold."

"You can't prove that I won't win the lottery. There's always a chance. You can't win if you don't play."

That is, we slant the amount of evidence to fit in with our pre-dispositions. We require a mountain of evidence to make us doubt something we already believe, but we require only the slightest of evidence to make us more sure of it. Even our own ingenuity can work against us. No matter how bizarre or farfetched a point of view is, if we become convinced that it is true, our ingenious minds can almost always construct at least *some* evidence in its favor.

How should we make judgments? If we are interested in accuracy, in knowing the truth or what is likely to come closest to the truth, we should go with the *preponderance of evidence*, regardless of whether we started out for or against a particular conclusion. That is often extremely difficult to do because decisions can be made below the level of our awareness and because our beliefs are so often bound up with our egos and developmental ways of thinking. We can increase our awareness and open-mindedness by using critical thinking.

This is also true when we are basing judgments on personal experience. Personal experience gives us a valuable supply of information, one that we can use to draw conclusions, make decisions. One of the main ways teachers get students to think critically about a discipline is by asking them to relate the discipline's concepts to their personal experiences. No one would deny the value of personal experience in critical thinking.

However, personal experience can also be an impediment to critical thinking. That's particularly true of vivid personal experiences, the kind that are unusual and imprint themselves on our minds. For each of us, our personal experience is limited. If we make generalizations from it that go beyond what we are acquainted with, we stand a good chance of drawing distorted conclusions. Your own experience has far more impact on you than the experiences of a hundred other people you hear about. But, if you want to draw accurate conclusions about what is likely to happen, then (other things being equal) you should put more faith in the experiences of a hundred people than in the experience of one—even if that one happens to be you.

What do you need to do to broaden your knowledge-base so as to take account of a wide variety of experiences and conclusions beyond your own? You should look at reputable books, studies, journal articles, sources that gather and assemble information from a great variety of human experience. If you own a Kia that repeatedly gives you trouble, that is an excellent reason not to trust that car in the future. But if you want to make a wise decision about whether the next car you buy should be a Kia, your personal experience is too limited. It would be wiser to consult *Consumer Reports* or some other neutral agency that evaluates cars.

How Deep Is Our Need for Critical Thinking?

One of the great things about critical thinking is its versatility. It is valuable at all levels of our thinking.

At the Level of Practical Decision Making

Critical thinking helps when we are simply trying to deal with ordinary tasks: how to study more efficiently, find a strategy when we are stuck in an airport, decide what kind of clothes to buy. This is thinking about the means to use to accomplish our goals. It is problem solving of the most authentic kind. This is an important level of critical thinking, one that addresses all those ordinary decisions we make.

Developing thinking skills helps you envision alternative paths you could take. It helps you identify and discard outdated assumptions you may be making. It helps you anticipate some of the consequences, both positive and negative, of decisions you or others may make. It helps you keep your goals in sight and think of more effective means of achieving those goals.

At the Level of Meaningfulness

Learning to think critically also helps people deal with the much larger issues of living their life. Critical thinking frees people, the way nothing else really can, from habits of thinking they are often ruled by. Not completely of course, but substantially. Critical thinking opens up other viable courses of action that leave people far more fulfilled, paths that otherwise might never occur to them. Finding a life partner or a new occupation; incorporating the profound knowledge that's available in your courses into your way of thinking about your life; developing reasonable attitudes toward self, toward others, toward your values, toward all the things that make life meaningful for you—all of these can be made richer and more attainable when you examine them thoughtfully.

At the Level of Concepts

We think in terms of concepts, and these inevitably shape our life to a considerable degree. Very often the concepts we think in terms of are ones we accept uncritically. We may understand what love is from movies and from the way we feel. We may understand what freedom is simply by having heard the word over and over and making vague associations with it. We may grow up thinking justice means getting even. We all have concepts of what it is to be a student, a teacher, a woman, a man, a religious person, an atheist, a scientist, an artist, a professional in the field we are studying. We have concepts of what it means to be brave, to be treated fairly, to be intelligent, to fit in, to be anything you can name or describe. We can reach a deep level of critical thinking by examining our concepts critically, becoming more aware of the way individual concepts help us or hurt us, limit us or free us.

Even aspects of ourselves that are distinct from thinking are heavily influenced by our concepts. Desires, for instance: If you like something, or hate it—a person, a movie, a subject in school, a kind of car—the liking or the hating is not itself an instance of thinking. Rather, the liking or hating is influenced by the concepts you use in your thinking. It is only recently that anyone thought suntans were beautiful, that beaches were a desirable place to spend a vacation, that thinness in men and women was attractive, that wilderness held value, that toleration was a virtue, that democracy was workable, that it was unhealthy to be a caretaker in a relationship. Our standard concepts for each of these key terms has changed, becoming strikingly more positive or negative. The concepts may well change again. It can be liberating to step out of the fads that come and go with respect to what is desirable. Re-examining the concepts you have of the things you desire will help you rise above the fads.

Similarly, your concepts have an immense influence on what you are afraid of and what brings you joy. If you are afraid of the dark, afraid of math, or even afraid of dying—these are not universal fears. There are many people, not very different from you, who don't share these fears. Some people feel safe in the dark, delight in math (even if they are not very good at it), and find peace and acceptance in contemplating death. We fear things in part because of the concepts we have of those things, because of how we classify them and think about them.

Emotions are not really under our direct control, though how we act on those emotions often is. Many of the ways people try to gain direct control over their emotions actually hurt. If you are afraid of speaking in public, for example, but feel you shouldn't be afraid of it, you can try to suppress the fear. Maybe you can even force yourself to speak in public, or pretend to yourself that you are not afraid of it. You can reason as follows: "It doesn't make sense to feel fearful of speaking in public. There's really nothing to be afraid of. Therefore, I am not afraid of speaking in public." This is called *denial*. Denial is when you keep yourself from seeing something you know is true. The classic case is alcoholics who refuse to see that they are alcoholics. Many people confuse denial of this sort with being rational. Neither suppression nor denial is very healthy. Neither is very effective either, at least not in the long run. Both have high psychological costs.

Though our emotions are not under our direct control, we can indirectly affect them by addressing our concepts. You can work on

Many people automatically assume that bravery is good. But here are some possible examples where bravery makes a situation worse, where being brave does damage:

- Someone who is brave but a Nazi

- A sports figure who bravely plays despite a serious injury

- Criminals who bravely risk their lives in committing their crimes

- Achilles, the hero of *The Iliad*. Did his bravery accomplish what you would call worthwhile purposes?

Plato would say that these examples are not part of the concept of bravery at all. How might someone believe that?

In your view, are these examples of bravery, or of something else? Why? If they are examples of bravery, would you admire the action in each case? Or would you say, "We would all be better off if these people were not brave?"

your concept of public speaking and try to understand why you see it as fearsome. You can admit and honor the fear that arises. You can investigate what its roots are, what associations you have with it that generate the fear, and build new associations. You can rethink the concept over time, and usually this will be effective in changing your reaction to it.

The Experience of Learning to Think Things Through

You may already be good at thinking critically. In some areas, you may be very good at it. In fact, in some areas you may be so good at critical thinking that it occurs naturally—you no longer even recognize it as good thinking. For example, suppose you are driving down a street and a ball bounces out in front of you from between parked cars. You instinctively put your foot on the brake; you instinctively look around, searching for the child who might dart out. Another example: There's a sudden accident in the cars ahead of you. To get out of the way, you instinctively pull to the right rather than to the left.

These *seem* instinctive, but they're not. You've *learned* to do these things by reflecting on likely consequences. You've internalized the critical thinking so well that it seems natural, instinctive. But these actions are still the product of critical thinking.

As you work your way through this book, you can be confident that your thinking skills will improve significantly. Of course, it's not enough *just* to read the book. You have to engage in the activities, try them out in this class, in other classes, and in your life outside school. If you *do* the critical thinking, your skills will improve.

The trouble is, you may not *feel* as if your skills are improving. The improvement is unlikely to be obvious. Many people have the opposite reaction. They feel they are getting worse at reasoning as they work through a course that emphasizes critical thinking.

That happens for a number of reasons. First, working through a disciplined process of critical thinking will slow your thinking down. A problem that you once effortlessly thought your way through will now take much longer. You will have to focus on all the parts of the thinking that you previously took for granted.

Second, questions will start to arise for you where none arose before. "Am I being clear?" "Is this really an implication?" "Maybe I'm jumping to a conclusion here." "How can I check on this?" Questions are a sign of growth, of opening to new ways of thinking. But we often believe that questions are a sign of *not* understanding, that it is better to have no questions at all. Critical thinking lives in questions.

Third, the reflectiveness of critical thinking can cause you to start second-guessing yourself, especially at the beginning, or when you are feeling down on yourself. Before, you might have confidently asserted an answer; now, however, you might reflect, "Wait a minute, maybe I'm jumping to a conclusion here," or, "Is this really an implication of this author's position? Maybe I'm being unduly influenced by the fact that I disagree with her."

Fourth, some of your certainty about things can be a bluff to cover up the threatening fact that you really don't know, or don't know for sure. The main person you are bluffing may be yourself. Studying how to think critically often calls your bluff. You start asking, "What assumptions does my automatic response rest on?"

Finally, as Michael Scriven explained in a classic text on reasoning, if you are a swimmer or a tennis player and you start studying with a professional coach, you'll find that you have to change many of the ways you do things, unlearning certain moves and learning others. This will feel awkward, and it will slow you down—at first. But that slowing down is really the only way to build up proficiency and reliable speed. "Speed builds slowly."[4]

Here is a list of reactions many people have to studying critical thinking. You should not be surprised, or troubled, by experiencing many of them. (In fact, as a teacher I would be troubled if you experienced none of them.)

- Difficulty applying critical-thinking terms in practice
- Not being able to tell if you have applied them correctly
- Becoming very concerned with how concepts overlap
- Becoming confused about things that seemed clear before
- Persistently doubting that you will ever improve
- Having initial confidence in an answer, followed by nagging doubt
- Feeling that your teachers are not teaching enough because they generate more questions than answers

Again, when trying to learn to think critically, what's important is to engage in the activities of critical thinking, including getting feedback, and to be open to how they can enrich your life.

Getting Started: Clarifying with SEE-I

As we have seen, critical thinking begins with asking the questions you need to ask. Asking questions is a way of starting to get clearer: by formulating questions you are focusing your mind on what you need to address. In general, a good way to begin any critical-thinking process is by *clarifying*, by making things clearer.

A very useful process for clarifying almost anything is called **SEE-I**. This book contains many critical-thinking processes that accomplish far more than you would ever expect at first glance, and SEE-I is one of them. The letters stand for four steps that help make whatever you are working on clearer:

S: State it

E. Elaborate [explain it more fully, in your own words]

E. Exemplify [give a good example]

I. Illustrate [give an illustration: maybe a metaphor, a simile, an analogy, a diagram, a concept map, and so forth]

Statement

To **state** something is, essentially, to say it briefly, clearly, and as precisely as possible. Sometimes it means constructing a good definition, but it can also mean stating the thesis of a chapter by trying to capture the heart of what the chapter is saying in a single, clear, well-formulated sentence.

Elaboration

To **elaborate** on something is to expand on it, to explain it in your own words, at greater length, so that the reader gets more of the fullness of what is meant. For instance, I can **state** the law of conservation of energy; I can then **elaborate** on it, explaining it in more depth, in greater detail, spelling out what it is saying. You can begin your elaboration by saying, "In other words, ..."

Exemplification

Here, the goal is to give a good **example**—not just any example, but a well-chosen one, one that will clarify for yourself or for a reader what you mean. Usually, it should be your own original example, not one from the book or the teacher, and it should fit well with your statement and elaboration. Thus, I might try to clarify the concept of *falling in love*: first I would try to **state** in a sentence what *falling in love* is; then I would **elaborate** on it; and then I would give a good **example** of falling in love, one that the reader can connect with. (Romeo and Juliet come to mind, but it could be a personal example as well.) You can begin your exemplification by saying, "For example, ..."

Illustration

An illustration is literally a picture (as in "an illustrated book"). To clarify something, it helps to give readers something they can picture in their minds. Sometimes, it can be an actual picture (Figure 1.2 on page 36 of this book is a visual illustration of the process of critical thinking). In some cases, it can also be a graph, a diagram, or a concept map. More often, your illustration will be a picture in words: an analogy, simile or metaphor that captures the meaning. For instance, Rush Cosgrove was clarifying the concept of *civil disobedience*. He stated his definition of it in a sentence; then he elaborated on it; and then he gave a good example of civil disobedience. (His example was Rosa Parks refusing to sit in the back of the bus.) Then he gave an **illustration**: He said that civil disobedience was like being a cliff at the edge of the ocean—the waves crash against it, but the cliff remains there. To me, that illustration captures vividly what Cosgrove means by *civil disobedience*. You can begin your illustration by saying, "It's like... ."

There are two aspects of clarifying something. The first is getting clear in your own mind; the second is communicating clearly to

When students are assigned a five-page paper to write, they often have difficulty "filling up" the five pages. (Teachers are often amazed by this because teachers usually have the opposite problem: they have difficulty "cutting down" what they want to say to five pages.) Using SEE-I gives you a way to "fill up" those pages—but without just adding filler. With every major point you are making in your paper, you can state it, elaborate on it, give examples, and top it off with an illustration that conveys the point. This will "fill up" your paper with writing that is clear and directly relevant to the development of your paper (see pages 33–34).

others, so that they understand you well. SEE-I works well for both of them. You can improve your writing in a major way by taking each main idea and developing it in your paper with an SEE-I. The result, with practice, can be a smooth flow of richly understood and well-communicated ideas. SEE-I can make both your thinking and your writing dramatically better. It is also a way of testing your understanding of what you learn (and is thus a valuable way to study for exams). If you can accurately S, E, E, then I a concept or a principle in a course, it means you almost certainly have a good grasp of it, that you understand it to a much greater degree than if you are merely able to state it. Similarly, SEE-I is a method your teacher may use to test your understanding, to assess how clear you are about concepts and issues in the course.

The Flexibility of SEE-I

All of the critical-thinking processes in this book are flexible and adaptable. They can be shaped to a great variety of circumstances that call for critical thinking. Critical thinking is seldom simply a linear activity. That is true for SEE-I also: it is not a rigid process. For instance:

- Though the idea is to go step by step—*first* state, *then* elaborate, *then* give an example, *then* illustrate—you don't simply finish one step and then you're done with it. You will find that as you *elaborate*, you will often need to revise the *statement* you formulated in step one. Similarly, both your example and your illustration may cause you to refine or even change your mind about the earlier steps.

- An ideal clarifying statement is a single, clear, well-formulated sentence. But in some cases it may take two. Similarly, you will usually elaborate in one or two paragraphs—but with complex ideas, more elaboration than that may be needed. The point is not really *how long*—the point is to capture the *essence* in a **statement**, and to explain it in its *fullness* in an **elaboration**.

- Sometimes you can skip the illustration-step with very little loss. Often, though, a striking illustration will make the subject suddenly come into focus. It allows your creativity to come forward.

- In exemplification, you give an example. But sometimes what really clarifies the issue is to give both an example and a **contrasting example**. Thus, with civil disobedience, I can say that Rosa Parks is an example of it, but that cheating on my income tax in order to protest tax laws is *not* an example—it is doing something self-serving under the guise of civil disobedience.

- Much of the time, the statement-part of your SEE-I will be your own formulation, a definition or thesis statement that you yourself construct. But sometimes it is beneficial to take the statement-step from some authoritative source, such as your teacher or the textbook. You then clarify your understanding of that statement in your elaboration, give a good example of your own, and an illustration that conveys it well. Thus an Anatomy and Physiology text gives a definition of "anatomy" as "the study of internal and external structures of the body and the physical relationships among body parts."[5] Writing out this statement does not, of course, show that I grasp what anatomy is, or how it is different from physiology. But I can clarify my understanding of it in my own mind, and convey that understanding accurately to a reader, by elaborating on that definition in a paragraph or two, by giving a good example of an anatomical structure (and maybe a contrasting example of a non-anatomical process), and by giving an apt illustration of anatomy.

SEE-I IN THIS BOOK

STATE

A **statement** of what *critical thinking* is can be found on pages 1–2. In fact, there are three statements of it there.

ELABORATE

Pages 3–4 are an **elaboration** of what *critical thinking* is. Pages 5–12 are another elaboration.

(continued)

SEE-I IN THIS BOOK (Continued)

EXEMPLIFY

There are many **examples** of *critical thinking* in this book. One is on a reasonable way to deal with math anxiety on page 8; another is reasoning out the fairness issue on page 10. More extended examples are Chris's analysis of marriage (pages 71–75) and the analysis of the logic of earth sciences (pages 96–97). Other examples will come from you: Any of the outcomes listed at the end of any chapter in this book are examples of critical thinking. Some **contrasting examples** (examples of *not* thinking critically) are also found throughout this book: for instance, the bulleted list on page 9. Examples of non-critical-thinking standards are listed on page 151.

ILLUSTRATE

There are several **illustrations** of critical thinking in this book. A picture of critical thinking is given on page 36; a visualization of thinking through the elements of reasoning is given on pages 63–64. But I could also say, as an illustration, that critical thinking is like a pair of binoculars: it allows you to get up close, explore detail, put what you see in context, and understand more of what you are seeing. That is an analogy. It is not an example of critical thinking; it is something that critical thinking is being compared to. Another illustration: when people give me a ride someplace in their car, or if I follow GPS instructions, even if I pay close attention I usually cannot find my way on my own next time. If on the other hand, I figure out my own way there, maybe using a map, I can almost effortlessly retrace my path every time. It stays with me indelibly. The illustration: critical thinking is like figuring out your own way there.

Critical-Thinking Template

Here is a simple critical-thinking template, which can be applied in any area where you and others are trying to think things through:

- Find four or five other people who are also trying to think critically about this area. (This can be done in person or on-line.)

- Figure out the three most central organizing concepts or ideas that underlie the area. (For example, the three main concepts in a chapter you are studying for this course.)
- Begin with writing an SEE-I: State, elaborate, give an example of, and illustrate each of the three concepts.
- Next, write a paragraph or so explaining how the concepts fit together, how they operate in the world, in your life, in the subject matter. Duplicate both pieces of writing so that everyone has a copy. (It is important that your responses be written, even if they are just jotted down. Written responses are concrete and allow you to confront your thoughts in black and white.)
- Critique one another's thinking. (Remember that critiquing is not the same as criticizing or finding fault.) In the critique,
- Focus on the elements from Chapter 2. Does the writer specify the purpose behind the concepts? Identify key assumptions? Look for consequences, for alternatives? and so on.
- Focus on the standards from Chapter 4. Are the ideas clear? Are they accurate? Do they explain what is most important? and so on.

An Overview of the Book That Lies Ahead

Here is the basic model of this text, in a nutshell.

When people engage in critical thinking, they start off with some question. They try to answer it by reasoning their way through it.

1. **There are elements of reasoning**. The elements are the basic building blocks of reasoning or thinking. *Assumption* is an element. When people reason things out, they make assumptions. So one way to examine their reasoning is to focus on that element of their reasoning: *assumption*. We can ask, "What assumptions are they making?" (The elements are explained in Chapter 2.)

    So if the question is Q, we can picture the reasoning process thus far as shown in Figure 1.1.

2. **There are also standards of reasoning**. They can also be called "standards of critical thinking." These standards determine whether people are reasoning through the question well or not. *Accuracy* is an example of a standard. So one way to examine how well they have reasoned it out is to focus on that standard of reasoning: *accuracy*. We can ask, "Are the assumptions they have made accurate?" (The standards are explained in Chapter 4.) You can picture the standards as a set of filters as shown in Figure 1.2. They are used to filter out reasoning that doesn't meet the standards.

FIGURE 1.1   *The process of reasoning.*

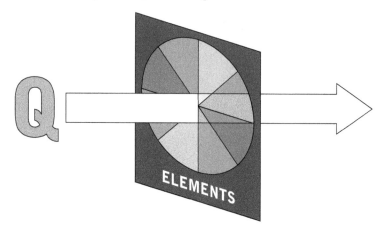

3. Suppose the question being addressed is one **related to the discipline or field you are studying**. Maybe it is a question your teacher has assigned; maybe it's from the textbook in the subject; maybe it's your own question.

There are ways of thinking that lie at the heart of the discipline you are studying. These include fundamental and powerful concepts, and central questions of the discipline. Disciplines are not bits and pieces; they are not assemblages of facts. Instead, there is a logic to thinking in each discipline. For example, in biology, the goal is to think biologically, to think the way a biologist thinks. In history, the goal is to think historically.

The concepts will differ from field to field. *Social patterns* is an example of a fundamental and powerful concept in sociology. So one way to examine how well people have reasoned out a question in the discipline of sociology is to focus on that fundamental and powerful concept: *social patterns*. We can ask, "Have they drawn conclusions,

FIGURE 1.2   *The process of critical thinking: reasoning through the elements and standards.*

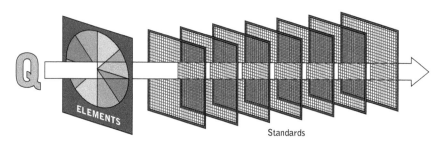

Standards

FIGURE 1.3 *The process of critical thinking in a discipline.*

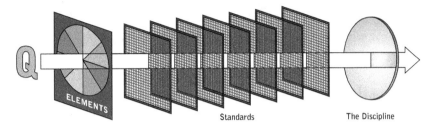

Standards   The Discipline

accurate conclusions, in terms of what we know about social pat-terns?" (Critical thinking in a discipline is explained in Chapter 3.)

You can picture the discipline as a lens or set of lenses through which people reason. Figure 1.3 gives us a full picture.

Some Outcomes

At the end of this chapter . . .

1. You should be able to run your finger slowly down the table of contents and identify the main concepts of Chapter 1:
   - reflective thinking; reasonable thinking
   - misconceptions about critical thinking
   - the role of emotions in critical thinking
   - impediments to thinking more critically
   - and so on

2. With the book closed, you should be able to state, elaborate, exemplify and illustrate each of these concepts, using examples from your own life, learning and experiences. You should be able to give contrasting examples as well (e.g., of unreflective thinking, or of a mistaken idea of the role of emotions in criti-cal thinking).

3. You should be asking more questions—about your thinking, about the discipline you are studying, about everything. You should also be reflecting more on your reasoning.

4. You should be able to identify which aspects of critical think-ing are getting clearer for you and which are still unclear.

You should not expect to achieve the outcomes listed above in a way that is perfect. But you can expect to be improving in them, to find them increasing in your behavior. Not all of these will be directly observable by your teacher. You yourself may often not notice them. Changes in critical-thinking abilities are usually gradual and subtle.

Ideas for Writing

Here are a few ideas for writing. They are aimed at some of the main themes in the chapter. There is a lot of flexibility in what you write in this section. Depending on what you decide or your instructor assigns, you may write a paragraph, a page, or something larger. (If it's a deeply interesting question to you, you may want to consider pursuing that question in your later research and education, possibly even becoming a professional who focuses in that area.) The writing may be for a take-home assignment, for a term paper, or something you write in your journal. Your teacher may assign some of these ideas (or similar ones) to write on, but you might also choose to write about some of them on your own. Also, after you've read the chapter, you may want to construct some ideas to write about that interest you personally. Since this is the work of critical thinking, explain your ideas in enough detail for a reader to understand you well.

1. In your best judgment, what role should questions play in the way people live their day-to-day lives? What role should they play in school? What role do they play in learning a discipline?

2. Pick one emotion to reflect on (anger, for instance). State what that emotion is, elaborate on it, and give a good example of it. Then explore in writing how that emotion interacts with critical thinking. When might it help, and when might it hurt?

3. What are some widespread misconceptions people have about critical thinking? How are they misconceptions?

4. Suppose there is a centrally important idea in one of your courses, and many people in the course do not understand the idea well enough to be able to SEE-I it. Is it possible for them still to get a good test grade on a question about that idea? If your answer to that is "Yes," the next question is: *Should* it be possible? Should education work that way? Or should good grades be achievable only to the extent that the person actually understands the idea?

5. Near the end of this book (pages 175–176), some critical-thinking character traits are described briefly. Even this early, though, you should feel your *intellectual perseverance* being challenged: there is a lot to revise in your thinking. In your judgment, to

what extent is intellectual perseverance essential for becoming better at critical thinking?

6. Create your own ideas for writing about an aspect of Chapter 1.

Tell Your Story

The "Tell Your Story" section of each chapter asks you to reflect on your personal history, especially with respect to aspects of critical thinking that have been involved in your life long before you took this course. The kind of thinking you do is strongly influenced by your life so far—the people you've associated with, your family, the values you've grown up with, the activities you've grown to like, and so forth. Your personal history, "your story," also influences the way you do critical thinking, the aspects of it you respond to or don't respond to. The idea behind this section, then, is to become more consciously aware of "your story" and how you've been shaped by it. That then lays a foundation for you to become more intellectually autonomous, to gain substantially more ability to shape your own present and future through critical thinking.

1. How do you feel about asking questions? (The answer may be different in different contexts.) What aspects of your personality or experiences have led you to feel that way? How comfortable are you with the idea of reasoning things out?

2. What has been your attitude toward the topic of critical thinking before you began this course? Where did you acquire that attitude? Do you think you are open to changing or modifying your attitude toward it?

3. Think of your life as a whole. How has your own native egocentrism changed in your life from childhood to the present?

4. What are some impediments to critical thinking that affect you? Reflect on how they have operated in your personal history.

5. When you have had an important decision to make in your life, how did you go about it? (Be sure not to describe here how you think you *should have* gone about it, but how you actually did.)

6. At this point, how open are you to critical thinking, to letting it become an important part of the way you live your life?

CHAPTER I Exercises

Some of the questions in this and later chapters call for the straight-forward application of concepts from the text, but some are more than that. Some ask you to extend concepts in the text to new areas and then to think critically about these extensions. Some of the exercises are designed to teach new concepts. Answering them is part of learning to think critically.

Starred exercises (★) are ones that have answers (or at least responses) at the back of the book. The responses there are not necessarily complete. Sometimes they are very sketchy. Often they simply point out one dimension it would be wise to consider when answering the question. Sometimes the starred response will contain additional questions as well.

I.I What are some "good questions" you have about this course? Ask some good questions in each sense (ones that open up central areas and ones that you really want to know the answer to). What are some "bad questions" you could raise about the course (bad in the sense of superficial or bad in the sense that you don't really care about the answer)? Compare the questions you raise here with those you raised on page 8.

1.2 Envision a prospective employer who might hire you after graduation. What are the most important understandings he or she would want you to have learned from your college education? How does this relate to critical thinking?

1.3 Go back to the box on page 22 and look at the responses you gave about advertising, conformity, and driving. Now turn the question to yourself: To what extent are *you* influenced by advertising? To what extent do *you* conform to roles dictated by society? Are *you* a better-than-average driver?

1.4 Raising central questions. Here are some "facts" or alleged facts. Formulate good questions about each. Explain why each is a good question.

a. The U.S. is #1.

b. In 1996, "Dr. Ian Wilmut of the Roslin Institute in Edinburgh, Scotland, cloned the first adult mammal, the famous Dolly."[6]

c. "Art is not a luxury, as many people would have us believe, but an integral part of daily life.... We feel better about ourselves when we are in environments that are visually enriching and exciting."[7]

d. Smoking causes more deaths per year in the U.S. than alcohol, illegal drugs, murder, suicide, and AIDS all together.

e. Our stereotype of Neanderthals as "dim-witted, ugly people who are like apes" or "shambling cave people" comes from "mistaken studies of Neanderthal skeletons.... In fact, the Neanderthals were strong, robustly built humans.... There is every reason to believe that they were expert hunters and beings capable of considerable intellectual reasoning."[8]

1.5 Review the definition of denial and the examples given there. (Here's another standard example: Smokers who deny that smoking causes early death.) Identify three of your own examples of denial. (they can be from your own life or someone else's). Explain how denial can appear "rational" to the person engaged in it.

1.6 A woman goes for a haircut at a national hair-cutting chain. The hairdresser asks her what brand of shampoo she uses. He then puts some of her hairs under a microscope and shows her that there is a white film on the hairs. He recommends that she buy the store's brand of shampoo rather than the one she has been using.

What would be some good questions for her to ask herself about this situation?

1.7 **Group activity.** Individually write out some factors that you see as impediments to developing your own critical-thinking skills. Then, prioritize the list, choosing that factor that is the greatest impediment for you.

Sit in groups of four. Person A begins, explaining how that factor is an impediment for him or her and giving a good example. Proceed through person B, C, and D in the same way. Discuss the extent to which all four share the same impediments.

Then, the whole group should focus on Person A's impediment. Together, try to devise a practical strategy to counteract some of the influence that impediment has on critical thinking. Do the same for each group member.

1.8 Without looking back in the book, explain how SEE-I works to make your thinking clearer.

1.9 On page 2, you described a situation in which you thought through something critically, and another in which you did not think through something critically.

For each, what criteria did you use to decide? That is, what earmarks of the first situation told you that it was an example of good thinking? And what earmarks of the second situation told you that you did not think it through critically?

1.10 Look back at page 21, at the list of educational practices that the text says discourage critical thinking. Which of those practices seem "right" to you? That is, which of them seem to you to be a genuine way education should be? Why?

Then address this question: How could the practices listed actually get in the way of learning to think better within the discipline?

1.11 Name three things you have seen in movies that tend to give people a distorted view of the world. Discuss how they are misleading. Give an example of each.

Now, name three things you have seen in movies that have been seriously misleading for *you*. Explain briefly how they were misleading.

1.12 Watch a segment of a news program on TV or look at the news section of newspaper. Make a list of the news events reported there. Now make a list of events that could have been reported on, but weren't. In your best judgment, what criteria did the news compilers use to select the particular events they reported on?

1.13 It is one of those days when people seem to be driving erratically. Far more than usual, people are cutting you off, slamming on their brakes unexpectedly, or driving too slow. What are some good hypotheses to explain the way people are driving?

1.14 **In the discipline.** Look again at the impediments to critical thinking discussed in this chapter. (Eight major ones are listed.) Choose three and describe how they might be impediments for learning the discipline or subject matter of this course in a critical-thinking way.

1.15 In a book about how the sense of taste and smell work, the author explains that if you get sick and nauseated after eating a certain food, you will probably have an aversion to that food for a long time afterward. She notes that this is true even if the food you ate had nothing in fact to do with your getting sick. She says: "Intellectually knowing that it isn't a particular food that has made one sick does not override the instinct to avoid it .... The 'irrational' override of intellectual knowledge is based on our primeval past."[9] *Is* it "irrational?"

1.16 The topic of Chapter 2 is the elements of reasoning. Three of those elements are *conclusions*, *assumptions*, and *points of view*. Think of a difficult situation in your life, a problem in your relationship with someone, a decision you have to make, or something important about this course. Formulate three good questions about that situation, using each of the three elements listed. Then answer the questions, as well as you can.

1.17 Near the end of this book (pages 175–176), there is a brief discussion of some of the traits that are part of being a critical thinker. Read the descriptions of the traits there, and then focus on intellectual courage. Go deep: Look for a good example of how intellectual courage will be needed for you to think critically within the discipline you are studying, an example of when it will require courage for you to take ownership of some of the concepts or conclusions or points of view in the discipline. If you find a good example, describe it, including the role intellectual courage would play. If you can't find an example, write a paragraph considering the possibility that you are not taking the discipline seriously enough to believe the results.

1.18 **Work in pairs.** Each person chooses one written answer to an exercise in this chapter. (Alternatively, you could choose a written answer you gave to a critical-thinking problem about the discipline.)

Exchange papers with the person next to you. Each of you then writes comments on the reasoning in the other person's paper. Return the papers.

What can you learn about your paper from what the other person has said? What can you learn about what the other person values?

1.19 Group work. Use the template on pages 34–35 to address the topic of critical thinking as you understand it so far.

- Gather with four or five people to discuss the topic critically.
- In a discussion, figure out the three most central organizing concepts that underlie the conception of critical thinking being presented in this book. Try to come to consensus, but if you can't, use your own.
- Write out an SEE-I for each and a paragraph on how they work and fit together. Make duplicates for everyone.
- Each person critiques the responses of the others in the group. Focus on two standards: → (a) Are the responses clearly stated? → (b) Are they accurate?

DAILY PRACTICE
At incorporating critical thinking into your life and your learning

Two of the difficulties in learning to think critically are dramatically different from one another. The first is how to do it: how to acquire the skills of asking good questions, reasoning your way through them, and believing the results of your reasoning. One way to look at this book is as a guide for developing those skills.

The second difficulty is deeper, harder to reckon with: as you learn *how* to do it, you actually have to *do* it. Even *after* you acquire skills, your tendency may well be to let them slide, to engage in them only when given a specific assignment.

A subsection of the exercises at the end of each chapter is designed to help you incorporate critical thinking into your life and learning in a more ongoing way. (Here, it's Exercises 1.20 through 1.24.) The key to these is to do them as often as possible, daily if you can, in small repeated intervals, rather than in a single big burst of effort. It's like daily exercise—only this is mental exercise. Thus, spending ten intense, focused minutes per day on practicing applying the critical-thinking concepts to your life and learning will be more effective than spending the same number of minutes all crowded into a single day.

1.20 **Engage with questions.** Spend some time just noticing questions, and then writing them down in your journal. You can notice (a) asked questions: ones you ask, other people ask, questions in print or on TV. Get a feel for the places and times where people ask questions and the kind of questions they ask. But notice also (b) the questions that are not asked: write down examples you come across where questions would have made a difference, where they should have been asked, but weren't. That includes places where you should have been asking questions.

1.21 **Engage with reasoning.** Again, this is an exercise in noticing, and then in critical writing about what you notice. In your journal, write down examples of good reasoning, bad reasoning, and non-reasoning that you come across. Again, these can be on TV, in ads, in what people say, in what you say, anywhere. The goal is to start using the concept of reasoning as you observe what's around you.

1.22 **Engage with believing the results.** Spend some time noticing and recording examples where people (including you) don't believe the results of their reasoning. These will usually be most apparent when people's actions are at odds with what they say they believe.

1.23 **Confront the impediments to critical thinking.** Over a period of a number of days (say, two per day for four days), practice noticing and overcoming the impediments. There are eight major ones mentioned in this chapter. Start with one of them (such as "Forming a picture of the world on the basis of the news media") and identify that kind of thinking when you come across it. But more than that, search out examples: watch the news, ponder how people internalize it and take it for normal; notice things that people say that reflect a view that's based on the news media. That means you will spend at least part of the day being on the alert for that impediment. That's a major part of the exercise. Keep a journal of the examples you find.

Then, do the same with another impediment.

1.24 **Engage with SEE-I.** As you work through this book, you
will often be asked to write out an SEE-I. Extend this idea
on your own. That is, when you are reading this book and
you come across something that is important for critical
thinking, state, elaborate, exemplify and illustrate that point
without being asked to. Do this with other books also, in
other courses as well as this one.

Then extend it farther. Use an SEE-I in some other class
where there is written work. It can be a paper you are writing, an essay exam response, a presentation you are making.
Try actually using the key words: after you state a point you
are making, say "In other words ...," "For example ..." and
"It's like ...." Notice how it makes your writing richer, more
substantive, and clearer.

Chapter 2
The Elements of Reasoning

Critical thinking is not the same as thinking. Thinking is any activity in which you process things with your mind. So, forming a closely reasoned judgment after paying close attention to the evidence is an example of thinking. But so is jumping to a conclusion without considering any evidence. Similarly, weighing both sides of an issue and carefully checking for biases are both examples of thinking. But so is stubbornly holding on to prejudices and using stereotypes to judge people.

Although all four descriptions are examples of thinking and reasoning, only the first and third are examples of *critical* thinking. Two conditions are necessary for critical thinking. First, the thinking has to be reflective; it has to involve thinking-about-my-thinking. Second, this reflective thinking must meet high standards; it must be reflective reasoning that is done well. This chapter focuses on the elements of our thinking. When we reflect on our thinking, the elements are what we reflect *about*.

The Nuts and Bolts of Critical Thinking

There are at least two or three dozen basic concepts in critical thinking, maybe as many as 50. The most central concepts number around 20 and can be grouped into 8 categories. These are called the *elements of reasoning*.

Some of these concepts map out very different aspects of critical thinking; some overlap and are closely related to one another. Being able to think critically means being able to use these elements as tools in your thinking—being able to use them with sensitivity and the knowledge of how they interact. By using them with the standards described in Chapter 4, you can produce thinking that is reliable and trustworthy (though not infallible).

Let's look briefly at an example of an element: conclusions. This is a central concept of critical thinking. When we reason, we draw conclusions. We want to draw reasonable conclusions, not unreasonable ones. That is, we want to draw conclusions that are *accurate*, that have *sufficient* evidence to back them up, and that are *relevant* to the issue we are investigating. (Accuracy, sufficiency, and relevance are *standards* for using the element *conclusions*.)

Notice how thinking in terms of *conclusions* changes our thinking, makes it more reflective, more critical. It starts to lead us logically from step to step. Someone says something and you realize, "That's a conclusion." Then you are led to the next question, "Well, since it's a conclusion, what is it based on?" When you ask that, you don't necessarily mean to be skeptical. The conclusion might be based on excellent evidence. But calling it a conclusion brings home the idea that it's not an absolute, not a given. It is a result of human reasoning and based on some evidence, some information. Now, that leads you to two more questions: "Well, since it's a conclusion based on evidence, is that evidence accurate?" and "Is the evidence it's based on enough to support this conclusion?" Just thinking it out this far puts you deep in the process of critical thinking.

The Elements of Reasoning

Figure 2.1 is a chart of the elements of reasoning.[1] (Compare it to the overview in Figure 1.3 on page 37.) Each of the eight wedges shown in Figure 2.1 is an element of reasoning. Whenever we reason through anything, all eight are always present. Thus in any piece of reasoning, you can reflect on any or all of those eight and be assured of finding them there. In addition to the eight elements, the chart also contains *context* and *alternatives*. *Context* is the background to the reasoning rather than being literally an element in

FIGURE 2.1   *The circle of elements.*

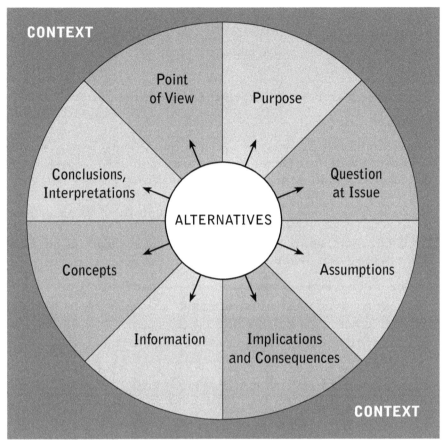

it, and *alternatives* encompass the different choices that could be made in the reasoning. Whenever we reason through anything, there is always a context in which the reasoning takes place, and there are alternatives that shape it.

The eight elements plus context and alternatives are called the 8+ elements. They are arranged in a circle, but they are not numbered because there is no required order. The order in which it is most beneficial to apply them depends on the question being addressed.

For each of the 8+ elements, this book will be saying roughly the same three things. It will first introduce the element and give you a sense of how that element is present in all our reasoning. Second, it will illustrate how identifying that element in many contexts is essential to thinking critically. Third, it will describe briefly a number of other critical-thinking activities that center on that element.

The initial description of each element is abstract, but the examples that follow will make the abstract more concrete. Try to get a feel for each element, for its flexibility and usefulness. Each of the elements is essential, and each can furnish you with insight into the heart of the subject you are reasoning about.

Purpose (objectives, goals, desired outcome, intention, function)

Whenever we reason, we do so with a purpose. People have goals and objectives in all their activities, in their reading, writing, decision making, in the things they make intentionally (books, theories, equations, cars, advertisements, etc.). All have purposes. Therefore, it's always relevant to ask, "What is the purpose in that?" You can identify the purpose of anything that involves reasoning.

Flexibility: Here is a small selection of areas where you can identify purpose. For example, you can:

■ Identify the author's purpose in an assigned essay
■ Identify your own goals in reading it
■ Ask, "What is the purpose of this experiment?"
■ Identify the purpose of all homework assignments
■ Ask why this case study is being presented
■ List your main goals in a term paper you are writing
■ Figure out your goals in your relationship with a close friend

Notice how it is always relevant and central to ask questions like these. With practice, thinking about purpose can become a constant in your reasoning, and it will often bring insight.

Question: What is the *purpose* of the course or discipline you are studying?

All the examples just listed have to do with *identifying* a purpose in something. But the concept of purpose has other uses as well. You can not only identify your purpose:

→ You can keep it firmly in mind as you work through a whole host of details. That can be difficult to do—seeing the forest while looking at the trees.
→ You can question your purpose, or an author's purpose, asking whether it is worth achieving, and at what cost.
→ You can compare my goals to yours, or one textbook's goals to another's.

Thus, purpose serves as a center for asking a host of relevant, reflective questions, as well as for performing a large number of higher-order thinking activities.

Question at Issue (problem, topic, "the point," "Q at I")

Whenever we reason through something, we are trying to answer some question or address some problem. So in any act of reasoning, ask, "What is the question at issue? What is the problem being addressed?"

If *purpose* is what you are trying to accomplish, the question at issue (q at i) is the more specific question you are addressing to achieve that purpose. The purpose of this book, for example, is to guide people to think their way critically through a subject. By contrast, the question at issue is "What is the best way to help people accomplish that?" Since all reasoning is about some question, it's always relevant to ask what is the question being addressed.

Flexibility: Here are some areas where you can identify questions. For example, you can:

- Ask, "What is the question at issue this author is addressing?"
- Ask, "What, specifically, is the problem being addressed in this piece of art criticism?"
- Identify the major questions at issue in this math problem, in this marketing strategy, in this physical education exercise
- State the question at issue you are addressing in writing a term paper
- See the point of a cartoon

Questions are vital to all critical thinking. The central question of a course (see pages 106–109) is vital to critical thinking in a discipline.

Question: What are two important questions at issue in the course or discipline you are studying. What is a question about your life that the discipline may help you understand?

Notice that in any area that involves thinking, there is a question at issue, and you can identify it. In addition, after you *identify* a question at issue, you might have to go further:

→ You can ask, "What *other* questions at issue need to be addressed? What major questions have been left out?"
→ When you identify the question at issue in a term paper you are writing, also be mindful and stay focused on that question all the way through.

→ You can create a set of guideline questions on a topic or for reading a chapter.

→ A good pro-active question to ask is, "If I try to solve this problem this way, what further problems are likely to arise?"

All of these are rich ways to explore your thinking and the thinking of others, and all of them revolve around the element *question at issue*. As with each of the elements, to learn how to answer questions like these is to develop a range of higher-order thinking skills.

Assumptions (background theory, what is given or what is taken for granted, axioms)

Whenever you reason through something, you always have to begin somewhere. You can't "begin at the beginning" because there is no beginning. What you begin with are your assumptions, everything you take for granted when you think through something. Sometimes people can state their assumptions up front. More often, though, the most crucial assumptions we make are those that are unstated. In fact, it is often a major insight to identify assumptions an author may be unaware of even though they underlie his or her reasoning.

Any area where reasoning is taking place is an area where it is important to identify assumptions. If you are having an argument with your friends, maybe a heated argument, a good question to ask is, "What are their main assumptions?" But it is at least as important to ask, "What are my own assumptions?"—and to hold yourself to the same standards you apply to your friends.

If you're doing a writing assignment, it is crucial to ask, "What assumptions am I making about the person who will read this?" Whether you ask this question or not, you automatically do make assumptions about the reader. The critical-thinking question is not whether you *make* assumptions—we all do that all the time. The critical-thinking question is whether you are *aware* of the assumptions you're making. Only by becoming aware of your assumptions can you then evaluate them, so you can be more in charge of your thinking.

Flexibility: You can find (or identify) assumptions in anything that involves reasoning. For example, you can:

■ Identify the assumptions an author is making

■ Ask, "What is the background theory to keep in mind while formulating this political science questionnaire?"

■ Identify the assumptions behind the famous Milgram experiment

■ Describe your assumptions in designing a health plan

■ With your family, identify your mutual assumptions about how and when it is appropriate to express anger with one another

Question: What are two important assumptions in this course? If you take the discipline seriously, is there a personal assumption you make about your life that might be challenged?

So far we have been talking about *identifying* assumptions, but you can reflect critically on assumptions in any number of other ways:

→ You can evaluate people's assumptions in the light of evidence.

→ You can compare your assumptions to other people's.

→ You can put people's assumptions (including your own) in a larger context, asking how they are rooted in their upbringing or their cultural background.

→ You can seek out others with different assumptions as a way of becoming more aware of your own.

Assumptions, then, like all the elements, serve as a core idea around which to investigate a large number of critical-thinking questions.

Sometimes we are told, "Never make assumptions," "Don't assume anything," or "When you ASSUME, you make an ASS of U and ME. So don't assume."

But that advice makes no sense. We *have to* make assumptions. The speaker of the advice above is *assuming* that the hearers follow the play on words, that they care, that advice can help, and so on. It is *impossible* to avoid making assumptions.

We don't need to stop making assumptions: we need to check our assumptions to see if they are reasonable.

What are two areas of your life where you need to check your assumptions?

Implications and Consequences (what follows, costs and benefits)

Just as your reasoning has to begin somewhere, it also has to end somewhere. The area *beyond* where it ends constitutes the implications and consequences of your reasoning. To ask about the implications and consequences of a piece of reasoning is to ask, "What *follows* from it?" If you have a certain position on capital punishment, you need to ask, "What are the implications of that position?" That is, what further things must I adhere to if I hold that position? What further beliefs does this commit me to?

Flexibility: Consider a few of the many areas where you can identify implications and consequences. For example, you can:

- Identify the consequences, both positive and negative, of making this decision rather than that one
- Ask, "What are the costs and benefits of implementing this marketing strategy?"
- List the implications noted by the authors of a case study
- Identify the implications of creating a design, of not following a schedule, of consistently being late for classes

Question: What are two implications or consequences of the discipline you are studying? How might your learning in this course have implications and consequences in your life?

But to think critically, you need to become skillful at handling implications and consequences in ways that go beyond simply identifying them:

- In most real-world situations, consequences are seldom automatic, so you need to do something more subtle: not just *identify* consequences of an action, but *assess* the likelihood of various possible consequences, few of which are certain.
- Because many decisions have both a plus-side and a minus-side, you need to be able to weigh the costs and benefits of decisions.
- You sometimes have to accept the unwelcome implications of your positions.

Focusing on the element of *implications and consequences* allows you to see aspects of situations and thought processes that, previously, you saw only occasionally, in a hit-or-miss sort of way. This element allows you to focus on something that is one of the keys to reasoning well, to taking charge of your thinking.

Each of the elements in fact functions in this way. As you get better at internalizing them and using them, they will change how you

CRITICAL WRITING: SEE-I.

You have just read through sections on four of the elements of reasoning (purpose, question at issue, assumptions, implications and consequences). Close your book. For each element, write out an SEE-I: state, elaborate, give a good example, and illustrate it.

think about your life as well as about the subject matter you are studying in school.

Information (data, evidence, observations)

Whenever you reason, you use information. Therefore, it always makes sense to ask, "What information is relevant to this issue?" You might ask, "What information do I have, and what information do I not have, but *need*?"

Flexibility: Here is a sample of ways you can look for information. For example, you can:

- Identify the information the author of an article supplies and the information the author omits
- List the data an experiment yields
- Ask, "What evidence do I have to back up my claim?"
- Describe what you observe about these cells in the microscope
- Identify the main observations you've made about the children in this special education setting

Question: What are the main sources you will use to gather information in this course or discipline? What is another reliable source you *could* use (but won't)?

Notice that people use information even when they reason badly through an issue. People who draw prejudiced conclusions often base their reasoning on incomplete or incorrect information. So you often need to do more than simply identify the information in a piece of reasoning:

→ You need to be able to evaluate both information and sources of information.
→ You need to distinguish information from your interpretation of that information.
→ You need to decide when you need more information to draw a reasonable conclusion.
→ You can learn how to find other reliable pieces of information on a topic.
→ You can organize information in a coherent way, and present it clearly.

Information is an essential element of reasoning. But information by itself is seldom enough to decide important issues. We need the other elements of reasoning just as much. If you know some information, but you don't know its implications, you can be seriously misled even by the facts. If you know some information, but you don't know the questions at issue that the information is relevant to, then the information just floats in your memory, like pieces of trivia.

Concepts (organizing ideas, categories)

All reasoning exists in terms of concepts. If you are reasoning about democracy in America, you have a concept of *democracy* that is operative in your thinking. It is part of being reflective to ask, "What is my concept of *democracy*? What is my understanding of that term?" If you are trying to figure out whether an office is running efficiently, it helps to step back from that question and ask, "What is my concept of *efficiency* here? What earmarks do I use to decide whether an office is running efficiently?"

The same is true with less familiar concepts like real numbers, or cognitive dissonance, or iambic pentameter. A major goal of courses in a field is to help students grasp its most important concepts. Teachers and texts often try to accomplish this by using definitions. Thus an environmental science text defines *biotic potential* as "Reproductive capacity—The potential of a species for increasing its population and/or distribution."[2] But it's important to realize that the definition is a means to an end, not an end in itself. To grasp it, you must understand both how a species increases its population or distribution, and how that increase is limited by factors such as food, water, predation, and disease. Thus a good question to ask yourself about important but unfamiliar terms is, "What is my *understanding* of the concept that term represents?"

One helpful way to look at concepts is to describe them using a word or a term rather than a sentence. Thus *honesty* is a concept, whereas "Honesty is the best policy" is an assumption rather than a concept. The *Treaty of Versailles* is a concept (of course, it is also a document), whereas "The Treaty of Versailles formed the peace terms of World War I" is a piece of information rather than a concept. Why is that important? Because that difference is the feature that allows concepts to be so versatile, to be usable in a wide variety of contexts. You can use the concept of honesty or the Treaty of Versailles to think through hundreds of important problems. The sentences containing these concepts, however, are far more specific and therefore usable in a much more limited set of contexts.

It is a considerable skill to learn to identify the main concepts in our reasoning. It is very similar to identifying assumptions, and it is difficult in much the same way. Just as we tend to make unexamined assumptions, we use unexamined concepts also. If I have the inner conviction that I've been treated unfairly, it doesn't often lead me to ask, "What is my concept of fairness? What do I mean when I classify this action as unfair?" For example, I can feel an action to be unfair simply when I've been hurt by it. If I don't then go on to explore the concept of fairness that is at work in my reaction, I may continue to draw the conclusion that I've been unfairly treated even when it is just bad luck.

Flexibility: Consider some areas where you can identify *concepts*. For example, you can:

- Identify the concepts that an argument turns on
- List the main concepts in a scientific theory
- Spell out the key concepts that define historical or artistic epochs
- Identify the most fundamental and powerful concepts in the discipline you are studying (see pages 101–104)
- Identify your concept of being a loving father, mother, daughter, son, spouse

Question: What are three main concepts or organizing ideas in this course or discipline? How might one of these concepts give you insight into your life?

In addition to identifying concepts,

→ You can refine your concepts.
→ You can compare and contrast different concepts.
→ You can amend your concepts in response to new situations.
→ You can create concepts to cover new cases.

Notice again that concepts are always present in everyone's thinking. Every single thought you have is guided by concepts. The question for the critical thinker, then, is not whether you are using concepts, but whether you are aware of the concepts you're using.

Conclusions, Interpretations (inferences, solutions, decisions arrived at)

To think about the world you live in is to interpret it, to draw conclusions about it. So it's always relevant to ask, "How are you interpreting this?" "What conclusions are being drawn?"

Flexibility: There are conclusions to be found in all reasoning. For example, you can:

- Identify your interpretation of this situation, this poem, this philosophical issue, this equation, this anything
- Clearly state the conclusion of an argument you are making

- Ask, "What is the inference this author is making?"
- Figure out solutions (or partial solutions) to problems in your life

Question: What are two major conclusions experts have come to in this discipline? If you took the subject matter in this course to heart, how might you interpret events in your life differently as a result?

It is often vitally important in critical thinking to distinguish information from someone's *interpretation* of that information. We see people's faces (information) and we interpret the look we see there as anger, maybe as anger at *us*. But we can easily be mistaken in that *conclusion*. The person may be feeling sad or tired rather than angry, or the person may indeed be angry but at something that has nothing to do with us. People who diagnose patients need to be constantly aware of the information they are receiving about the patient and also of their interpretation of that information. They then need to reflect on their interpretation and question whether alternative interpretations are more plausible.

In addition to *identifying* interpretations and conclusions, to be an effective critical thinker you need to develop other skills centering on this element:

→ You need to compare your interpretation of a situation to the interpretations given by others.
→ You need to decide which interpretations are most reasonable.
→ You need to be able to contextualize interpretations: the distinction between information and interpretation depends heavily on context. (For example, when a beginner looks through a microscope, the data might be the fuzzy orangish blob she sees, and the interpretation might be that it is a cell. For a more advanced practitioner, the data might be that she sees a cell, pure and simple, and the interpretation might be that the cell is beginning to undergo mitosis.)
→ You can group a set of interpretations to see how they all follow from an underlying background system. (For example, evolutionary biologists interpret the hibernation of bears, the day-long lifespan of a mayfly, or the shape and size of a palm frond—indeed, almost all plant and animal characteristics—in terms of how that characteristic increases the organism's chances at reproductive success.)

You are constantly drawing conclusions—so is everyone else—based on what you observe (information), on the beliefs you carry (assumptions), on what you think will happen (implications and consequences). Conceptualizing your own thoughts (and those of others) as conclusions gives you an insight into what those conclusions are based on.

Point of View (frame of reference, perspective)

Whenever we reason through something, we do so within some point of view. So it always makes sense to ask, "From what point of view am I addressing this issue?" Addressing the same question from a different point of view can produce a whole different set of purposes, assumptions, conclusions, and so on.

It is sometimes difficult to distinguish point of view from assumptions. Indeed, the two often overlap. For example, to have a conservative's point of view on a political issue is to make certain assumptions about the importance of promoting free enterprise and reducing the role of government. But point of view is often quite distinct from assumptions. For example, consider psychological point of view: if you write your name in the blanks below, you'll end up with an accurate (and sometimes profound) sentence:

_____ is at the *center* of my point of view. Everything I think about is from the point of view of _____'s mind.

But the uniqueness of your psychological point of view does not necessarily mean you making the assumption that your point of view is more valid than other people's.

At least one point of view is distinctly relevant to the course you are taking, and that is the point of view of the discipline itself. If it's a course in sociology, you will be expected to address most questions from a sociological point of view—not, usually, from a biological, religious, personal, business, or even an ethical point of view. These may be relevant, and they may well be extremely important. But they are different points of view from a purely sociological one. It is important to think about sociological findings from an ethical point of view, and in many cases, sociologists contend that an ethical perspective should in fact take priority over a sociological one. However, the two points of view are distinct, and you should be able to think in terms of either. Learning to think from the point of view of a discipline is one of the most valuable outcomes a course in the discipline can provide (see pages 112–114). The goal of a course is not simply to provide you with new facts to fit into your old point of view; it is to provide you with new perspectives, fresh and reputable points of view you can use to see things in a way you couldn't before.

That is not the end of the matter, however. Part of being a critical thinker is having the ability to bring to bear a variety of relevant points of view. This is addressed directly in multidisciplinary courses, which explicitly require thinking from the points of view of several disciplines. But identifying multidisciplinary points of view is valuable even within a course in a single discipline.

Flexibility: Consider places where it would be useful to identify points of view. For example, you can:

- Identify the points of view of different characters in a drama or story
- Identify the audience's point of view in a report you are writing
- Ask, "What is my teacher's point of view on absences, academic integrity, completing homework assignments?"
- Describe an argument from your spouse's (parent's, child's, friend's) perspective

Question: How would you briefly describe the point of view of the course or discipline you are studying? How could you use this course to enrich your personal point of view on the world?

In addition to identifying points of view, you need to develop other, related skills:

→ You can think within someone's point of view, applying it to new situations.

→ You can contrast the nursing point of view with the patient's point of view—also with the point of view of the doctor, the hospital, the patient's family, the insurance company. Some of these are always relevant. Others are relevant in one case but not in another.

→ A major critical-thinking skill to develop is the ability to evaluate points of view. Clearly it is not enough just to know what my point of view is. Bigots, for example, sometimes openly admit that they look at things from a bigoted point of view. (They sometimes even seem proud of it!) Obviously, that is not

CRITICAL WRITING: SEE-I.

Close your book. For each of the four elements you have just read about (information, concepts, conclusion, point of view), write out an SEE-I. This may reveal to you what you are clear and unclear about.

an example of critical thinking. Once I've identified a point of view on an issue, my own or anyone's, I need to evaluate how plausible it is, how well it fits the evidence, how biased it is.

Alternatives (other possibilities, options, choices)

Whenever you reason, there are alternatives. One of the great benefits of learning to think critically is that you gain the freedom of having alternatives to your normal ways of approaching things.

Flexibility: The search for alternatives applies to each of the elements we've discussed.

- If you have a purpose, ask, "What alternative purpose should I be trying to accomplish instead?" or "What other purpose can I accomplish *in addition?*"
- If you are reasoning through a question at issue, ask, "What other questions at issue should I be considering?"
- You can also ask, "What alternative assumptions could I make?" "What other sources of information could I consult?" and so forth, for each of the elements.

Each of the elements of reasoning is empowering, but thinking about the elements in terms of *alternatives* is empowering in a more direct way. *Thinking outside the box* means envisioning alternatives where before there seemed to be only the sides of the box. Getting in the habit of searching for alternatives allows us to see many potential paths ahead of us, where before there seemed to be only one. Both psychologically and practically, this is empowering:

- You can identify alternative ways of reasoning through experiments, health-care issues, information systems, math or business problems—through anything.

    Question: What are two alternative paths or choices you could pursue within the course or discipline you are studying? What alternative choices in your life might this course open up for you?

For most people, simply *seeing* alternatives (where there seemed to be none before) opens paths for them, puts doors in the sides of the box. But, in addition to *identifying* alternatives:

- You need to be able to think your way down alternative possible paths, and then compare them before deciding which path is the best one to follow.
- You need to cultivate the ability to live with ambiguity, realizing there are multiple paths you could follow.

■ You need to see that you can combine alternatives, that a third possibility might allow you to accomplish both of two seemingly irreconcilable courses of action.

For example, it often seems as though we have to choose: either fight for our own point of view or give in to the other person's. There are, however, usually alternatives that are different from either choice: discuss the issue; ask for what we need (rather than demanding it); compromise; find the good in the other person's point of view; take turns; seek arbitration; let the other person prevail, but do so out of generosity rather than giving in.

There is also something else to live with once you start taking alternatives seriously. In all major events in your life or in your thinking, there are likely to be alternative reasonable paths to follow, and each one will have its own consequences, both positive and negative. Therefore, it is unusual for any one path to accomplish all you wish for. If you choose to major in English, you give up other fields you may well be interested in. If you have a long-term relationship with X, even when you find a good deal of happiness, you automatically give up other possible futures. When doctors operate on patients unsuccessfully, the consciousness that other paths could have been followed can be a source of deep guilt (even if they chose the one that was most reasonable beforehand). It might be nice if we didn't feel guilt or regret or the loss of other directions our life might have taken, but that's not the way our minds work. We humans do have such feelings. And telling ourselves that we shouldn't feel what we in fact do feel is unreasonable—both because it's unproductive and because it involves denying reality. So:

→ We need to develop the ability—one that involves emotions in a strong way—to give up desired alternative paths, accepting that it's often important to grieve for paths we could not follow.

Context (setting, background)

We do not reason in a vacuum. Our reasoning always takes place in a context, and the question at issue always exists within that context. So it is always relevant to ask, "What is the context in which this reasoning is being done?"

Flexibility: It is beneficial to identify context in innumerable areas. For example, you can:

■ Identify the personal histories that led writers to produce their work
■ Identify the path that brought you to your present point of view
■ Ask in what context a drama is being performed, an experiment is being carried out, a managerial decision is being made

■ Describe some of the different backgrounds of students in a diverse classroom

Question: What are two contexts that are relevant to understanding the course or discipline you are studying? How could you incorporate the findings of this discipline into the context of your life?

In addition to identifying the context, you may need to exercise other critical-thinking skills as well:

→ You can gather more information about the context.
→ You can compare the political backgrounds of John Adams and Thomas Jefferson.
→ You can spell out the context to someone who is unfamiliar with it.
→ You can ask, "How does the context of the writing make the writer *not* address certain questions?"

The following is a list of some of the main contexts that you may need to consider when reasoning through a particular question:

■ historical   ■ scientific
■ economic   ■ personal
■ cultural   ■ social
■ linguistic

This completes the quick survey of the 8+ elements from the circle shown in Figure 2.1. A major critical-thinking activity is to *go around the circle*: that is, to analyze a question, problem, or topic in terms of the 8+ elements and synthesize them to see the logic of how they fit together.

A Visualization

Here's a way to visualize the elements. It's only one of many you could construct yourself.

You are on a journey. Picture yourself walking down a path. It is the path of inquiry.

Ahead of you, where you can see it in the distance, is your *purpose*.

You think about why you are headed there, how far it will be, whether it will be worth it: your *questions at issue*.

Behind you, where you came from, are your *assumptions*.

Your mind-set, as you walk the path, is your *point of view*—it's the frame of reference you use to view the things around you.

The whole environment around you is the *context*.

As you walk, you gather *information* about the world—about the path ahead, about the forests and mountains you see, about the breeze you feel, about the friends you meet on the road, the beautiful places and the obstacles that lie ahead.

You gather that information by taking your impressions and classifying them according to the *concepts* you carry with you: "path," "mountain," "breeze," "friend." Some parts of the landscape you conceptualize as "places of beauty" or as "obstacles."

What will happen to you as you journey down the path can be pictured as *implications and consequences*: you will reach your goal, or you won't; you'll travel on afterward; you'll feel tired; you'll be excited; you'll encounter old friends.

You draw *conclusions* as you travel: you conclude you will reach your goal before nightfall, that the path will be longer than you assumed. You *interpret* your journey as an important one in your life.

You think of all the other paths you could be walking, the other goals you could be heading toward, the *alternatives* that still lie before you.

Three Additional Elements of Reasoning

Three other elements must be mentioned. They are not explicitly in the circle because they overlap categories. Still, they are important concepts in critical thinking.

Reasons

Reasoning can be defined as drawing conclusions on the basis of reasons. So, reasons are always present when someone is reasoning. It's crucially important to identify reasons: "What reasons do I have for my beliefs on this issue?" "What reasons does this author give for her conclusions?"

Reasons is a much broader category than the other elements of reasoning. Reasons can include pieces of *information, assumptions*, and *interpretations and conclusions* someone has come to on other grounds—almost any of the elements.

Claims (judgments)

People who teach courses specifically on critical thinking tend to emphasize the word *claim* a great deal, and it's a useful term to get in the habit of using. It is a very general word. It has roughly the same meaning as the term *judgment*. The terms *claim* and *judgment* overlap all the other elements. When I say, "This is my *purpose*," "This is the *question at issue*," "These are the *assumptions* I am making," and so on—all of these are *claims*. People can make claims about anything, and (except for questions and commands) most of what you read and hear consists of claims.

Aristotle says that humans are rational animals—that is, he makes the *claim* that humans are rational animals. Notice how explicitly calling it a claim—rather than just describing it as what Aristotle says—helps you think about it in a slightly different way. Calling it a claim holds it up before your mind as something to be wondered about: What reasons did Aristotle have for making that claim? Is it true that humans are rational animals?

To call something a claim does not necessarily call it into question, but it does leave the statement *open* to question. It reminds us that we can ask further questions about the evidence for believing the statement, how to interpret it, and what significance it has. That is why *claim* and *judgment* are such useful critical-thinking terms.

> Run your finger down three or four pages in your textbook. Pick out some sentences that are important. (Don't pick incidental statements or mere examples the author is providing.) Describe those sentences to yourself as *facts*. Then describe those sentences to yourself as *claims*. When you describe them as claims, you should notice that you no longer take the statements as absolutes. What questions about those specific sentences arise in your mind when you call them claims?

Hypothesis

The term *hypothesis* is a central part of reasoning in the sciences. It does not play such a prominent role in other fields (though perhaps it should). A hypothesis is a type of assumption that I make or a conclusion that I draw, usually about the way a situation will turn out, but I hold it tentatively while waiting to see whether the situation will turn out the way I thought it would, waiting to see whether my hypothesis will be confirmed or disconfirmed, often by experimentation.

This is a fairly formal use of the term *hypothesis*, but actually we form hypotheses all the time in our thinking. We may not call them hypotheses, but we make predictions about how things will work out, and then we check to see if they do work out that way. If they do, then we usually conclude we were right; if they don't, we (at least sometimes) conclude we were wrong.

Being reflective means recognizing the hypotheses you are making. When you read a novel or watch a movie, you make predictions about what will happen and how characters will change. When you read a textbook attentively, you do the same kind of thing: you have a tentative awareness of where you think the book is heading. When you write, you make hypotheses about how the reader will understand what you are saying. So critical writers pay a lot of attention to feedback about their writing because that allows them to refine their writing in the light of whether their hypotheses were confirmed.

We are unaware of most of the hypotheses we make in our day-to-day living. A major part of becoming a critical thinker, however, is becoming aware of how you think. That is the process of reflection. Reflection helps you take control of your habitual patterns of thinking, rather than letting the habitual patterns control you. John Maynard Keynes said, "When somebody persuades me that I am wrong, I change my mind. What do *you* do?"

A Misleading Element: Facts

The term *fact* is not in the list of elements. Facts fall under information, but habitually using the word *fact* can do a disservice to critical thinking. Pieces of information we are very certain about we often call "facts." We believe they have been proved. These are usually pieces of information that seem to us to be completely unproblematic. For example, it's a fact that Neil Armstrong was the first person to walk on the moon, that smoking causes lung cancer, that Michelangelo sculpted the statue *David*, that Lee surrendered at Appomattox, that I like chocolate ice cream, that A got angry when B insulted him. There is nothing automatically uncritical about using the word *fact*, as long as we do it carefully.

Still, it's a term that tends to shut down inquiry rather than promoting it, and it tends to conceal problematic aspects of those claims that are labeled facts. In the previous list of facts, all are (as far as I know) true, but the second, fourth, and sixth facts have something problematic about them. Smoking does cause lung cancer, but calling it a "fact" may hide the *statistical* nature of the claim; it does not necessarily mean that everyone who smokes will get the disease, and therefore it cannot be refuted by giving examples of people who managed to smoke to a ripe old age. It means that a significant percentage of those who smoke will have a greater chance of developing lung cancer, and at an earlier age, than those who do not smoke. Similarly, it is true that Lee surrendered to Grant at Appomattox, but surrendered *what*? The statement, though true, is elliptical: It leaves out an important part and can easily be misleading. Many people draw the conclusion that Lee surrendered the *Confederacy*, but that is not true at all. Similarly, it may be a fact that A got angry when B insulted him. It may be true as far as it goes. However, it may be a *superficial* truth and therefore misleading. We often get angry at insults because the insult connects with some fear we have about ourselves, often a childhood fear. It may be more beneficial to A for him to realize that B's remark tapped into his own pre-existing fears in some way. But if A calls it a *fact*, he tends to close off further exploration of what is really going on inside him.

It is probably better to think of facts as pieces of information that we assume do not require questioning or clarification in the context of a particular discussion.

How to Analyze a Piece of Reasoning Using the Elements

The reasoning you are trying to understand may be written: an argument, a news story, a chapter from a textbook, a novel, a poem, a text message, almost anything. Or the person doing the reasoning may instead be speaking to you. It could be someone you know or someone giving a lecture. The person whose reasoning you are trying to understand may be you.

The point of analysis is to understand, in a fairly deep way, just what the person is saying, how he or she is reasoning through an issue.

The following questions are *guides* only. Sometimes you will have to be flexible and adapt a question to fit the piece of reasoning you are trying to understand. (For example, you may often have to change the singular to the plural, and vice versa. If the questions are phrased one way to understand an argument, you may have to ask them somewhat differently to apply them to a novel or a chapter in a text.) That flexibility is also part of learning to reason well. Sometimes you may need to do an analysis in greater depth and detail, or you may need to focus on different aspects of how the elements enter a piece of reasoning. So some further analysis questions are suggested in parentheses after the basic ones.

Going Around the Circle: The Basic Process of Analysis

1. What is the person's main *purpose* in this piece of reasoning? (Also, what other goals or objectives does the person hope to accomplish in this piece of reasoning?)

2. What is the key *question* or problem the person is addressing? (Also, what are two or three of the most important subsidiary questions at issue?)

3. What is the most important *information* the person is using to reason through this issue? (Also, what other information or data does the person need in this piece of reasoning?)

4. What are the person's major *conclusions*? How is the person *interpreting* this issue? (Also, how does the person answer the main question at issue? What solutions are being offered?)

5. What are the main *concepts* the reasoning depends on? (Also, how does the person understand those concepts? How do those concepts fit together in the person's reasoning?)

6. What are the main *assumptions* the person is making in this piece of reasoning? (Also, what are the crucial stated and unstated assumptions the author is making?)

7. What are the main *implications and consequences* of the person's reasoning? (Also, what are some of the unforeseen consequences of this line of reasoning?)

8. From what *point of view* is the person addressing this question? (Also, what other points of view are necessary to understand this piece of reasoning? What discipline's point of view is being used to address this issue? What other disciplines would help illuminate this reasoning?)

9. What is the *context* of the issue the person is addressing? (Also, what circumstances led up to the issue and to this person's reasoning? What is the background in the discipline [scientific, artistic, cultural, business, sociological, etc.] in which this issue is being addressed?)

10. What *alternatives* are there? (Also, what alternative answers could you reasonably give to the preceding questions? What alternatives are there to the person's reasoning?)

Working with the Elements: The Logic of Something

Becoming a critical thinker means becoming adept at using the elements explicitly and reflectively in your thinking. This involves being able to take a piece of reasoning, your own or someone else's, and analyze it using all 8+ elements from the circle in Figure 2.1. It may seem unrealistic to go through all 8+ elements with respect to every reasoning problem you encounter, but it's a good way to become more proficient in using the elements (and you will quickly get faster at it).

There is another benefit to analyzing a problem in terms of the 8+ elements. Going around the circle displays the *logic* of that problem. The elements, after all, are *parts* of a *whole*. You may notice that as you go around the circle, your responses to the different elements will gear together. Sometimes they will almost seem to repeat the same set of themes. Though the elements are valuable individually, they are even more valuable when you think through a question in terms of how they fit together. So going around the circle involves not just analysis but *synthesis* as well: not just breaking an issue down into its component parts, but also seeing it as an integrated whole.

Some things, however, do not have a logic to them. Their parts don't fit together to make a coherent whole. You can't figure such things out because there is no rhyme or reason to them. Maybe the best you can do in such cases is to memorize individual bits of information. People's first names are like that. You can't look at someone intently and then figure out that her first name is Janis. In cities and towns, street names may or may not have a logic. If Oak Street is followed by Main, that gives no clue as to what the next street is. There is no logic to it. Sometimes, however, there is a logic: if 24th Street is followed by 25th, it doesn't take much effort to figure out what the next street is likely to be. In that situation, street names have a logic.

> Find two examples of topics that have no logic to them. Find two examples of topics that do have a logic to them.

Any reasoning topic has a logic to it, however. This will be especially important to grasp when it comes to analyzing the logic of a discipline (see pages 93–99). Going around the circle is versatile: it applies to any topic, question, or problem in the discipline. Indeed, a central part of understanding a field is developing the ability to think through topics like the following in a deep and thorough way:

- supply and demand
- how to prepare and give a speech
- plate tectonics
- what will happen as global warming continues
- the way the concept of "the frontier" has shaped Americans' view of their country.

Similarly, thinking critically about your personal life means that you think through topics like the following, grasping the logic of them:

- taking this course
- how fears get in the way of your personal growth
- the most effective way for you to study for exams
- why your boss repeatedly takes his anger out on you
- adolescence, gender, race.

In working through the elements, you may need to adapt the way a particular element fits in with the demands of the question being considered. In the previous lists, the items are described in different forms—questions, concepts, topics, incidents, fragments of a thought process—to emphasize how versatile the circle of elements is. There is no magic formula for how to apply the elements uniformly to any question that arises. Making that adaptation is also part of thinking critically.

Analyzing Positions You Disagree With

Sometimes you will be called on to analyze a position that you disagree with deeply. That's an important part of critical thinking because

Take some point of view you deeply disagree with:

- communism,
- al-Qaeda,
- atheism,
- conservatism,

- capitalism
- patriotism
- religion
- liberalism

Analyze it. Go around the circle. Be sure to analyze it in a fair-minded way.

Apply the three tests, especially the second one: An advocate of the point of view (a communist or whatever) should be able to say, "Yes, you have captured it well. That is exactly what I believe in."

before you can evaluate a position reasonably, you have to understand it accurately. Here are three quick tests of whether you have given an accurate, fair-minded analysis of a view you disagree with.

First, no words of evaluation should lurk beneath the surface of your analysis.

Second, a person who holds that position should be able to say, "Yes, you have captured it well. That is exactly what I believe in."

Third, a neutral critical-thinking observer, reading your analysis, should not be able to tell if you agree or disagree with the position. If anything, because you have been empathetic in your analysis, the observer's suspicion should be that you advocate the position (even though, in fact, you may disagree with it deeply).

Example: Thinking Through the Logic of Getting Married

Chris and Sean are considering getting married, and Chris tries to think through the question as deeply as possible. [The italicized remarks in brackets are a critical-thinking commentary on Chris's reasoning.]

Chris starts by asking questions based on each of the elements.

- What is the purpose of marriage?
- To live as full and as satisfying a life as possible, for both of us.

    [*Notice that this would not be everyone's purpose in getting married. Chris's response did not mention children, for example, and the purpose of marriage for many people includes children. Also, notice that Chris could have listed more purposes, not just that one.*]

- What is the main question at issue?
    - Should I marry Sean?
    - Should I marry Sean now?

    [*Chris could have asked other questions, and these might influence subsequent answers: Do I love Sean? How can I tell whether marrying Sean would help us live the happy and satisfying life I want? How can I tell this with good reason, not just an impression?*]

- What are the main assumptions I make about marriage?
    - That it's a commitment to monogamy.
    - That marriage is a lifelong commitment.

    [*This assumption leads Chris to identify a different kind of assumption:*]

    - That we will both grow older, and our looks will change.

    [*Chris is not going through the elements mechanically, without thinking, but as part of a process of genuinely thinking through the idea of marrying Sean. Therefore, Chris takes the time to notice an implication of the last assumption: That though how they look may*]

*be important to both of them, it should not be the crucial factor
if marriage is a lifelong commitment and their looks will change
over time.]*

- What are the main implications and consequences of marrying?
  - First, there is the implication already mentioned, that marriage should not be based too heavily on how we look.
  - There are many legal consequences of marrying someone.
  - Children may or may not be a consequence.

  *[This leads Chris to notice another question at issue: Should
  Sean and I discuss our attitudes toward children (including, maybe,
  adopted children) before we address the question of marriage?]*

  - There will probably be conflicts of interest in the future. In fact, there will probably be some serious conflicts of interest. → It would be especially good to have some psychological tools available to deal with these conflicts when they arise.

  *[Chris wonders if the statement about future conflicts of interest is
  a consequence or an assumption, and decides that in a way it is both:
  The conflicts of interest themselves are a consequence; the claim there
  will be such conflicts of interest is an assumption.]*

- What information do I have (or need to have) about marrying Sean?
  - I have a lot of information about myself: about my likes and dislikes, about my long-term goals, about how I see marriage, about my religious beliefs, about how I was raised.
  - I have a lot of information about Sean as well, but not nearly as much as I have about myself. fi Maybe we should talk about this.
  - I have heard that certain kinds of dysfunctionality run in families. My father was an alcoholic. I really don't know much about Sean's childhood. It would be a good idea to get more information about this so that we know how to deal with problems stemming from our backgrounds as they arise in our marriage.
  - I know I have a certain amount of fear about committing to marriage. → I assume Sean does too. → We should talk about this. We both need more information.
- What are the main concepts I use when I think about marriage?
  - Well, the main one is the concept of marriage itself. What is my idea of marriage? What is involved in being married for me? What is Sean's concept of marriage?

■ What is my concept of *loving someone*? My concept of being *in love*? What do I understand by those terms and how they apply to us?

■ Is *being a friend* part of being married to a person? What do I understand by being a friend?

■ One thing I want with the person I marry is to share unconditional love. But what is unconditional love? Does that mean that I would love the person *no matter what*? That's an extremely broad commitment, and—once I start imagining possible scenarios—a scary prospect to me. Is it even possible to love people no matter what they do?

[*Concepts often influence our behavior below the level of awareness. That is why it's so important to identify the concepts that operate in us. Suppose Chris and Sean had radically different concepts of marriage and were unaware of this. One might have a concept of marriage as, for example, a union that links two whole families, while the other might think of it as being only between two individuals, with their families being completely irrelevant. Because of their different concepts, Sean's behavior with respect to their families might be completely inexplicable to Chris, and vice versa. Both may see their own behavior as entirely appropriate— and the other's behavior as entirely irresponsible.*]

■ What conclusions should I draw? What interpretations am I using?

[*Chris has already come to a number of conclusions while reasoning out the elements so far: the importance of talking about their attitudes toward children, getting some information and tools for conflict resolution, and acknowledging the potential effects of having an alcoholic father. Chris may also be coming to a tentative conclusion (a hypothesis, maybe) that the concept of unconditional love is one that does not apply in marriage.*]

■ Whether to get married to Sean or not is the main conclusion I am trying to decide. But there are more specific conclusions and interpretations as well.

■ That Sean is a loving, caring, affectionate individual.

[*Notice that Chris calls this an interpretation rather than information. Chris's information may be that Sean has acted in a loving, caring, affectionate way before marriage. This is often very different from being a loving, caring, affectionate individual.*]

■ That this is the right time for me to consider marriage seriously.

- That our interests, personalities, and the way we view life are compatible.
- What points of view should I consider?
  - My own, of course: the point of view of someone who has had a certain kind of upbringing, in the society we live in, who has certain expectations and hopes about the future.
  - Sean's.
  - Are there male and female points of view on marriage? → I don't know. Maybe that's just a stereotype.
  - Our families' points of view.
  - Is it important for me to consider society's point of view, or a legal point of view, or a psychological point of view?

    [*It is important to consider other points of view if they are relevant, and if they are likely to give a person insight into the problem being reasoned out. This is often difficult to decide beforehand.*]
- What alternatives are there?
  - Continue as we are now.
  - Decide that marriage is not in the cards for us.
  - My Al-Anon book talks about not forcing solutions: "Instead of redoubling my effort, I can slow down and reassess the situation."[3] That seems reasonable under the circumstances. So we could defer the decision to the beginning of next year when some of the uncertainties in our lives will, I hope, be sorted out a little.
  - Consciously decide to enter into some new relationship with one another. → Each of these brings up a host of new possibilities and new feelings as well. Those are all alternatives to the main question at issue I'm addressing. But there are also alternatives to the other elements I've just gone through:
  - I've thought a lot about my concept of marriage, and the legal point of view just entered my mind. Does my concept of marriage automatically bring with it the idea of legality? → Could we have a relationship with one another that we would consider being married, even if it was not legally binding?
  - An alternative source of information: I should buy a good book that deals with the decision to get married. I know I can't learn everything I need to know from a book, but I don't want to be afraid to consult books either, especially about such an important decision. I can probably learn some things I haven't considered at all. And all I stand to lose is a little time.

[*Chris could also have considered alternative purposes, conse-quences, interpretations, and so on.*]

- In what context is this question being addressed?
  - Well, it's a real context for me. It's not a problem in a text-book where filling in an answer merely results in a grade. This is my life I'm talking about. If I don't carefully consider the important parts of the decision to get married, it may have an impact on the rest of my life.
  - There is the context of where we are in our relationship, how long we've been together, our ages and backgrounds, the influence of friends, family, and society (and some influ-ences I may not even be aware of).
  - I realize that the issue of same-sex marriage is one that is very serious to a great many people. I have put off consider-ing it until now, maybe because I have such strong views about it. So does Chris. Still, it is part of the social, ethical and legal context in which we live, and it has consequences for how we feel about the institution of marriage.
- Should I have addressed context first, before I did any of the other elements?

  [*Remember, there is no right order to apply the elements. The most useful order may vary from question to question. Many people have the experience that no matter which one they start with, it feels as if they should have done another one first. It often helps to describe the context at the beginning, so we can anchor the problem in its actual setting and not let it become an abstract puzzle.*]

Context, purpose, and *question at issue* are often good places to start. So is *point of view,* for example when you are reasoning within the point of view of a particular discipline. But keep alternatives in mind as you go through each element. It is good to revisit alternatives at the end of your analysis to open up new insights you may have overlooked.

Trusting the Process

You may have a number of concerns as you finish Chapter 2, partic-ularly if you have tried to work through the elements in the subject you are studying. You may be concerned with how the elements fit together. You may see that they sometimes overlap, that their appli-cation is not always completely clear, that what you thought was an *assumption* may be an *implication* or a *point of view* in another con-text. You may find yourself concluding from concerns like these that the elements are confusing. These are natural concerns. They are a part of many people's reactions.

A good thing to do is give the elements a chance to develop in you. Trust the process—maybe not completely, but give it a chance to take hold. The benefits start to come when you get familiar enough with the elements to use them in your day-to-day practice of thinking, both inside the course and out. That takes some time. Expect to feel some resistance inside you. Most of us have a strong tendency to continue down more familiar paths. It will probably feel unsafe to have your thinking process slowed and broken into parts. It will likely feel unsafe to face the multitude of questions and doubts that may arise as you go through this process.

Some Outcomes

At the end of this chapter . . .

1. You should be able to state, elaborate, exemplify, and illustrate what is meant by "the elements of reasoning" and "analysis."
2. You should be able to name most of the elements of reasoning without looking back at the list. (You should be able to do this not by having memorized them, but by seeing how they are involved in reasoning and then by using them in practice. A future outcome: By the end of the course they will start to become spontaneous parts of your thinking.)
3. Running your finger slowly around the Circle of Elements, you should be able to give a clear explanation of each of the elements.
4. You should be able to give your own examples of each element and to show how each can be used in different contexts.
5. You should be able to apply the elements to almost any question or problem. Your application will of course not be perfect. You should be able to apply some of the elements easily in some contexts; other elements, or other contexts, may be far more difficult.
6. At this point you should be alert to the elements. Thus, in your life, in the coming pages, and in the course you should be able to identify which elements are occurring ("Here the writer is drawing a conclusion").
7. You should be asking more questions about the elements.
8. You may be confused where before you didn't always even realize there was something to be confused about. (As paradoxical as it sounds, sometimes confusion indicates progress.)
9. Look back at the outcomes listed for Chapter 1 (page 37). They are not over and done with. You should be able to elaborate on them in a somewhat deeper way now because you can fit them in with the elements. You should also be able to give new examples.

Ideas for Writing

(General guidelines for "Ideas for Writing" are on page 38.) The elements of reasoning are the *parts* of thinking, and that gives them an almost unlimited applicability. Ideas for writing about them are also almost unlimited. Writing about them at this stage requires you not to be a perfectionist: your understanding and practical use of them are not as sharp as they will become. With that in mind, you can try writing about any **one of the elements** (for example, assumptions: How do assumptions work in people's lives or in disciplines?); about **inter-relations between pairs** of them (for example, How do the questions you ask shape the conclusions you come to? And how do the conclusions you come to shape the questions you ask?); about **how to transfer them** from one course to another; about **applying them** (or some of them) to life issues you will face (such as your own thinking about marriage or your choice of an area of study to pursue in school); about how developing your skills with them helps develop **critical-thinking character traits** (see pages 175–176); about **problems** you face in taking ownership of them.

Tell Your Story

(The idea behind "Tell Your Story" and some suggestions about responding to it are on page 39.) Think about and discuss your personal history—your story—in relation to the elements of reasoning. For example:

> **purpose**: How have your goals and purposes changed over the course of your life? What influenced you to take on those goals in the first place, and what influenced you to change the ones you have changed? How do you anticipate your goals changing in the future?

> **questions or problems**: Contrast the questions that were most on your mind five years ago with those that are most on your mind now. How have you changed? Or: What are some of the major problems you have faced, ones that may have shaped who you are today?

In a similar way, tell your story with respect to the main **assumptions** you have made in your life, to how you have gotten in touch with the **consequences** of your actions, and so forth. Telling your story in relation to the elements can give you an insight into your life you often cannot get any other way.

CHAPTER 2 **Exercises**

These beginning exercises will help you become familiar with going around the Circle of Elements.

2.1 Choose some problem or question you have. It can be in the field you're studying, but it may be better to begin with one from your personal life.

Think through each of the elements with respect to the problem or question you have chosen. Go around the circle as Chris did with respect to marrying Sean.

(It is best to begin with a problem that's familiar to you and not too difficult. The purpose is to become familiar with identifying the elements. Also, note any questions you have about how the elements apply.)

2.2 Go around the circle again. This time take a question from the field itself. Again choose one that you feel comfortable with; don't choose one that requires you to stretch too much in your thinking. The goal here is to become comfortable thinking with the elements. (After you are finished, again note any questions that arise in you about how the elements apply. Compare the questions with the ones you identified in Exercise 2.1.) Try to pinpoint areas where the elements are not clear to you.

2.3 Go around the circle again. This time choose a problem in the way you relate to the subject matter you're studying. For example, "Why am I studying anthropology?" "How does this course in communications fit into my life?"

The following exercises deal with individual elements rather than with going around the circle as a whole, but remember that the elements do not operate in isolation. Instead, they fit together to form the logic of the problem or question. (There will be more exercises on the elements when you are ready to apply them more directly to the field or discipline you are studying [Chapter 3] and to put them together with the standards of critical thinking, at the end of Chapters 4 and 5.) Each question in Exercises 2.4 through 2.13 is about one element. Each contains a list of topics, situations, excerpts, or questions. Identify that element in each of the items listed. (Your instructor may have you do some of these exercises as critical discussion in groups, rather than as individual written responses. If so, he or she may ask you to write a brief report on the discussion.)

2.4 Purpose.

    a. Identify the purpose of three important regular activities in your life.

    b. What is the purpose of Chapter 1 in your textbook?

    c. What are your instructor's goals for you in this class? Be specific.

    d. Try to identify an activity in your life where you do not entirely know your purpose.

    e. Pick out three activities you engage in regularly where you tend to lose sight of your purpose.

2.5 Question at issue.

    a. Identify the main problem in how you get along with someone you are close to.

    b. What is the question at issue in Chapter 2 of this critical-thinking text?

    c. What are three main problems experts are addressing in the field you are studying? (Though these may not be problems you will actually be studying, they will be problems at the cutting edge of the field.) If you don't know, describe a realistic way of finding out.

    d. Here is part of a table of contents for an art book[4]:

CHAPTER 6. SPACE

Geometric Projections 143

Scientific Perspective 144

Atmospheric Perspective 156

Space in French Impressionism 160

Cezanne's Perspective of Color 162

The Uncanny Space of Cubism 164

On the basis of this very limited amount of information, try to identify three major questions at issue to be addressed in the chapter.

e. Using only the table of contents, apply Exercise 2.5d to a chapter from a subject-matter book in this course.

2.6 Assumptions.

a. Identify assumptions you make about someone who is important in your life.

b. Identify assumptions that person makes about you (check with the person afterward).

c. Identify a theory that is important in the field you are studying. (Write an SEE-I for it.)

d. Try this exercise even if you know very little about economics. Identify two assumptions in this excerpt from an economics textbook:

> The concept of "needs" encourages all-or-nothing thinking. That's why economists prefer the concept of *demand*. Demand is a concept that relates *amounts people want to obtain to the sacrifices they must make to obtain these amounts*.[5]

e. Identify two assumptions from an important paragraph near the beginning of your textbook.

2.7 Implications and consequences.

a. Identify some implications and consequences of the syllabus for your course.

b. What are some implications and consequences of an important decision that is coming up for you?

c. Here are three claims from a psychology text: "Probably the best-known herbal remedy for memory is ginkgo . . . . Americans spend several hundred million dollars on it per year. Yet controlled studies comparing ginkgo with a placebo show that its effects on memory in normal individuals are minimal, even non-existent."[6] Use your best judgment to identify some important implications of that claim.

d. Choose three important sentences from your text. Identify the implications of each.

2.8 Information.

a. Focus on an important decision you need to make: what information do you have about it?

  b. For the same decision, what information do you need?

  c. Identify the five most important pieces of information from a chapter of your text (or some other reading). Describe how that information fits together.

  d. Summarize and describe the subject-matter information you will need to do well in this course.

  e. Describe a situation in your life where you made a bad decision because you lacked information that was readily available to you.

  f. Describe the research (information gathering) it is appropriate for you to engage in as part of being in this course.

2.9 Concepts.

  a. Focus on a relationship you have with someone, a relationship that has a specific name (e.g., sister, mother, friend, business partner, teammate). What is your concept of that relationship? (e.g., What is it to be someone's sister?)

  b. Describe your concept of "learning the subject" in the discipline you are studying.

  c. Think about the concept *animal*. That seems like a straightforward concept: We all know what an animal is. But consider this:

  Until 2008, cockfighting was legal in Louisiana. In cockfighting, two roosters are placed in a ring. They violently peck and gouge one another until one dies. Onlookers cheer. Louisiana also has a long-standing law prohibiting cruelty to animals. Before 2008, the attorney general reconciled these two laws by ruling that cockfighting is permissible because roosters are not animals!

  Of course that's ridiculous. Of course the attorney general knew that roosters are animals. What he ruled was that when lawmakers prohibited cruelty to animals, they did not intend for it to apply to roosters. So, roosters are not *legally* animals.

  Your state has a law prohibiting cruelty to animals. What are some animals that you are legally allowed to kill with a painful death? So what is the concept of *animal*, legally, in your state?

  d. Identify the three main concepts in Chapter 1 of your textbook.

2.10 Conclusions, interpretations.

  a. Identify three conclusions you have drawn about the importance of critical thinking in classes.

b. In your book, find an example of an interpretation the author is giving. Describe the information that the interpretation is based on.

c. After some careful reflection, give an example of when you have seriously misinterpreted another person's behavior. What information did you base your interpretation on? How should you have interpreted that information?

d. A psychology experiment was performed to see when people would violate a cultural norm against littering. Robert Cialdini and his colleagues tested the conditions under which drivers would litter a parking lot:

> Specifically, when the experimenters had previously littered the parking lot with fliers, the majority of the drivers simply followed suit—probably thinking, "After all, if no one cares about the cleanliness of the parking lot, why should I?" Interestingly enough, people were much less likely to litter if there was one piece of litter on the ground nearby than if the parking lot was completely free of litter. The reason is that seeing one piece of litter reminds us of litter—and shows us that the vast majority of people are subscribing to that norm. If the parking lot is free of litter, most people probably do not even think about the norm and, therefore, will be more likely to litter mindlessly.[8]

What part of the excerpt is information, and what part of it is interpretation?

2.11 Point of view.

a. Describe the difference between your instructor's point of view on the subject matter of this course and your point of view on it.

b. Describe two prominent points of view within the discipline you are studying.

c. The editors of an anthology in social ethics describe the views of Peter Singer, a famous advocate of animal rights:

> Singer rejects speciesism, which he defines as a prejudice or attitude of bias in favor of the interests of members of one's own species and against those of members of other species. In his view, speciesism is analogous to racism and sexism. Just as we have a moral obligation to give equal consideration to the interests of all human beings, regardless of sex or skin color, so, too, we have a moral obligation to give equal consideration to the interests of animals. Insofar as animals, like humans, have the

capacity to suffer, they have an interest in not suffering. Not to take that interest into account is speciesist and immoral.[9]

Describe Singer's point of view in your own words (not in the editor's words).

d. In a single paragraph, succinctly describe the point of view of the discipline you are studying.

e. Describe your point of view on the issue of memorization versus critical thinking in your courses.

2.12 Alternatives.

a. Identify some goal you want to achieve in relation to this class. Describe a way you can achieve that goal. Then, describe another way to achieve that goal. Then, describe yet another way.

b. Look back over the responses you've given to any of the questions before this. Pick out two that you are least satisfied with. Describe why. Revise them by writing alternative responses.

c. Focus on an important decision you have to make: Identify two (if possible, three) realistic choices you have?

d. Describe how thinking in terms of alternatives is important within the discipline you are studying. Give clear examples.

2.13 Context.

a. Describe how the field you are studying fits into the context of other closely related fields (e.g., if it is a social science, how is it similar to and different from the other social sciences?).

b. Describe the historical background of the field you are studying.

c. Identify an area or activity that is important to you, maybe the kind of music you like, the kind of sports or leisure activity you engage in, the kind of occupation you are interested in, the kind of books you read. Sketch out as well as you can when that particular area or activity was invented, discovered, or became widespread. Try to get a sense of how ancient or how recent it is.

d. Read the first chapter of your text and describe how it sets forth the context of the field you are studying.

e. Describe a situation where, because of your personal history or your cultural background, you were unable to grasp something important that was going on. Then, describe a situation where your history or cultural background gave you a deeper insight into what was going on.

2.14 Try the outcomes (page 76). Just go through the list of outcomes and see how many of them you understand well with your book and notes closed.

2.15 Look on pages 175–176 for a brief description of some critical-thinking character traits. Describe how *fair-mindedness* is important in thinking things through using the elements of reasoning.

DAILY PRACTICE
At incorporating critical thinking into your life and your learning

Before you start Exercise 2.16, look back at the instructions on pages 44–45.

2.16 **Spend a day on an element. Keep a log.** Pick one of the elements. For example, spend your day looking for assumptions. Write down any of them you can find. Note whether they were assumptions that were clear in the person's mind or ones the person was unaware of. Look for assumptions underlying your own statements and those of other people, in the way software works (or doesn't work), in advertising, in classes, everywhere. Feel free to ask people, "Excuse me, but I'm doing a critical-thinking assignment. I just heard you speaking. Are you making the assumption that _____?"

In your log, write down any questions that come up for you about assumptions. Those may be questions you'll want to ask in class, of your teacher, or of a classmate.

Wait a few days. Then choose another element to spend a day on. Go through all of them, including context and alternatives. By the time you have finished, you should be significantly better at identifying the elements and using them in practice.

2.17 Group work. Answer with an element. Sit in groups of four people, A, B, C, and D. Everyone takes turns asking questions of A. The questions can be anything, but try to ask different kinds. Before actually answering the question, A identifies the element he or she is using. Afterward, switch roles: everyone quizzes B, then C, then D. For example:

Question: What's your name?

A: A piece of information. My name is A.

Question: Where do you live?

A: Another piece of information (it's getting boring). My address is . . .

Question: Why are you taking this class?

A: My major purpose is . . .

Question: What is this stupid exercise for?

A: The question at issue, from your point of view, is "What is this stupid exercise for?"

2.18 In the Discipline: Metacognitive Discussion. Choose one element per class. Discuss how that element is important in the discipline. Do some pre-thinking and pre-writing the night before as homework. Have concrete examples of that element to share.

Chapter 3

What Is Critical Thinking within a Field or Discipline?

H ow can you learn to think critically in a field or discipline? That is, how can you start "learning the discipline" in a deeper, more thoughtful way–not just memorizing information, not just engaging in discussion or debate about it, not just defending your own firmly held beliefs?

One straightforward way you have already begun to try out is to take the elements of reasoning and use them to think through all aspects of the discipline itself. Since the elements are the nuts and bolts of reasoning, to reason within a discipline is to reason out questions within it using those nuts and bolts. When applied to the discipline itself this is called *the logic of the discipline*. But the elements apply equally to all aspects of study in the field: reading in it, writing in it, doing research, analyzing and evaluating positions, theories, arguments, strategies, artworks: all the topics that the discipline addresses.

CRITICAL WRITING

Pre-think what your course will be about. Begin by writing the name of the course (e.g., "Peoples of the World" or "Instructional Management in Special Education"). Write a paragraph or two on what you believe the course will be about: What are the goals of the course? What are the main questions you will address? How will the course fit in with other courses? What implications does it have for your life?

Next, write the name of the discipline that course is in (e.g., *anthropology* in the first case, *special education* or *education* in the second case).

1. Clarify your concept of the discipline by stating it, elaborating on it, exemplifying, and illustrating it (SEE-I).

2. Describe a situation in which you thought through something critically using some of the main concepts in the discipline.

3. Describe a situation in your life (one that actually occurred) in which it would have made sense to think it through critically using the concepts of the discipline, but you didn't.

Definitions and Parts of Critical Thinking: Applied to a Field

So, what *is* critical thinking in a discipline? What is it to think critically in a field such as biology or math, physical education, or nursing, or writing?

One way to approach these questions is by taking the definitions of critical thinking from Chapter 1 and applying them to specific fields. For example, apply Robert Ennis's definition to the field of biology:

> Critical thinking in biology is reasonable, reflective biological thinking that is focused on deciding what to believe or do in biology and in the relation between biology and the world at large.

Similarly, we can apply Matthew Lipman's definition to the field of history:

> Critical thinking in history is skillful, responsible thinking that is conducive to good historical judgment, because it is sensitive both to historical contexts and to other contexts which have a relation to history; it relies on historical criteria, and it is self-correcting.

The re-written definitions may be a little cumbersome, but it is worthwhile taking time to ponder what makes thinking in the field you are studying *skillful* or *responsible*. What is involved in being a *reflective* nurse or psychologist? What is it to think in a *reasonable* way in music or political science? What are the main *contexts* a critical-thinking engineer or writer must be sensitive to?

We can also take the three parts of critical thinking discussed in Chapter 1 and apply them to learning a subject. Critical thinking in a field involves asking good questions, reasoning out responses, and believing the results of our reasoning.

Asking the Question

If I am a student thinking critically in a field, I will find myself asking questions in the field: questions about the reading, about what I hear from teachers as well as from other students, about the subject matter, and about my own beliefs and understanding. I won't necessarily ask them out loud, and I will not expect them all to be answered, but with practice, and once I start freeing myself from a passive model of what it is to be a student, I will probably be flooded with questions—far more questions than I can answer.

In fact, that is a good rough-and-ready test of whether you are becoming more of a critical thinker in the field. You will see complexities beneath the surface, ones you never noticed before. You'll notice a lot more places where things are not as clear to you as they seemed before. You may find yourself confused in cases when previously you would not have understood enough even to be confused: before, you would simply have taken notes.

To begin, identify the most central ideas in the course—maybe from the name of the course—and ask yourself, "What are they?" For instance, "What *is* abnormal psychology?" "On the deepest level I can think at, what makes something abnormal?" "What is the purpose of psychology?" In a management course: "What is it to manage an office?" That is a *deep* question, one that you can ask yourself at different points in your life and come up with differing and deeper answers every time. You cannot be an effective office manager unless you re-answer that question when business conditions change, the office changes, or you yourself change.

In a physics course, you can ask, "How does an object get from point A to point B? How does it *do* it? How do forces work? How does energy get transferred?" Don't allow questions like these to be answered simply by definitions the text gives. Definitions are an *aid* to thinking through the question and answer. They are not, by themselves, "the answer."

When Richard Feynman, the Nobel laureate in physics, was a boy, he noticed the ball in his wagon kept rolling even after he stopped the wagon. He asked his father why that happened. His father gave him a profound answer, rooted in a spirit of asking questions: "The general principle is that things which are moving tend to keep on moving . . . . This tendency is called 'inertia,' but nobody knows why it's true."[1] Feynman points out how the answer, inertia, could have been used to stifle the wonder behind the boy's question. But the answer his father gave, promoted further questioning.

It takes practice to improve at critical thinking. That is particularly true of learning to ask questions. If you are like many other students, when you read a paragraph in your text or you listen to a lecture, no questions come up for you at all. As you work on your critical thinking, though, that will change. But guard against the idea that having no questions shows you understand something. For any subject matter that is at all complicated, the opposite is the case: if no questions arise for you, it probably means you do not understand it deeply enough to see the many paths of questioning that arise.

Reasoning It Through

Reasoning in a field can be difficult. Initially, it requires you to recognize both what you know *and* what you need to know but don't. Additionally, it means being able to draw conclusions on the basis of reasons.

Think of the difference between memorizing a list of the causes of World War I and reasoning those causes out. The historians who first formulated the thesis that the war came about as a result of entangling alliances *reasoned* this out as an answer, and so do all the people who rethink this answer for themselves. They re-examine how adequate it is, whether it's deep enough as a cause. They amend it, add to it; some of them end up rejecting the idea that entangling alliances were a major cause of WWI. Jennifer Reed, a history professor, regularly asks her students to work through not just a single set of causes of WWI, but also causes that are geographic, political, economic, social, technological, and personal. She helps students reason out what combination of these causes was necessary and sufficient for the event.[2]

That is an example of reasoning in the field of history. It is entirely different—different in kind—from merely repeating what someone else said about the causes of WWI. In its fullest sense, reasoning in a field involves being able to use the elements (Chapter 2) and standards (Chapter 4) of critical thinking in the subject matter.

Take a paragraph or two from your text, selected by you or your teacher. The paragraphs may be largely composed of factual material; they may also contain reasoned judgments. But in either case, they are the product of *reasoning*. So picture them as *conclusions*, conclusions that people have drawn from a long process of reasoning. Try to describe the process of reasoning that might have led to these conclusions.

The paragraphs may contain:

■ A set of definitions or classifications → Can you describe the disorganized state of affairs that existed before these definitions and classifications were formulated?

■ Factual matters that are the results of tests or investigations (these may not even be mentioned) → Can you determine the kinds of tests and investigations that led to these results?

■ Biographical or background information → Can you describe the kinds of primary sources that this information is derived from?

Believing the Results

It may seem that, as you become more adept at asking questions in the field and then reasoning through the answers, you will automatically believe the results of your reasoning. But believing the results of your reasoning—or acting on that reasoning—may not follow.

Here is a personal example. I learned in school that heavy objects and light objects fall toward the earth at the same rate. Everyone learns this. It is a scientific law. And, of course, I know that law is true. I learned it many times in school; if you ask me on an exam, I will give the right answer. But despite all that, I strongly suspect that I don't really believe it! That is, in my heart I probably don't believe it: If I had to bet my life on the outcome, without a lot of time to think it over, I'm afraid I might bet that the heavy one would hit the ground first (even in a vacuum).

Here is another example, a far more serious one. One of the hardest things to teach student nurses and other health-care practitioners to do is to wash their hands between patients. It is easy, however, to get student nurses to *say* they will wash their hands. If you ask on a test, "It is important to wash your hands: TRUE or FALSE," they will always get the right answer. They can also correctly explain why hand-washing is necessary. What's difficult is getting them to learn to *do* it.

A few years ago, there was a conference in New Orleans for experts on infectious diseases. These were doctors, not nurses. Some graduate students stationed themselves in the restrooms and counted how many of these doctors washed their hands after using the restrooms. They found that 13 percent of the women and 44 percent of the men

---

Give some examples of findings in the field you are studying that you don't believe.

These may fall into two distinct categories. The first is where you straightforwardly *disagree* with claims or positions in the field. You may or may not have any of these. If you do, write some of them down.

The second category is much harder to identify. It is where the findings in the field subtly conflict with background stories or accounts you already have in your head. (See pages 115–117.) These background stories may not be fully formulated in your mind; they may not be conscious at all. (My example of heavy versus light objects is an example of this.)

It is especially important to look for this second category as the course progresses. Why is that important? Because if you don't, you won't really be taking the subject matter seriously—and *not* because you disagree, but rather because you have an unexamined story guiding your thoughts. And it may well be a story that you will reject once you have thought about it.

---

did not. And these were experts in *infectious diseases!*[3] Every one of these experts would tell you that hands are the single main vector for passing infections—but the "knowledge" still didn't work its way into their actions. This strongly suggests they have not completely internalized their thinking about the importance of hand-washing.

Thinking Biologically, Thinking Sociologically, Thinking Philosophically, Thinking Musically . . .

Here is another way to describe what it is to think critically in a field or discipline: The discipline works as a set of lenses through which you can see the world in a more focused way. (Look back at Figure 1.3.) You can picture the discipline's lenses as like the ones inside a microscope or telescope: they let you look more deeply into events or see the distant up close.

Critical thinking in a field is thinking things through *in terms of* the concepts of the field. Critical thinking in biology is *thinking biologically*. Critical thinking in the field of anatomy is *thinking anatomically*. Critical thinking in geography is taking any problem having to do with the spatial ordering of the earth and *thinking it through geographically*. Notice how broad the application of such thinking is: it goes far beyond those problems brought up in the course.

Not all fields have a convenient adverb attached to them, such as "biologically." We can't say someone thinks "nursingly" or "literarily." But we can still use the idea: Critical thinking in nursing is thinking the way an observant, informed, reasonable nurse thinks. Critical thinking in literature is thinking the way a knowledgeable, sensitive, reasonable literary reader thinks.

So what is it to think biologically? Here is an example that gets at it, at least in a negative way. In my critical-thinking course, virtually all students have taken a course in biology, either recently or in the past. So for several years I gave a quiz (not for a grade) in which I asked students to define 10 biological terms. I chose ordinary terms, such as *cell*, and some more specialized terms, such as *mitochondria* or *endoplasmic reticulum*. As you might guess, students' ability to define them differed widely: Some were able to define many of them and some only a few or none. Students did better defining ordinary terms like *cell* than they did defining terms like *mitochondria*. Keep in mind that the course has nothing to do with biology. Several weeks later I gave another quiz and asked students to write a paragraph or two in response to questions like these:

> What happens when you cut your finger and get an infection?
>
> How does a person catch sexually transmitted diseases?
>
> What happens when someone gets cancer?
>
> How are babies made?
>
> Why is it harmful to get a suntan?

Students answered these questions in various ways. But in two years of classes, virtually no student's response ever used the word *cell*. And this was the result *whether or not* the student had defined *cell* correctly on the earlier quiz. I conclude from this informal experiment that the term *cell* had not become a significant part of the way these people thought through questions. My judgment is that the students answered these questions in the same way they would have if they had never taken a biology course at all. The concept of cell had not become internalized.

But *cell* is an important concept. It is different from *mitochondria*. For most of us who are not professional biologists, we will probably never confront a problem for which thinking in terms of mitochondria will help us make better choices. But that is decidedly not true of cell: cell is a *powerful* concept. Thinking in terms of cells gives insight into how to answer the ordinary questions we confront daily.

You can think biologically at any level of educational expertise, in high school, in college, as a graduate student in biology, as a professional biologist. At each level, though, you need to incorporate the concept of cell into the way you habitually think through questions. You need to apply that concept not just to questions specifically asked in the course, and not just to those that are labeled "biology questions," but to any question about our life processes where the concept of cell will yield insight and promote better choices.

One of the main goals of a biology course is to help you internalize the most central biological concepts and to learn to think through questions in your life using those concepts. That is what it is to think biologically. Similarly, thinking mathematically is, in a way, seeing the world in terms of quantity. Thinking historically is not the same as knowing a hodgepodge of events and persons from the past. Rather, it revolves around a central question: How are events made meaningful by the past they grow out of?

The Logic of the Field or Discipline

What Is a Field or Discipline?

A common impression is that a field consists essentially of a body of information. It is as if geology were equivalent to all the information we have acquired in geology. But that is an inaccurate and misleading view of a field. True, geologists, professional or amateur, have a good deal of information. But a field is far more than that. Fields are dynamic: they change, grow, evolve. Fields embody a distinctive way, or set of ways, of looking at the world. The perspective of geology is different from the perspective of geography or sociology or psychology.

Practitioners in a field—at whatever level of education—do not simply possess information. Rather, they know how to use that information as well as the concepts that structure it. They are able to apply both of those to new cases. They know how to synthesize the information. They know how to think *about* the field, and they know how to think *within* the field.

The Concept of the *Logic of a Field*

Almost everyone has experienced learning *parts* of a subject, but with no idea at all of how those parts fit together. Though this can happen in any field, it is dramatically true of many people's experience of algebra. You can learn how to solve quadratic equations by factoring, by completing the square, or by applying a theorem for solving radical equations, and not have any idea of how these methods fit together—or even that they *do* fit together.

Similarly, you can learn parts of a subject with no idea of how those parts fit into *the whole*. That also happens with algebra. Very few students finish a course in algebra with an idea of what the whole of algebra is. Many students' experience with a history course is learning lists of events, dates, people, and the relations among them, but with very little idea of what the history of that time and place was *as a whole*.

If you have had that experience, what you were missing was *the logic* of that subject matter. Understanding a whole is not the same as understanding the parts. It is not even the same as understanding all of the parts. Instead, it is understanding parts as they fit together with one another and form a coherent whole: a logic.

Thinking critically in a field is getting hold of the logic of that field. The concept of "the logic of" something is one of the most important concepts in learning to think critically.

Take the U.S. Constitution. You can memorize the entire Constitution (preamble, 7 articles, 26 amendments) and still not know the Constitution in any real sense. Professors of constitutional law probably never memorize it at all. They know the Constitution in quite a different sense. They understand, for example, how to extrapolate from constitutional principles to situations that did not exist at the time the Constitution was written. They understand alternative ways it can be reasonably applied in an era of nuclear secrets, Miranda rights, and responding to terrorist threats. They understand *the logic of* the Constitution. To call it "the" logic does not mean there is only one such logic—there are several in fact. But it means there are coherent ways of thinking through and in terms of the Constitution. It means the Constitution has a distinct set of purposes, which fit together with the assumptions, implications, alternative readings, interpretations, central concepts, key questions at issue, and distinctive points of view embodied in it—all the elements of reasoning, working together. Understanding the Constitution is understanding the logic sufficiently to be able to reason within it.

You can also approach the concept of "the logic of" by considering what you do when you forget something you have learned in a field. Suppose you have memorized something in a course—the dates of the Civil War, for example, or Hobbes' second law of nature, or whether a U- or a V-shaped valley is the result of glaciation. And then you forget it. Because you learned it by memory, you have no recourse but to look it up and then memorize it again. But people who know the logic of a subject won't have to look it up if they happen to forget a detail. Instead, they can *figure it out*. ("Figuring it out" is almost a synonym for "critical thinking.") They can figure it out from the events they know led up to the Civil War and the other events they know followed from it, or from understanding Hobbes' idea of a state of nature and the social contract. They can figure out the shape of a glaciated valley by envisioning how glaciers move, and drawing conclusions.

The subjects taught in school are almost never composed of unrelated individual bits of information. If it seems that way to you, that's only because you have missed the logic of that subject. (There are a few exceptions to this rule; e.g., the keyboard skills used in typing have no logic.[4] But such exceptions are rare. And it is no coincidence that there is no *field* of typing.) In fact, a rough test of whether you grasp the logic of a field is to see how much you feel the need simply to memorize bits of information. The more you feel that need, the less you grasp the logic of the way it all fits together.

What Does the Logic of a Field Consist Of?

Ultimately, we can display the logic of a field by analyzing it in terms of the *elements of reasoning*. A field or discipline embodies a distinctive range of problems and questions. It involves a set of purposes, key assumptions about the world, key concepts and models that people in the field use to gather and categorize information and trace out its implications. It involves a unique and fertile point of view in which people draw conclusions that could not be drawn without the discipline. A good way to describe practitioners is to say they have ownership of the logic of that field.

Here are two abbreviated examples of an analysis of the logic of a discipline. The first is an analysis of earth sciences, and as you read it, notice how the earth-sciences student has a grasp of the field as a whole. She analyzes the field—breaks it down into its essential parts—but she also synthesizes it. This is, of course, not *all* there is to earth sciences. And it is not the only version of a logic of earth sciences. But it assembles fundamental parts of the field for us, displays a vision of the whole, and shows how the parts are interrelated. The second example is a shorter one on the logic of a literature course.

AN ANALYSIS OF THE LOGIC OF EARTH SCIENCES

The main <u>purpose</u> of earth sciences (geology, physical geography) is to explain the composition of the earth, its history, and the physical/geological forces that made it this way. Another goal is to help us locate natural resources so we can use them while also preserving the environment.

The main <u>question at issue</u> in geology is "What is the earth like and how did it come to be this way?" Other important questions: How did the movement of tectonic plates produce the physical features of the earth (mountains, rivers, volcanoes, etc.)? What makes rocks? What is the future of the earth? What can we learn from geology about global warming?

The geological processes on the earth take place within the <u>context</u> of the universe as a whole: the big bang, the birth of our galaxy, the formation of our sun and solar system, including planet earth. Geology as a field fits in the *context* of the natural sciences: physics, chemistry, biology, astronomy.

The <u>information</u> geologists use comes from observations and tests on the composition of rock, air, and water, from precise observation and measurement of natural features, from the fossil record and from stratification.

Geologists make the <u>assumption</u> that we *can* find out about what happened to the earth in the past, that scientific method helps us put natural resources to new uses, and that the earth is best understood by observing data and gathering evidence. A major assumption of earth sciences is that plate tectonics explains the physical features of the earth *[but maybe this is a <u>conclusion</u> based on a huge body of evidence]*.

Some <u>implications and consequences</u> of earth sciences: The geological processes that formed the earth are still going on and will continue into the future. Plate tectonics results in predictions about where various natural resources will be found. Natural resources are limited.

The <u>point of view</u> of geology is a scientific one, based on observation, careful measurement, theory construction, and tests. The geological point of view is characterized by seeing the earth as something to be preserved and nurtured because it is the result of eons-long processes.

The main <u>concepts</u> of earth sciences include plate tectonic theory, convection heat systems, continental drift, subduction; the rock cycle, the hydrologic cycle; geological time.

<u>Conclusions</u>, <u>interpretations</u>: Geology allows us to <u>interpret</u> the land around us as the result of the movement of immense tectonic plates that have shaped the planet. Now when I look at mountains, rivers, or the ground under my feet, I draw <u>conclusions</u> about how they were formed, and that lets me see them in a different way. An important conclusion to draw from studying earth sciences is that the government should consult the geological community about the use of natural resources.

There are <u>alternatives</u> to looking at the earth geologically: some people believe that the earth has always been the way it is now, that it is basically unchanging, or that science and religion are opposed, and we should look at the earth from the point of view of religion only. Some people think the earth was given to humans to use as they see fit.

The value of analyses like these does not consist so much in reading them as in creating them, in thinking them out. Once you have constructed your own analysis, your understanding of details will fit into this logic in a coherent way, and as your understanding deepens, the logic will grow deeper as well.

LOGIC OF A LITERATURE COURSE

- **Purpose:** To think the way a literary reader thinks about his or her life

- **Question at Issue:** How can I think in a deep literary way about stories and about my life in terms of those stories?

(continued)

LOGIC OF A LITERATURE COURSE (*Continued*)
Assumptions:

- That I can learn about life by reading stories deeply
- That I will connect more deeply to stories by seeing them in terms of character, conflict, change
- That a story can be like an old friend—in which I can always find new and worthwhile things

Implications and Consequences:

- That my reading of stories will become deeper during the course
- That I will apply stories to my life in a richer way at the end of the course than at the beginning
- That stories help me understand aspects of my life; that stories also keep aspects of my life hidden from me

Concepts:

- Character
- Plot
- Theme
- Conflict

- The concept of *story* itself → What makes something a story? Just because you write stuff down about things that happened doesn't make it a story.
- Meaningfulness

Information:

- The actual stories we will read in the course
- Sometimes, information about the author, or the context in which the story was written

Conclusions/Interpretations:

- Conclusions about specific stories (e.g., how Holden Caulfield has changed)

- Conclusions I will draw about my life on the basis of the stories: Am I a catcher in the rye too?
- Interpreting items in my life in a different way: the way when you read a book (Shirley Jackson) or watch a movie and you can *see* the world in terms of the story

Point of View:

- The points of view of various characters: What does the story look like from their point of view? (e.g., the kid that Holden Caulfield can't stand)
- Also: developing empathy with alien points of view

Context: I am reading these stories as someone of a certain age, of a certain gender, with a personal history, in a society, in a culture—and all of these shape the stories I read and the way I interpret them.

Alternatives: I have choices—alternatives—about which stories I will let influence me.

Learning the Vocabulary of the Discipline

How can you begin to think in terms of the logic of the discipline you're studying? A good place to start is learning to use the discipline's vocabulary. This is a minimal condition, and it is easy to confuse means and ends. Learning the vocabulary in a field is *a means* to an end. It is an essential means for learning to reason better in the field. But be careful not to think that learning the vocabulary—learning the *names* for concepts in the field—is somehow the *point* of studying in the field. It isn't. Teachers don't stress terminology because it's the purpose of the course. Rather, it's that the purpose cannot be accomplished without the essential terminology. Learning the parts of a flower in a botany course is important, but it is seldom an end in itself. (It is for some people. Some people find value in knowing the precise names of things.) For most people, the vocabulary is important because it increases their ability to think clearly about flowers, to communicate clearly about botany, to gain precision in their observations. These abilities in turn provide insight beyond flowers, insight into how things grow, into fundamental processes of life.

What Is It to Think in a Discipline's Vocabulary?

Of course, thinking in a discipline's vocabulary is not the same as merely memorizing definitions. Haven't you often memorized definitions of terms without really having a handle on what they mean, without being able to use them intelligibly? Disciplines are integrated wholes, and their vocabulary reflects that. Vocabulary in a discipline is like a web: it's interconnected. Thinking of one vocabulary word brings up its connections to other words in the vocabulary. It starts you thinking in terms of logical connections, rather than in terms of fragments. It also brings up the connections between the concepts that lie behind the words. For example, the term *force* in physics should lead you naturally, almost automatically, to think about *mass* and *acceleration*. In an English literature course, the term *stream of consciousness* should bring James Joyce's *Ulysses* to your mind, at least as a background, ready to be applied. In social work, when you think about "enabling behavior," your mind turns naturally to dysfunctionality, control, needs, and a web of other terms.

There is another advantage to learning the vocabulary of the field. Your present vocabulary is saturated with the point of view you grew up with. It has its own connections, and often these run counter to the more accurate, precise, and important connections that have been discovered in the discipline. So, if you think in your present vocabulary of something *in motion*, you are liable to connect to the idea of "something else that puts it in motion" (a force). That's natural, but it is the direct opposite of what we learn from Newton. In Newtonian theory (and in reality), "being in motion" connects to the idea that *nothing* is moving it (*no* net forces); in reality, things that are moving simply keep moving. (Only when they turn or move faster is there a connection to the idea that a force is moving them.)

The concept of *enabling* in social work is a dramatic example. We often think of helping people who are in a recurring state of need (e.g., helping an alcoholic make it home) as a *good* act, as an act of mercy or unselfishness. Thinking in terms of *enabling*, though, shifts these connections and calls them into question. Now, connections are made to how the one who seems to be helping may be perpetuating a *dysfunctionality* in the person, and how the *enabler* may be *controlling* the situation to meet his or her own *needs*.

To change your way of thinking, you need to change the vocabulary of your thinking.

Fundamental and Powerful Concepts

Here are two basic questions about learning a discipline:

1. If I take a course in a discipline, how can I think critically *within* that discipline?
2. How do I learn to think critically while also amassing the large amount of information—often misleadingly called the content—I may need to learn in the course?

When confronted with these questions, students, and sometimes teachers, often phrase them in terms of a false opposition. They think they have to choose *either* to learn critical thinking *or* to learn content—as if the two were opposed.

They are not at all opposed. Learning content *is* learning to think. If I learn content, but I don't learn to think in terms of that content, then it's not *content* at all. It's just *words*, memorized and soon forgotten words. If I learn that for every action there is an equal and opposite reaction, but I can't explain what that phrase means when given the example of a man pushing against a wall (what is the reaction?), then all I have is a singsong slogan. That is not *content*. Content is not repeating formulas or slogans, nor is it memorizing long lists of information. Rather, I have ownership of a course's content when I *understand* the course concepts, see their implications, relate them to other concepts; when I can raise relevant questions about them, when I can apply them to new situations.

The answer to both questions 1 and 2 has to do with fundamental and powerful concepts.

Understanding Fundamental and Powerful Concepts

What are fundamental and powerful (f&p) concepts? A fundamental and powerful concept is one that can be used to explain or think out a huge body of questions, problems, information, and situations. All fields have f&p concepts, but there are a relatively small number of them in any particular area. They are the most central and useful ideas in the discipline. They are to be contrasted with individual bits of information, or with less general concepts. In the earlier example, "cell" is a far more fundamental and powerful concept than "mitochondria." The idea, then, is that if you can understand the f&p concepts in a deep way, you are in a position to understand a great deal of the rest of the course. You need to learn to think in terms of the fundamental and powerful concepts, to use them to think through any new problem or question that arises.

For example, when I was in college, I liked poetry, particularly the Romantic poets: Keats, Shelley, Wordsworth, and Coleridge. So I took a course in the Romantics. Here is all that I remember from the course: *Michael*, 1800. That is, I remember that Wordsworth's poem *Michael* was written in 1800. That is the sole remnant left from more than 200 names of poems and dates I memorized in that course. This is an example of the opposite of an f&p concept. It is a detail, and it illuminates nothing, not even itself (I don't even remember what *Michael* was about!). What would be an f&p concept in that course? Well, one would clearly be the concept of *romanticism* itself. Romanticism involves a whole way of looking at life: a feeling of deep yearning, a longing for the unknown, the richness of imagination and strong emotions, an intense love of nature, especially for the mystery of nature, for the faraway and the unattainable.

What makes romanticism a fundamental and powerful concept is that once you grasp it deeply, you acquire a concept for understanding and appreciating many Romantic poems. You can then take almost any poem written during that period, understand it as an expression of romanticism, and think it through using the concept of romanticism. That gives you an insight into those poems that you would not have without that concept. Additionally, if you have questions about how those poets lived—about their attitudes toward politics, love, drugs, or religion; or about novels and essays written at the time—you can now think through any of these questions using the concept of romanticism. It is a *powerful* concept.

But the case is far stronger than this: If you can learn to think in terms of f&p concepts—in this case, *romanticism*—then not only are many questions in the course illuminated, but also any number of questions beyond the course, ones that arise long after the course is over. How does romanticism apply to later poets you may read? How does it apply to your own poetry? How about movies? The topics can go on and on. Romanticism is powerful as a concept because it continues to illuminate, far beyond the subject matter of the course. How do you look at *your life* in terms of romanticism? How about the romanticism of science or the law? What are the romantic aspects of your choice of profession, your choices in romantic relationships (the other sense of "romantic"), your self-image? How does the concept of romanticism help you understand yourself and others?

The concept is *fundamental* because it forms the foundation of our understanding of that era and of a great many forms of life that extend beyond that era. It is *powerful* because it is useful in understanding a wide range of questions and problems, issues, and situations.

Although fundamental and powerful concepts are important in *understanding* certain phenomena, they are just as important in fields that emphasize *doing*.

Take the nursing concept *asepsis*. There are many antiseptic procedures, both medical and surgical, some suitable in one situation, some in another, and each one has a subset of steps associated with it. But as a student nurse, you can spend so much time learning these individual procedures that you lose the forest for the trees. It's easy to become engaged in parroting and carrying out rote procedures rather than assessing what to do in a situation by thinking it out. Every nursing teacher has scary stories of nurses unthinkingly carrying out one procedure even though it's obvious the patient is in desperate need of another. So the idea is: Take any situation that arises and think it out with the idea of *asepsis* in mind. How can this situation be made aseptic? With that in mind, you can identify the specific antiseptic procedures called for by a specific situation. If you have to adapt the procedure to an unusual situation, you have a way of doing so—namely, thinking in terms of how to achieve asepsis. It is not a surefire way, of course. But it is a good way, a reasonable way. If, however, all you have done is memorize the specific procedures, you can't determine which part you've forgotten, and you have no insight into why a particular procedure is appropriate for an unusual case. In fact, you may have no real grasp of what a procedure is *for*: it may be just a procedure you follow blindly. When new procedures come along, long after graduation, you have no broader concepts through which to understand them.

To think critically through a course, the f&p concepts need to be learned in a *deep* way. Almost certainly, the teacher of the course I took in Romantic poetry did define romanticism. But it remained just that—a definition. For me, the student, it was one more detail, on a par with "*Michael,* 1800." By contrast, fundamental and powerful concepts should constantly return throughout the course as part of the explanatory context whenever new material is introduced. Given any new material, always raise this question: How is this illuminated by our small stock of f&p concepts? Occasionally, it may be that some new material is not illuminated at all by one of the f&p concepts. That's okay. You should recognize that too. Maybe you should ask about it in class. But what you are aiming for is to make those f&p concepts part of *the way you think*.

All courses have f&p concepts: *Homeostasis* in biology is an example, the concept of *the audience* is one that is central to all writing courses, the concept of *what is justifiable* is at the heart of any ethics course. Most courses and fields have more than one, but not a large number. If you start thinking in terms of 10 or 15 concepts, or more,

IDENTIFYING FUNDAMENTAL AND POWERFUL CONCEPTS

Depending on how far along you are in your course, you may not yet be able to identify the fundamental and powerful concepts. Your teacher may have told you the f&p concepts. If so, do not treat that as just another piece of information. Rather, take those concepts and use them to think out every single important topic or question that arises in the course.

If you are far enough along:

1. Focus on the course as a whole, not on individual parts.

2. Identify three f&p concepts that underlie the whole course. Do this by first identifying *one*. Only then, go on to identify two others that stem from that one. (Use the concept map in Figure 3.1.)

3. Share and discuss the f&p concepts with other students. How do they underlie the field or course as a whole? Are they fundamental enough? The concepts each class member identifies should be similar.

FIGURE 3.1 *A concept map.*

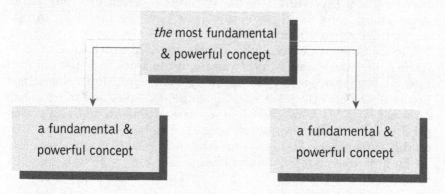

you are already going beyond the fundamental ones to narrower, more specific concepts. Focus instead on a smaller number, trying to get at what is most central:

- To identify the f&p concepts
- To understand how they fit together
- To learn them in a deep way

- To use them in your thinking about every important question or problem that arises in the course
- To use them to begin to think through questions that lie beyond the scope of the course

Using Concept Maps to Display Logical Connections

Concept maps are a useful way of showing the logical connections that exist between concepts (see the example in Figure 3.1). For instance, the field of clinical psychology trains therapists to deal with the psychological disorders of patients. When clinical psychologists work they focus on diagnosing the client, identifying the major causes of the psychological disorder in that client, and carrying out a course of treatment. We can identify five main concepts, then: *clinical psychology, psychological disorders, diagnosis, causes,* and *treatment.* A concept map of these might be drawn as in Figure 3.2.

That's not the only way to map out these concepts, however. You may reason instead that the treatment a clinical psychologist recommends for a patient is not *separate* from the diagnosis and causes, as portrayed in Figure 3.2. Treatment *depends* on the diagnosis the psychologist gives and on the causes of the disorder in that patient. Such reasoning might be depicted as in the map in Figure 3.3. The concept map reflects the system of thinking, the logical connections between concepts.

FIGURE 3.2   *A concept map for psychological disorders.*

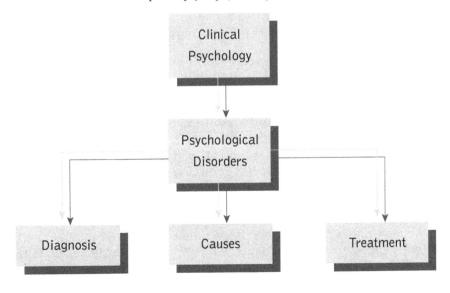

FIGURE 3.3   *An alternative concept map for psychological disorders.*

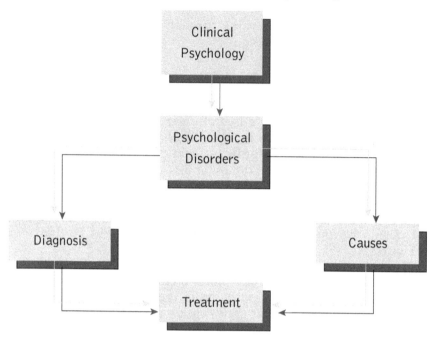

The three concepts, *diagnosis, causes,* and *treatment,* are f&p concepts in clinical psychology. That means that, as you learn to think the way a clinical psychologist thinks, you can reason out virtually any question in the field in terms of how to diagnose it, what its causes are, and how it should best be treated.

The Central Question of the Course as a Whole

Another important way to keep your thinking in the course on track, to grasp the logic of the field, is to think in terms of the central question of the course as a whole.

A course in a field has a central question that it revolves around. It is the unifying question, and everything in the course fits into that question. The way to understand every item in the course, to see how it all fits together, is to understand it in terms of that central question. Take this book. This is the central question it addresses: *How can you learn to think critically in a field or discipline?* Every topic discussed in the book is an aspect of that central question. So, if you have difficulty understanding how implications fit with assumptions, or if you wonder, "How do the impediments discussed in Chapter 1 fit with the standards in Chapter 4?", the way to think it out is to ask, "How do these fit together to help me learn to think critically in the field?" That central question forms the unifying center around which all other topics and questions are organized. Without keeping that central question in mind, the parts of a book (or a course) fall apart into separate and unrelated pieces.

One problem with describing a central question is that it can seem so simple. And it *is* simple—simple in the sense of uncomplicated, not in the sense of easy. Insights that are simple in that sense are often the things most worth saying.

Picture yourself taking a course in educational psychology. You are deluged with educational theories, countertheories, procedures, statistics, case studies, definitions, objectives, and a hundred other items. All of them seem important. This one relates to that one, this other one doesn't. This theorist says X, this other theorist says Y, and a third says Z. In such cases, it sometimes seems almost heroic to see the forest for the trees.

What is the central question? It is, *How does a student learn? And how can I help students learn?*[5] That is what educational psychology is all about. Everything in the course is geared to that one question. You are taking the course in education to get a richer, fuller understanding of how students learn, and how you as teacher can help them learn. To think through any issue critically during the course means to think it through *in terms of* how it contributes to answering that central question. That question provides the structure through which everything else is understood.

There can be more than one central question in a course. It is usually helpful to assume there is only one because it unifies your vision of the course and the field. But you may have to suspend that assumption. For example, the central question in a literature course might be *How can literature enrich and deepen the way I live my life?* That is a profound and far-reaching question. The whole course, every assignment, every poem, drama, or story, and all class discussion, can be seen as addressing that single, central question. But that same course might have another central question. It might focus on the *craft* of writing: *What do writers do to make literature effective?* That is also a central question, one that directs your attention to how writers accomplish what they accomplish: how they use characters, theme, plot, conflict, and literary forms. A third central question might focus on the interaction necessary to make meaning: *How do writer, reader, and society together create meaning in literature?* This too is a question that may underlie the entire course. It directs you to ask, whenever you read *any* piece of literature, in the course or long afterward, *How do we, together, make this work of art?*

Thinking in terms of central questions can change your whole understanding of a course. A good candidate for a fundamental and powerful concept in physical education, for example, is lifelong fitness.

A central question is *How can I promote lifelong fitness?* That is, the suggestion is to think of every activity in a physical education course in relation to how it promotes, or detracts from, lifelong fitness. You can now think through nutrition, sports, and exercise in a different, more global way. Notice how thinking in terms of that central question—and lifelong fitness—can change your perception of potentially damaging sports like football or boxing, at least as part of a physical education program.

Here are some examples of central questions for a few courses:

- **Chemistry:** How are you and the world around you created by chemicals?
- **Composition:** What *is it* to write an effective essay?
- **Economics:** How is society shaped by the decisions people make on the basis of expected costs and benefits?
- **Philosophy:** How can you make sense of your life and of the world around you?

Thinking in terms of the central question may sound easy, but it's actually difficult. The goal is to use the central question in your thinking at every point in the course. Doing so, even some of the time, takes practice and focused attention. It doesn't come naturally. Think about other classes you have taken, and notice how many of them you sat through, from beginning to end, without ever asking yourself the central questions underlying the class, without ever understanding that there even *was* one.

CRITICAL WRITING

Write down, as well as you can at this point in the semester, the central question of the course you are taking. Do this by writing *three* versions of it. With each one, approach it as if it is *the* one and only central question of the course. When you are done—when you have three different questions written down, each attempting to capture the most central question—choose the one that, in your judgment, captures it best. (At a later time, you may well choose a different version.)

A central question is difficult the way a mission statement is difficult. A business, a university, a hospital, or an organization may formulate a mission statement. Many individuals also formulate a personal mission statement. It is a way to keep themselves focused on what is important and allow what's less important to drift away. A person's mission might be "My mission is to respect myself, others, and all things." It is often difficult to formulate a mission statement that captures what you truly think is important, what you think your mission is. By the same token, though, formulating it can be deeply enlightening.

What's even more difficult, however, is keeping the mission in front of you as you go through life: remembering it, keeping it fresh, not letting it become an empty formula, reviewing it as you mature, actually living your life, as much as possible, in accord with it.

The central question of a course operates the same way as a mission statement, and it is difficult in the same way. Like a mission statement, it is a question you can ask yourself over and over. As your education and understanding increase, the depth with which you answer that question will also increase.

- Formulate the central question(s) of the course as a whole.
- Break it down into two or three subsidiary questions. Then figure out how they fit together within the central question.
- Look at every topic in the course and ask, "How does it fit into the central question? How does that topic contribute to answering the central question?"
- Remind yourself of the central question frequently, especially at times when you feel overwhelmed or when you find yourself just going through the motions.
- Reformulate the central question from time to time.
- Push the envelope. Ask, "How is that central question important for my life beyond the classroom?"

SHORT ESSAY

USING FUNDAMENTAL AND POWERFUL CONCEPTS TO THINK THROUGH A CENTRAL QUESTION IN AN INTRODUCTION TO SOCIOLOGY COURSE

Central Question: How do humans behave socially, and why do they behave that way?

If I had to describe how and why humans behave socially in just a few sentences, I would use three fundamental and powerful concepts: social forces, socialization, and norms/sanctions. I would say that "social forces"

(continued)

SHORT ESSAY (*Continued*)

act on people as they grow up and as they go through life. From these social forces, people learn how to behave. They learn which actions and values and things to do are acceptable and which are not. This process is called "socialization"—it is the way people become part of society. Societies have "norms and sanctions." That means a lot of the behavior we think of as individual free choices is brought about by cultural norms that we are taught unconsciously and accept automatically.

A major part of the social forces that influence us comes from the groups we belong to, including the social categories we are in. Some important groups that influence us socially are family, peer groups, our schools, and our religious groups. Social categories are things like a person's race, age, gender, and income level. Each of these groups has norms that tell us, "This is how you're supposed to behave in the group." And each of them has sanctions, meaning, "If you don't behave that way, you will be punished for it." One thing that was hard for me to get is that these norms and sanctions are things we're not aware of. It's not like anybody ever said to me (I'm a male): "Don't wear dresses!" and "If you do, we're going to punish you by laughing at you." It's just something you know as you grow up. You don't even think of people laughing at you as a punishment or "sanction." It's just what people do.

So the way sociology looks at people is very different from the way I looked at people before I began taking this course. I understood the behavior of my friends and family (and even strangers like sports figures and movie stars) on the basis of my personal experience and what I talked about with friends (in sociology, these are called "peer groups"). I also learned a lot from music and movies and TV. I was also brought up with certain values, like in my family they always talk about being a success. You just know things about people—like: you can trust your friends and you can't trust other people as much.

What I didn't think about was how I was "socialized" to take on these values and obey certain norms. I'm not saying that social forces *make* me have certain values, but I can see that they have a strong influence on me (as well as on everybody else). For example, I like football. I play sports sometimes, but what I like most is watching football on TV with my friends. We have a great time!

I always thought that I just liked football. I thought it was my individual choice and nobody else had anything to do with it. My friends and I even act like we are kind of being rebellious and nonconformist in the way we like football. I hate to say it, but we even look down on people who don't like football: I mean, what's wrong with them? But now I realize that there are social patterns to the way we like sports. What my friends and I do is *very much like* what thousands and thousands of other groups (mostly males, like us) do across the country. In fact, when I think about people who don't like sports at all (like maybe they like to dance or bird-watch), I now realize that they probably look down on my football group just the way we look down on them. (My group would be called an "in-group" in my social interactions, and they would be called an "out-group.") I go through some of my own values, and it amazes me how much they are like the values of the groups I belong to. Not all of them, but a lot more than I ever realized.

It's not just sports or movies. We begin to be socialized through our families. Then we continue to be socialized by our peer groups and the way we are categorized into race, gender, and age groups. We don't just learn to like football (if we grew up in England, my friends and I would probably be wild about soccer or cricket!). We are also socialized to take on deep values like being an individual versus following the crowd, or learning to do whatever it takes to succeed in life.

There are other ways someone could try to understand human social behavior—psychologically, economically, politically, maybe even biologically (maybe some of our values are in our genes). So a key to understanding human behavior sociologically is to look for "social forces." If there are a lot of groups that do the same things, have the same values, and follow the same norms, then we should look for the social forces at work making the groups conform.

The Point of View of the Discipline

Disciplines embody a unique way of looking at the world. The point of view (or perspective) of a discipline runs so deep that it can seem as if practitioners of the discipline are seeing a different world from yours, and in a sense they are. Sarah Blaffer Hrdy is a brilliant evolutionary anthropologist, and her description conveys beautifully what it is to think in terms of that field:

> For better or for worse, I see the world through a different lens than most people. My depth of field is millions of years longer, and the subjects in my viewfinder have the curious habit of spontaneously taking on the attributes of other species: chimps, platypuses, australopithecines. This habit of thinking about mothers in broad evolutionary and comparative—as well as cross-cultural and historical—perspectives distinguishes my examination of motherhood from those of the psychoanalysts, psychologists, novelists, poets, and social historians whose work I build on.[6]

This way of thinking is available not just to professional anthropologists like Hrdy but to almost anyone. It can open up clear, accurate, important perspectives for the way we conceptualize our lives. That happens because each discipline has a vision of the world that's embodied in its point of view.

What is involved in "seeing the world from the point of view of the discipline"? Three things (though they are not completely separate):

- Seeing the items in the *domain* of the discipline
- Seeing them in terms of the *concepts* and categories of the discipline
- Seeing the *connections* among those items

The place to begin is by recognizing there is a whole set of objects (or events) that the discipline investigates as its area of expertise. That set is the *domain* of the discipline. The items in that domain are ones that the point of view of the discipline can give you special insight into.

So a good first step toward taking on the perspective of the discipline is at least to identify its domain. Thus the domain of psychology is human behavior (and also the behavior of many nonhuman animals). The domain of chemistry includes chemicals and their interactions. The domain of art history includes artworks (as well as other objects and events that are made meaningful via artworks). The domain of nursing may be hard to describe simply: it includes "nursing situations"— those health-related situations where the field of nursing applies and gives understanding.

But you don't "identify the domain" just by saying the words. Seeing things from the point of view of the discipline involves *seeing* the things in our world *as* items in the domain of the discipline. It is essential not to wall off the domain of the discipline from our ordinary life ("school stuff": see page 117). The domain of psychology covers human behavior. But if I describe it that way I can easily miss its significance. The domain includes *all* human behavior, meaning it includes everything that anyone does or thinks. That's the domain that psychology can give us insight into. To "see" from the point of view of psychology, then, is to notice—consciously notice—those acts of human behavior around me. Similarly, the domain of chemistry includes "chemicals"—but *everything* is made of chemicals. If I describe the domain as "chemicals," I am probably blinding myself to what chemistry is actually talking about: it is talking not about some specialized thing called "chemicals" but

Think back on the visualization of the elements in Chapter 2 (page 63), the one where you were walking down a path, seeing the world in terms of the elements. The world you see as you walk down the path will be strikingly different if you are a geographer, a writer, an economist, an artist, a philosopher. It will be different in the objects or events you focus on (the domain), in the way you categorize them, and in the connections you "see."

Describe the path, as best you can, according to how it would look from the point of view of the discipline of the course you are in.

about the chemical make-up of *everything*. Thus, to "see" from a chemistry point of view is to look at the world around me—tables, books, chalk, blood, my dog, people—and to see them as assemblages of chemicals. In the same way, it's difficult to imagine an object or event that is *not* shaped and made meaningful by artworks, or any aspect of what we do that is *not* a "health-related situation." And I can "see" them that way.

Thus practitioners in a field don't simply see the same things you do and just call them by different names, as if what you see are some tall weeds by the side of the highway and ecologists merely supply the Latin name for them. That's just a trivial difference. In "seeing" objects and events, disciplines conceptualize them and categorize them in strikingly different ways from the ways we understand them without the discipline. For example, you may be highly aware that you and your fellow waiters at a restaurant are angry at your customers, but once you conceptualize that anger as "cognitive dissonance," suddenly a whole new way of thinking about it (psychology) becomes available to you. This happens because the point of view of the discipline allows us to see not only objects and events differently, but also the *connections* between those objects and events. Thus, when you see weeds, ecologists may see native grasses that are struggling against both crops and invaders from other continents, and managing to survive only because the grasses are located in a small habitat of untended land that humans have inadvertently allowed to revert back to a state close to the great prairies that once covered a huge area of the United States and Canada. You see weeds; ecologists see struggle, balance, succession, history, and loss of genetic diversity.

The same is true of all disciplines. The connections you start to see, as you take on the point of view of a geographer, a writer, an economist, an artist, a philosopher, will furnish a deeper understanding of the world around you. If you let it, this powerful point of view can become part of your standard way of looking at the world.

Impediments to Thinking Critically within a Discipline

The impediments to critical thinking mentioned in Chapter 1 are impediments to thinking critically within a discipline as well. For example, two of the impediments deal with forming a picture of the world based on what we learn from news reports or on what we see in movies, TV, advertising, and other fictionalized accounts. But these sources can also provide us with an uncritical picture of the subject matter in courses we study.

For example, space travel is presented matter-of-factly in fictionalized accounts (often at "warp speed," with stars streaking by, and the "noise" of booster rockets firing). We also see news reports of spacecraft sending incredibly precise data back from Mars or Jupiter. We also hear reputable scientists talk about black holes and the consequent possibility of wormholes through space-time. These are three separate sources of information that really have almost nothing to do with one another: fiction, news bites, scientific reports. But many people put them together uncritically and assume that space travel to other planetary systems is just around the corner. They form an unrealistic picture, one that can easily be an impediment to learning about science. Space travel beyond our tiny system of planets is unlikely ever to happen. Distances are simply too great, our highest speeds are infinitesimally small, and there are physical limits (not just practical limits) to what objects with mass can do. Human space travel beyond the solar system cannot be proved impossible, of course, but it's only a fantasy, probably no more likely than finding out leprechauns actually exist.

You can readily find examples of how the other impediments discussed in Chapter 1 can seriously interfere with your ability to think critically through the subject matter in your courses. Think of the common *fear* of taking math or science and how it interferes with reasoning through questions entirely within people's capacity; or the way we *stereotype* social scientists, nurses, professors, psychiatrists, and students; or the way even within a discipline people identify *egocentrically* with one position or another and go to unreasonable extremes to defend that position; or, *developmentally*, the way a need to feel safe can lead people to major in a subject where they feel in control, even though their real interest is in a different subject entirely.

Background Stories, Background Logic

There are other impediments to critical thinking in a discipline. We enter courses not as blank slates but with *background stories* and accounts already in place. These stories have a logic that shapes how we think within the discipline. We have a story, for example, about chemicals: Chemistry teachers sometimes despair at the persistent background story that if something is made of chemicals, it is therefore bad for you. Chemistry teachers respond to this background story by teaching that this can't be true because everything is made of chemicals. As a student, though, you can hear what your chemistry teacher says, you can write it in your notes, you can give the right answer on exams—and even after all that, once class is over, you can still believe chemicals are bad for you. It is extremely difficult, for example, to understand what it means when biochemists say that *life* is chemistry.

Though these examples are from science, background stories are strong impediments to critical thinking in all fields. You have in you right now, like a default program on your computer, background stories about how business works (including marketing, management, accounting, . . .), what nursing and education are (including all the specializations), how humans interact (psychology, sociology, political science, . . .), what other cultures are like (anthropology, history, . . .), what reality is like (philosophy, science, religious studies, . . .), and how to find answers (librarianship, methods courses, math, . . .). It is not so much that these background stories you have are false. Many of them *are* false, but even if the story has a lot of truth in it, it is probably a very limited truth, and the story will be deeply misleading when it is extended beyond the area where it works.

Even calling them "stories" is misleading because that implies the stories are easily supplanted with new information from your courses. But that doesn't do justice to how deep our background stories run and to how pervasive their influence is. It is hard for the account you learn in your course to get through. Background stories are deep and pervasive in part because they are unexamined and in part because they have *a logic* to them. That is, our background stories are not just stories; rather, they embody a whole way of thinking about things.

Here is another example. Most people have a picture of how evolution is supposed to work according to Darwinism. Yet, that picture is deeply misguided, often straight-out wrong. How many of the following do you think of as part of the theory of evolution?

- Life progresses by evolution.
- There are higher and lower forms of life.
- Evolution has something to do with how individuals adapt to their environment.
- The fittest organisms tend to survive.
- Organisms have a drive (or an instinct) to reproduce.
- Organisms also have a drive (or an instinct) for self-preservation.
- Evolution has something to do with whether an individual survives.
- Humans are more evolutionarily advanced than chimps.
- The better an organism is able to adapt to its environment, the more likely it is to evolve.
- We live today in the age of mammals; there was once an age of dinosaurs.
- Humans evolved from monkeys or apes.
- Humans are more fit to survive than dinosaurs.
- Humans are advancing evolutionarily in their intelligence.

Notice how these statements have a logic to them: we can reason from one idea to another. We can reason *from* progress *to* higher forms of life, *to* advanced ability to adapt, *to* greater survival, *to* humans as the high point of evolution.

But *all* the statements are deeply flawed. A few of them can be made to fit in with evolution, but only by wrenching them from their ordinary meaning. This whole way of reasoning seriously distorts what the theory of evolution is about. Yet, if you are convinced of any of the statements that make up this logic, you probably cannot get hold of how in the world it could be wrong.

Background stories are so difficult to counteract because they are virtually invisible. We don't see them as background stories at all. We see them simply as *the way things are*. As a result, the background stories influence our interpretation of everything we encounter. We don't even *hear* that the account we learn in our courses contradicts our background story.

Simply becoming aware of our background stories is empowering because it means we can now decide what we are going to believe, and, if we choose, we can decide that by reasoning things out.

School Stuff

Another impediment to critical thinking in a discipline can be illustrated by a couple of math problems Kurt Reusser asked fourth graders.[7]

There are 26 sheep and 10 goats on a ship. How old is the captain?

Most children *add* 26 and 10 to find the age of the captain! Not only that, but the better they are at math, the more likely they are to add to find the age of the captain.

Here is a second problem asked of the fourth graders:

A school is going on a field trip, and they need school buses. There are 140 kids in the school, and each school bus holds 30 kids. How many school buses do they need in all?

The children's answer is "Four, remainder 20"!

What is going on with these answers? It is not that the children cannot do the math. It's that, for the children, there is simply no link between math and reality. For them, math is something you learn in school, and it has nothing to do with real captains or real school buses.

Most of us have this category called "school stuff." It is the stuff we hear about in school, and we keep all this stuff in a special receptacle in our minds. We think, "I have to jump through some hoops to become a nurse, and one of them is taking courses in basic science. But there is no need for me to remember that stuff. It's *just science*; it's *not nursing*."

The temptation to isolate course material as merely school stuff is heightened by ingrained study techniques: passive listening, memorizing information rather than organizing and synthesizing it, simply repeating information from the book or a lecture, not formulating questions. If I think of what I learn in my courses primarily as stuff to be put into notes and regurgitated on exams, there is little chance I will learn much. I will leave class with the same unexamined background stories. These are difficult patterns to break, and it's difficult to make the leap of faith that using critical thinking as a study tool will actually result in better school performance.

TELLING YOUR STORY

It is important to take the subject matter as *your own*, to participate in the construction of your own knowledge.

With that in mind, review some of your personal history. Think back on courses you took more than two years ago:

- What is an example of something you learned in a course that still has major importance in your thinking or in your life?

- What is an example of a course you took that had *no* long-term influence on your life?

Now ask yourself, "How can I make this present course I am taking more like the first example? How can I use it to bring *value* to my life?"

Trusting the Discipline

Talking about trusting the discipline, in the context of critical thinking, implies two seemingly contradictory messages: first, that critical thinking encourages you to question the discipline you are studying; but, second, that it's reasonable for you to trust the discipline you are studying. Each message is reasonable, and each can be exaggerated.

Questioning lies at the heart of critical thinking, and a student in a discipline will be questioning many aspects of it: how to analyze the course material, how to apply it to cases, how to compare and contrast different theories, how to organize the main concepts, and how to evaluate positions in the discipline itself. In a political science course, for example, you may be asked to compare and contrast various political systems, to evaluate them, and maybe to reject one or another. In an ethics course, you may be asked to evaluate competing arguments about the morality of abortion or killing animals for food, and maybe come to a well-reasoned decision.

That questioning attitude can leave you with the impression that a goal of critical thinking is to be skeptical about what you learn in a discipline. This is particularly true when the course covers topics you've experienced firsthand—relationships, sports, dieting, family, power structures, art. It's easy to leave the course with your ideas about those topics completely unaffected. Or, having read competing accounts of marriage, you can come to believe that everyone in the field has his or her own theory about the subject. You can conclude that each account of marriage is just one of many, with no better backing than a host of others. Each account can become something to be doubted automatically, certainly no better than your own view of marriage or the one you were brought up with.

The idea that the subject matter is just "school stuff" can increase that skepticism. At the least, it can lead you to the impression that course content is not something to be taken too seriously. You can quickly say, "There are so many different views about political systems or abortion or marriage, that I am no better off than when I entered the course. It's all just a matter of opinion." But that would be a mistake.

To a great degree, the findings in a discipline, the material presented in texts and courses in that field, can be trusted. In fact, compared to other sources of knowledge in our society, the content of the disciplines studied in school can be trusted to a remarkable degree. Disciplines do have built-in sources of distortion, and you need to be aware of these. For example, experts in the discipline are much more trustworthy in their central results than they are in their application of those results to actual situations, especially complex situations. Thus in physics we know the laws that govern physical processes such as the weather, but that doesn't mean physics can tell us what the temperature will be a week from Thursday in Colorado Springs. It can't. (As paradoxical as it sounds, it seems that physics can be used to *prove* we will never be able to predict next week's exact weather on the basis of physics.)

Another source of distortion is that discipline experts are as human as anyone, so they can be guided by egocentricity and developmental factors just the way you and I can. A third source of distortion is actually rooted in a strength of the discipline: disciplines by their nature cannot pay attention to all factors that affect a situation. A discipline pays attention only to those factors that it studies. Thus, if you are studying adolescent development in a psychology class, you are learning to think the way a developmental psychologist thinks. You get insight into adolescents by looking at their patterns of physical, cognitive, social, and personality changes, based primarily on experiments and correlational studies. In thinking the way a psychologist thinks, you concentrate on the psychological factors in adolescent development, and not on the anthropological, legal, economic, medical, and literary factors.

It is important, then, not to accept the discipline without question. As a student, though, it is hard to appreciate how much emphasis is usually placed on critical-thinking standards by teachers in their presentations, by the authors of textbooks, by scholars in the field. Very seldom is a book used in a course "just someone's opinion."

Compare that to editorials or opinions on TV, newspapers, or on-line, or to politicians, lobbyists, advertisers and some other "advocates": Many of them (though not all) are actively trying to influence you to accept their own view of the matter. In contrast, virtually any text-book on controversial issues presents many different viewpoints. Authors of texts work hard to eliminate bias. (A frequent criticism of textbooks is that they *include too many* points of view rather than too few, that they are *bland* rather than biased.) Scholarly work is scruti-nized by others in the field who have extensive knowledge and skills (peer review). (One observation is that in science [in contrast to dog-matic areas] no one is praised more than someone who refutes accepted theories.) None of this implies that authors are always suc-cessful in eliminating bias or egocentricity. Of course not. But they are far more successful than people who don't even try to root out bias or who present only their own side of an issue.

Trusting a discipline, then, does not mean believing it com-pletely or automatically. It means taking it seriously, treating it as something to be learned from, rather than as something to be doubted automatically or put aside or rejected out of hand. After consideration, you may reject an idea or find it inadequate in one way or another. But to trust a discipline means to "try it on," to think in terms of it and see how it helps you understand the world in a new and richer way.

INTERNALIZING THE FIELD

Consider:

(1a) Suppose you are selling your car to a man who doesn't know much about cars, and he is willing to pay you much more than you know the car is worth. What should you do?

In many ways, this is just an ordinary everyday question.

Now consider something different. In ethics courses, two major ethical perspectives are usually addressed: rights theory and consequentialist theory. Rights theory directs you to ask, roughly, "Whose rights are being violated by the action? Is this the fair way to act?" Consequentialist theory directs you to ask, roughly, "What are the positive and negative consequences of the action for all concerned?" Thus a teacher, as part of an ethics course, might ask an essay question:

> (1b) Address the following from either a rights perspective or a conse-
> quentialist perspective, or both: Suppose you are selling your car to a man
> who doesn't know much about cars, and he is willing to pay you much
> more than you know the car is worth. What should you do?

So one way to bring the point home about internalizing the discipline and getting out of the grip of "school stuff" is to see that there is a strong sense in which questions (1a) and (1b) are virtually *the same question*.[8] Part of the point of any course is that we should look at ordinary everyday situations in terms of the central concepts in the discipline. The intent is for this to hold long after the course is over. If it doesn't, the course may have missed you.

It is reasonable to apply a similar degree of trust even in matters that are far more controversial and deeply personal. For many people, for example, understanding the Bible is a deeply personal and intensely significant part of their lives. But, if you want to find out what the Bible is saying, if that is important to you, a reasonable way to go about it is to take a course in biblical studies. The authors you are likely to read in such a course will be biblical scholars, familiar with a wide variety of viewpoints and interpretations—not just with others who agree with them. They have read primary sources carefully. They have come to reasoned conclusions about the dating of manuscripts, and when and by whom those manuscripts were written. Most likely they know the original languages. They are intimately familiar with both the historical periods and the archaeological record. Their writings have been subjected to peer review.

Such extensive research is not found in most other sources you might consult, such as television documentaries, websites, sermons by religious leaders, evangelists on the radio, or the newest *New York Times* best seller.

Of course, the trustworthiness of the field does not imply that scholars are necessarily *right*. They could be wrong for any number of reasons—and you should think critically about their conclusions and their evidence, their interpretations and the context, the assumptions they make and the alternatives they ignore. They *are*, however, the best source you are likely to find. Moreover, if they are later shown to be wrong, it will most likely be by a member of the same community of critically thinking historians and biblical scholars.

The same can be said for just about any topic, no matter how controversial or personal. In fact, the more important a topic is in

COMMON SENSE

One of the things disciplines often do is contradict common sense. If that happens, you should feel a need to question the common sense. Disciplines are full of carefully amassed evidence, reasoned argumentation, and critiques by others. Common sense is not subject to any of these, certainly not in any systematic way. It is not common sense that the desk you are sitting at is 99 percent empty space; that being cold and wet has nothing to do with catching cold; that ulcers are caused by bacteria, not stress; that, objectively, there is no such thing as color; that the vast majority of us are capable of acting the way the Nazis did. Though these examples contradict most people's common sense, all, according to the most complete evidence we have, are clearly true.

your life, the more important it is to take a course in it, to read a textbook in the area. Here is a brief list of topics that are important to many people, and those people would benefit tremendously by consulting and taking seriously the discipline's findings and viewpoints:

- dieting
- healthy attitudes toward death and dying
- causes of crime in the United States
- global warming
- cloning
- the morality of abortion, the rights of animals, sexual morality
- the causes of "terrorism"
- the efficacy of herbal remedies
- the litigious nature of our society
- parapsychology, telekinesis

When You Disagree

There may be inaccuracies in your text or in lectures. That is quite possible. But be wary of concluding too quickly that lectures or texts are inaccurate or biased. If what the book says is contrary to your own experience, carefully consider a number of questions before concluding that the text is off-base. For example:

- Did I understand clearly what was said and what was meant, in context?
- Is my disagreement based merely on common sense? What is the real evidence for the commonsense view?
- Are my beliefs based on sources I have accepted uncritically?
- Is my own experience limited? Is it applicable only in one area?
- Do I have a vested interest in disbelieving what is in the text? Is my ego bound up with accepting one view over another?
- Do I feel some fear I may be unaware of at having my worldview shaken up? Do the findings in the discipline make me angry?

Some Outcomes

The outcomes listed here may be premature at this point. You may need further practice (maybe a lot of further practice) to do them well. But you should be making a beginning.

At the end of this chapter . . .

1. SEE-I: You should be able to state, elaborate, exemplify, and illustrate what is meant by the main concepts in this chapter: "the logic of a discipline," "the importance of vocabulary in a discipline," "fundamental and powerful concepts," "the central question of a course," and "the point of view of a discipline."
2. You should be able to *analyze the logic of the discipline* you are studying in a clear and accurate way (although not necessarily in a way that shows a deep or broad grasp of the discipline).
3. You should be *generating questions* within the discipline using the elements of reasoning. ("What are the implications of calling this artwork baroque?" "What information and assumptions is this theory based on?")
4. You are beginning to *use the vocabulary* of the discipline when you describe problems or situations.
5. You should be able to think through at least some important problems using *fundamental and powerful concepts* in the course. You should be able to carry this through in a way that is reasonably clear and accurate, though again not necessarily with

the depth or breadth that will come as you apply those concepts to an ever-widening range of problems and topics.

6. You can *identify the central question of the course*, at least tentatively. You should be able to describe how virtually every
problem or question that arises in the course is an aspect of
that central question.

7. You should be able to *describe the point of view of the discipline*:
the domain, categories, and connections one sees when looking
at the world through that point of view. You should be able to
give your own examples of these. But more than that, you
should be starting to actually *see* the world with that point of
view.

8. You should be able to *state, elaborate*, and *give your own examples* of impediments to thinking critically within the discipline.

9. You should be able to *integrate* the outcomes of this chapter
with those from Chapters 1 and 2 (pages 37 and 76). You
should now be able to *explain* and *apply* those earlier outcomes
to the discipline in a broader, deeper way.

Ideas for Writing

(General guidelines for "Ideas for Writing" are on page 38.)

1. What role do *questions* play in the discipline you are studying?
How about *reasoning*? How about the challenge of *believing the
results*?

2. Think about the distinction between seeing the discipline you
are studying as a system of thinking versus seeing it as a body
of information. What would you say are the key differences
between the two? How might that affect someone taking a
course in the discipline?

3. On pages 175–176, there is a brief description of some intellectual character traits of a critical thinker. As well as you can at
this point in your learning, describe what it would be like for
someone to be *intellectually engaged* in the field you are studying? (For example, suppose you are in a writing course. What
would it be like for someone to be *committed* to being a
writer?)

4. There are any number of questions you can write about in relation to the discipline you are studying: What impact does the
   discipline have on the world? What impact should it have?
   What would be the implications and consequences if people in
   general took the findings or expertise of the discipline seriously? How do people often fail to take account of it in our
   political, social, legal, or educational institutions? How are the
   discipline's fundamental and powerful concepts, and the central
   questions it addresses, essential in the world outside school?
   How would young people benefit from thinking through the
   point of view of the discipline (at their level)? Generate some of
   your own ideas to write about in relation to the discipline you
   are studying.

Tell Your Story

(The idea behind "Tell Your Story" and some suggestions about doing
it are on page 39.)

1. What is your attitude toward the discipline you are studying?
   How has your attitude toward it changed over the years, maybe
   even before you ever took a course in it? What are some factors
   that might help you personally to become more open to it?

2. Have you ever thought about what it would be like for you to
   have a degree in the field you are focusing on in this course?
   Or, even more, picture what it would be like to be a professional in this field. What would stand in the way for you?

3. Do you have a category like "school stuff" in your mind? If so,
   how strong is it? To what extent does it prevent you from taking the discipline seriously?

4. Consider the central question of the course you are taking, and
   reflect on background stories you carry with you as "answers"
   to it. Because we are so unaware of our background stories,
   spelling them out is usually very difficult, but you may have
   some real insights here. To write on this question, you probably
   have to let go of some of the restraints you usually impose on
   your thinking. So, if it's a course in political science, how do

you think politics or government really works? If it's a course in nursing, what's your picture of how to treat people who are sick?) Adapt the question to the domain of the subject matter you are studying. Then reflect on how you acquired your background story.

5. Think of the fundamental and powerful concepts in your course or discipline. What was your idea of them before you ever entered this course? Even if the words in the concepts are unfamiliar to you, the concepts themselves may well have operated in your thinking all along, without your being aware of it. How have these f&p concepts had an impact on your life?

CHAPTER 3 Exercises

The exercises contain examples from a wide variety of disciplines. Few of these examples will be in the subject you are studying. But what the exercises ask you to do is directly relevant to the field you are studying. The exercises were chosen because they bring home important points about critical thinking in any field.

If possible, after answering the question as it stands, see if you can adapt it to the discipline you are studying.

3.1 Analyze the logic of a discipline-based course you are taking by "going around the circle" with respect to it. If you wish, you can use the "Logic of a Literature Course" (pages 97–99) as a model.

3.2 Here are two paragraphs from a composition text:

> Whenever you write, your goal is to communicate effectively with the people who are going to read what you write. These readers are considered your audience. Sometimes your audience might include specific people such as your classmates, your instructor, your friends, your family, or your boss. At other times, you might be writing for the general public that reads your local newspaper.

> As you write, ask yourself: Who is going to read this? How much do they already know about my topic? What are their attitudes about my topic? The answers to these questions can help you identify your audience. . . . Once you have analyzed your audience, you will be better able to decide on the content, vocabulary, and tone that are most suitable for your paper.[9]

a. Use the elements of reasoning to describe how the authors reason from point to point in the two paragraphs.

b. Do the same kind of analysis with different paragraphs from the readings in your course.

3.3 Critical thinking involves asking good questions: Write down five questions you have about the discipline you are studying. They should be good questions, ones where learning the answer is important to you. If you have trouble thinking of such questions, what conclusions do you draw?

3.4 With your book closed, write an SEE-I for the main concepts in this chapter: "the logic of a discipline," "the importance of vocabulary in a discipline," "fundamental and powerful concepts," "the central question of a course," and "the point of view of a discipline."

3.5 Critical thinking is authentic. Consider math problems. Students often prefer certain math problems because all they have to do is the computations or the calculator work. They hate word problems. That's natural. Computations have a much safer feel to them because you have a good idea of how to proceed. The problem does not look so open-ended. Critical thinking, however, applies to real-life problems with a quantitative aspect. Think them through mathematically, and only then do the computation or calculator work.

a. Having any realistic understanding of math shows that buying lottery tickets makes no sense at all. People in math often call lotteries "the stupidity tax." Why, mathematically, do you think that is?

b. Think of credit card debt: What exactly are you *buying* with the interest you pay?
→ What are some areas of your life where you need to think mathematically?

3.6 **Logic of a field.** What is the difference between thinking ethically and thinking legally? Give some examples to illustrate the difference.

3.7 **Vocabulary of the discipline.** As the course goes along, keep a log of terms you can define but still don't really understand. Keep a log of vocabulary words in the field that you can apply directly to your life as you live it now.

3.8 Look in the Table of Contents of a textbook in a class you are taking, and draw a concept map of the main themes of the book. Alternatively, make a concept map of the fundamental and powerful concepts for this course.

3.9 **Group work.** In groups of four, critically discuss the central question of the course. Try to come to a consensus on what it is, how it unifies the course as a whole, how it fits in with the central questions of other related fields. Then write down the central question of three other courses you are currently taking (or ones you have taken as recently as possible).

Compare the central questions to the one you identified for this course. How are they similar? What are the striking differences? How do they fit with one another?

3.10 Look back at the box on "Internalizing the Field" (pages 120–121), and adapt it to the field you are studying in this course. Take three or four questions as they might be asked from the point of view of the field you are studying. (For example, in a sociology course: "From the point of view of a structural-functional analysis of the family, what main roles do families play in human society?")

Next, ask the same question, but leave off the whole first half. Try to phrase it in ordinary non-academic language: "How do families work?"

How do the two versions of the question seem different to you? From the point of view of the field, to what extent are the questions the same or different?

3.11 **Critical writing for self-assessment.** Construct your own pre-test and post-test on critical thinking in a subject matter. Choose an important question in the course. It may not be the central question, but it should be very important. Maybe you can write it by adapting the title of a chapter or group of chapters in the text. Here are some examples:

Life sciences: How does the body work?

Education: How do children learn?

Geology: How do landforms come about?

Business: How does one manage a business?

Composition: How does someone write a good argumentative essay?

Write out an answer to this near the beginning of the course. You will be thinking it out as you compose your response. When your answer is written, put it away somewhere, and don't refer back to it. Give it time to sink into the background.

Near the end of the course (and without looking at your first answer), write out an answer to the same question.

Then compare the two, but not just with respect to the information each contains (this will obviously increase substantially by the time the semester is over). Compare them with respect to:

- How you have organized the information
- How well you have grasped the logic of the answer
- How well you are able to see the parts working together as a whole (synthesis).

You should also notice a marked improvement in the accuracy, importance, precision, and depth of your response.

3.12 As a study skill, memorizing does not work very well. What can you do instead? (Consider the effectiveness of your study habits for your coursework. Suppose you were going to a doctor for a serious medical condition. Would you want your doctor to have studied in medical school the way you study for your classes? Why or why not? How would you want your doctor to have studied?)

3.13 As an illustration, draw a concept map of critical thinking as you understand it so far.

3.14 Here is a concept map based on a new management paradigm in a management textbook.[10]

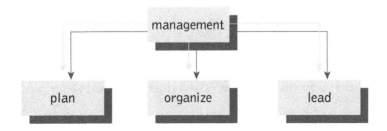

By thinking of the logic of this paradigm, can you see what is missing as a fundamental and powerful concept?

3.15 Impediments. Take each of the impediments listed in Chapter 1 (pages 16–25) and give an original example of how each might be an impediment to thinking critically in the discipline you are studying in this class. Be specific.

3.16 Why would you (or someone else) think that humans are more fit than dinosaurs? Evaluate the reasoning.

3.17 Group work. Focus on the background story you have for this course. (This is difficult work.)

Individually, take five of the most important concepts in the field. (A good place to get them is from the headings in the table of contents in the text.) Before you read anything about them in the book, write down your main ideas about them: how you understand them, how they work. For example, suppose it is a course in sociology and one of the chapters is entitled "Cultural Diversity." Explain what cultural diversity is, how it works, how it comes about, what effects it has, how you feel about it—whatever seems important to you. (Notice that this is an ill-defined question. You'll have to adapt it to your field.)

Now, discuss your responses in groups of four. Your aim in this is not to argue your points with others. It is to formulate a clear understanding of the background story that is operating in you.

Next, read the book and compare your story with the account in the book. Discuss this with the same group of four people. But your goal is not to find out if you were right or wrong. It is still to get a conscious grasp of your background story or logic, and to compare it to the logic of the discipline you are studying.

3.18 "We don't really know if the sun will rise tomorrow." Evaluate this statement.

3.19 Using fundamental and powerful concepts, write a short essay on the central question of your course. You can use the example on pages 109–111 as a model.

3.20 SEE-I. Look back over the contents of Chapter 3:

- Find a clarifying *statement* (or definition) in the chapter.
- Find an *elaboration* of an idea in it.
- Find an example; then find a contrasting example.
- Find an illustration.

3.21 Read the brief description of critical-thinking character traits on pages 175–176. Describe how intellectual empathy and intellectual humility enter into the learning of the discipline you are studying.

DAILY PRACTICE
At incorporating critical thinking into your life and your learning.

Before you start on Exercises 3.22 through 3.24, look back at the instructions on pages 44–45. Again, the key is to do the exercises as often as possible, daily if you can, in small repeated intervals, rather than doing them in a single big burst of effort.

3.22 **Engage with the fundamental and powerful concepts.** After you or your teacher have identified these in your course, spend a day in your life as usual, but as you do, start applying the fundamental and powerful concepts in a conscious, self-aware way. You don't have to be advanced as a thinker to feel the power of this. The exercise is to look for situations that can be understood better (or differently) by applying the fundamental and powerful concepts. Thus, if the concept is *romanticism*, I would spend intensive, focused time looking at almost everything—ordinary events, people, things, interactions—through the lens of romanticism. How can I use that concept to understand my quest for an education, my preference for driving versus public transportation (or vice versa), the people I choose (and do not choose) for friends, movies I like, books, anything?

3.23 Engage with the central question of the discipline. After you (or your teacher) have identified the central question in your course, spend a short period of time each day, for several days, asking yourself that question and applying it to what you encounter as you live your life. For example, suppose the question is, "What do writers do to make literature effective?" You could spend your day creatively applying this question in any number of ways: "How would a writer describe this situation effectively?" "How *have* writers I've read described this kind of situation effectively?"

Engage in this ongoing activity with the central question of your course.

3.24 Spend a day observing through the point of view of the discipline. At the beginning, you don't necessarily have to *explain* anything. Just *notice*, observe. (Observe not just visually, but with your other senses as well—and especially with your mind.)

Go through your daily life as usual, only notice—and write down—all the items you encounter that are in the domain of the discipline you are studying. Try also to observe in terms of connections—at least wonder about the connections between the objects and events you observe and other concepts in the field.

For example, suppose you are studying physics. You see leaves moving on a tree, and notice that you are seeing forces at work, energy being transformed. You see your hands writing in your journal, and you notice that you are seeing push–pull forces of muscles; you are seeing a lever at work as you get up from your chair, and so on.

Another example: Suppose you are studying the Impressionists in an art history course. You see colors and shapes dissolving as you look out the window, and that boundaries aren't nearly as exact as you thought they were; you see that shadows are blue or purple as Monet saw them, not really black at all; you see the effects of snow and how it turns things blue rather than white; you let your eyes unfocus and allow yourself to see black foreground and bright background switch places as Manet did.

In your journal, write down as many examples as you can (at least 12 to 15) of things or connections that you see differently when you are viewing them from the point of view of the discipline. Describe the differences briefly.

Chapter 4
Standards of Critical Thinking

T wo primary ingredients turn thinking into critical thinking. The first is that critical thinking is *reflective* thinking. It involves thinking *about* one's thinking, specifically about the *elements* of the thinking. The second is that critical thinking is thinking that is done *well*. It is thinking that meets high *standards* of thinking.

This chapter focuses on seven of the standards our thinking has to meet for it to be critical:

- Clearness
- Accuracy
- Importance, relevance
- Sufficiency
- Depth
- Breadth
- Precision

FIGURE 4.1   *The standards of critical thinking.*

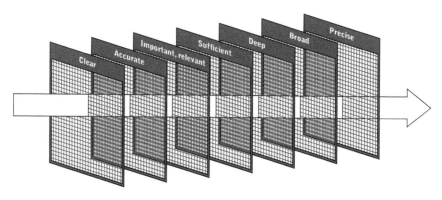

You can picture the standards as a set of screens or filters that screen out reasoning that is not clear, not accurate, or not sufficiently relevant, deep, broad, or precise (see Figure 4.1). An overall Standards Check appears on pages 158–159, at the end of this chapter.

Clearness

- Is the thinking clear?
- Is this clear in my mind?
- Am I saying this clearly?

Definition: Your thinking is clear when it's easily understood, when it's free from the likelihood of misunderstanding, when it's readily apparent what follows from it. Your thinking is clear when you can state your meaning exactly, when you can elaborate on it and explain it, when you can give good examples and illustrations of it (SEE-I).

Related terms: understandable, plain, clarifying.

Opposites: Your thinking is *unclear* when it is obscure, ambiguous, confused, easily misunderstood, or you don't see what follows from it. Your thinking is unclear when you cannot give an adequate SEE-I.

CLEARNESS AND CONCEPTS

One way to grasp the element concepts and the standard clearness better is to engage in a **conceptual analysis** that targets *implications*:

- Take a concept like "terrorist" and try to get clear about it by asking yourself about the *implications* of being a terrorist:
  - What would someone who is a terrorist do?
  - What would a terrorist refrain from doing?
  - Is there anything you can think of that people who are terrorists would *have to* do (if they didn't, they wouldn't be terrorists)?
- Next, list a set of related terms (such as violence, freedom fighter, innocent victims, political motives, martyr, and fanatic) and explain the similar and different implications of each.

Answering questions like these helps you to focus on the concept *terrorism*.

In the discipline. Do a conceptual analysis in your course by applying these questions to the fundamental and powerful concepts.

Discussion

Expressing Yourself Clearly and Thinking Clearly in Your Own Mind

There are two aspects to clearness. One is being clear in your own mind about what you mean; the other is expressing yourself clearly so the other person knows what you mean. Clearness as a critical-thinking standard is based on a metaphor, as when we say *water* or *glass* is clear: it means we can see through to the other side without anything getting in the way. In a clear picture or a clear diagram, we can readily make out what is going on. Similarly, you express yourself clearly when someone can see through your words directly to what you intended. Your thinking is clear in your own mind when you can see through to the implications of what you're thinking.

Unclear Expression.   There is an old joke about a father asking questions of his twelve-year-old son:

"Where did you go?"

"Out."

"What did you do?"

"Nothing."

That's unclear *expression*. The boy knows exactly where he went and what he did. He's just not telling.

Unclear in Mind.   You may not know what Kant means by "the transcendental unity of apperception." *Obviously* you don't if you haven't read Kant. But Kant is a tough philosopher to understand. Even if you have read his work, have studied it hard, you may still not be very clear about it. You may have only a vague, hazy understanding. You may not be able to state it in your own words, elaborate on it, exemplify it, or illustrate it. It's unclear in your own mind.

This can happen with familiar concepts also. All of the following concepts have a great deal of unclearness in them: freedom, patriotism, love, religion, philosophy, courage, wisdom. Even in your own mind you are probably not very clear about what they mean. If any of these concepts are important to you, it's worth the work to become clearer about them.

Most of the fundamental and powerful concepts in your course are probably closer to these than to "the transcendental unity of apperception." Fundamental and powerful concepts may be more or less familiar to you, but they are probably still not concepts whose full implications you know.

SEE-I and Clearness

A good way to get clearer in your own mind and to communicate more clearly with others is to get in the habit of using SEE-I often (pages 30–33). Good writers and clear speakers use SEE-I unconsciously a great deal of the time. They make their points succinctly (S); they elaborate and explain them (E); they give you examples to make their points concrete (E); and they give you illustrations so you can picture what they are saying (I). Even good writers and speakers, though, benefit from using SEE-I explicitly, reminding themselves of it, so they become clearer.

Clearness Is Context Dependent

What is clear in one context is not necessarily clear in another. Three important contexts where you may have to adjust your standard of clearness are audience, discipline or subject matter, and stage of thinking.

Audience.   To express yourself clearly, you need a clear idea of your audience. You must then choose your words appropriately. When explaining photosynthesis to a child, you'll use one set of words. When talking to a biologist, you will use a different set.

CRITICAL WRITING

One way students often fail to write clearly is by writing answers (in papers or essay exams) *for the teacher*—who already knows the material.

Take an important section of your text and explain in writing what it is saying. Write it as though you were explaining it to your teacher. Now, write it as though you were explaining it to a potential employer who does not know much about this subject. Your goal is to show the employer that you *understand* what you are talking about.

The two may be startlingly different.

Discipline or Subject Matter.   Different disciplines use the standard of clearness in different ways. What it is to be clear in describing the orbits of the planets may well be different from what it is to be clear when distinguishing the Renaissance from the baroque period or doing a sociological study of life in a Swiss village.

Stage of Thinking.   If you are thinking critically, your understanding of important concepts becomes clearer over time. For example, how clear a fundamental and powerful concept is to you at the beginning of a course will be different from how clear it is to you at the end. As you progress in a course in art history, your concept of the renaissance and the baroque should become clearer. It is sometimes important not to strive for too much clarity right at the beginning, instead allowing time for ideas to clarify themselves. For example, you may need to let your idea for a term paper mature.

Impediments: What's Difficult about Being Clear

- Saying what you mean
- Being clear in your own mind
- Anticipating what others will not understand

- Overcoming certain emotional, physical, and mental states that inhibit clearness. Depression, for example, influences us to believe some very unclear (and also inaccurate) generalizations. We look around and feel, "Everything is hopeless" or "My life is meaningless." Depression thrives on unclearness.

How to Become Clearer

Alone

- Get in the habit of using SEE-I, both for your own understanding and to communicate with others. As part of your SEE-I, give not only examples, but contrasting examples and hypothetical cases.
- Practice trying to refine both your thoughts and what you say. Remind yourself to be careful to choose the clearest words.
- Keep your audience in mind. Anticipate places where others may have difficulty following you.
- Restate what you mean in other words.
- Write down your thinking. Come back to it in a few days (when it is no longer so fresh in your mind what you meant) and see what it conveys to you.
- Use conceptual analysis (see page 135).
- Try out hypothetical cases and extrapolate to new cases.

With Others

- Ask others if they can state, elaborate, and give examples and/or illustrations of what you mean.
- Ask others in a group to paraphrase what you said or wrote. If they are easily able to paraphrase it, it is pretty solid evidence you were clear. If they are not easily able to say what you meant, it is some evidence you were unclear. (It is not strong evidence, however, because they may not be reading or listening attentively.)
- Get feedback from people outside your group and from those who don't look at the issue the same way you do. (Shared background makes it easier to take it for granted that people will understand you.)

Accuracy

- Is the thinking accurate?
- Are the statements accurate, true?

Definition: Aristotle gave one of the clearest definitions of the term *true*:

> To say of what is that it is, or of what is not that it is not, is true.

We could define accuracy in much the same way:

> My thinking and my words are accurate when they describe the way things actually are.

Related terms: true, well established, confirmed, corroborated, well authenticated, plausible.

Opposites: My thinking and my words are *inaccurate* when they are not in accord with the way things in fact are. Notice that my words can be inaccurate or false even if I *believe* that they are in accord with reality. What matters for accuracy is not whether I believe a claim, but whether that claim actually fits the way things in fact are.

Discussion

Philosophical Issues about Accuracy and Truth Arise for Some People.

Problems with the Term True.   Some people reserve the word *true* for situations where they are absolutely sure of something, or they reserve it for profound statements ("We hold these truths to be self-evident"). Notice that the word *true* as a standard of critical thinking is not used in either of those two ways. As a standard, it simply means your words describe the way things are. (For example, it's true that snow is usually white, that Caravaggio was a baroque painter, that objects fall toward the earth at 32 ft/sec^2.) A good deal of the information we all have is likely to be true (though of course not all of it is). The information we find in reputable textbooks and coursework, where authors have worked at presenting the most reliable, well-established findings and conclusions, is more likely to be true (though, again, not all of it is). But, if philosophical problems about the word *true* interfere with your critical thinking, use the term *accurate* instead.

Accurate versus "How Do We Know It's Accurate?"   To say something is true or accurate is not always the same as saying we know it's true or accurate. Take the idea of life on other planets in the universe: Either there is or there isn't. We don't know which. We may never know. Yet—independent of whether we ever know it—one side or the other is true.

Accuracy and Making Mistakes. You need to be reasonable. You need to judge accuracy and truth by doing the best you can, using your best reasoning and the most reliable sources. You may turn out to be mistaken, of course. But it's not critical thinking to hold yourself or others to unreasonably high standards. The fact that you possibly made mistakes does not show your reasoning is inaccurate. Only one thing shows that your most informed and reasoned conclusions are inaccurate: *better* reasoned and informed conclusions.

Impediments: What's Difficult about Being Accurate and Recognizing What's Accurate

- It is often hard to be open to the accuracy of things we hear, especially if what we hear is threatening to us.
- Inertia. It is more comfortable to keep the beliefs we have than to change them, even when we get evidence that our beliefs are not accurate.
- Wishful thinking and denial. We often let our desires or our fears influence our assessments of what's accurate. The desire to win the lottery blinds us to the fact that we have no realistic chance to win it. People often blind themselves to their own alcoholism and the alcoholism of those they are closest to.
- We often generalize too quickly, especially from vivid personal experience. This makes us less than open to findings that contradict our personal experience. (If I visit Chicago, all it takes is a few rude Chicagoans for me to conclude that Chicagoans are rude—even though I was mistreated by only three people, and there are 3 million other Chicagoans out there.)

  A good informal way to test the accuracy of a generalization is not to look primarily for corroborating examples, but to *look for counterexamples*. If I believe Chicagoans are rude, instead of looking for rude Chicagoans to confirm my generalization, I should look for Chicagoans who are *not* rude. Finding only a few reduces the credibility of my generalization. A good way to test for accuracy is to search hard for disconfirmation.
- We often believe our unexamined background stories and form an inaccurate picture of the world from news-media and fictional accounts.

Evaluate the *accuracy* of the Golden Rule: "Do unto others as you would have them do unto you."

You can probably think of a hundred examples in favor of this generalization. But that doesn't show the generalization is accurate pure and simple.

Think of a good counterexample: a case where it would be wrong for a person to do something unto others, even if the person would want others to do the same thing unto him or her.[1]

How to Become More Accurate

Alone

- Check out questionable information. Do the research to find out.
- Consult reliable sources.
- Test beliefs you hold. Treat them as hypotheses.
- Be on the lookout for wishful thinking.
- Get in the habit of reflecting on what you believe, read, and hear by asking questions that probe for accuracy:
  - Where did I learn that?
  - How reliable was my source in this context?
  - Do I believe this only because it "sounds right"?
  - How could I check it? How could I test it?
  - Can I think of counterexamples?

With Others

- Get feedback on what aspects of your thinking others consider doubtful or questionable.
- Get feedback on where they believe you need more reasons for what you say.

Importance, Relevance

- Does the thinking focus on what is important?
- How relevant, central, important is the thinking for the problem at hand?

Look at the syllabus for your course. Read it carefully. What are the three most important things you need to do in the course? Next, think about the content of the course ahead of you. What are the three most important things you need to do to think critically in the discipline?

Definition: To say something is important is to say it matters. If you're thinking about an issue, the thinking is important when it matters in deciding that issue. The thinking is important when it's directly relevant to addressing the problem at hand.

Related terms: main, central, essential, significant, crucial, critical, related.

Opposites: You are focusing on what is *unimportant* if it makes little or no difference in relation to the question you're addressing, or if you are focusing on a minor aspect of the problem. At an extreme, your thinking can be *irrelevant* to the problem at hand.

Discussion

Important *to*, Relevant *to*.   In critical thinking, relevant means relevant to a question at issue, with a purpose in mind and set in a particular context. It doesn't mean relevant in general. The same is true for the term *important*.

Everything is relevant to *something*, but that doesn't mean it's relevant to the problem at hand. When we evaluate a piece of reasoning, what we are interested in is whether that reasoning is relevant or important to deciding the question at issue. Many things are vitally important to me personally: my health, for example, or the well-being of my family, or the emotions I am feeling. It can feel insulting for someone to tell me that such considerations are irrelevant or unimportant. Yet those considerations can indeed be irrelevant to reasoning through a particular question at issue.

For example, victims of violent crime often have intense feelings of anger and outrage. However, those feelings are not relevant to the question of whether the person accused is guilty or innocent. In fact, the intensity of those feelings can even make the question of guilt harder to decide reasonably. Obviously, victims' feelings of anger and violation *are* important—important to them and important to us as empathetic fellow humans. But the feelings are not important when deciding whether someone is guilty. Only the evidence of the case (motivation, identification by witnesses, circumstantial evidence, etc.) is relevant to arriving at a just verdict.

Impediments: What's Difficult about Focusing on What Is Important

- Losing sight of your purpose in reasoning the question out
- Forgetting or ignoring the context of the question
- Missing the forest for the trees
- Thinking that everything in a course or subject matter is equally important
- Speaking just to be speaking; writing just to be filling pages; responding without reflecting
- Being threatened or preoccupied: this can make reactions seem relevant to the problem, even when they aren't

How to Focus on What Is Most Important

Alone

- Keep in mind the question at issue, your purpose, and the context in which the question is being asked.
- Take a step back in your thinking: try to get an overview.
- Ask, "How does this point relate to the topic at hand?"
- *Outline.* Outline what you read or hear or think. In your outline, distinguish between main points and subsidiary points.
- *Summarize.* Write a short summary of what you read or hear. (Then maybe make it shorter still.)
- Sketch a quick concept map. (See pages 105–106.)
- When listening or reading, focus on what is being said and put aside your *reaction* to what is said.

With Others

- Compare your outlines and summaries with those of other people in a group. Exchange honest but respectful feedback on what is relevant to a question and what is not.
- Practice picking out what is essential *to the other person.* Ask, "Is this the central part of what you are saying?"

Sufficiency

- Has this been reasoned out sufficiently?
- Have I reasoned this out enough to decide the issue reasonably?

Definition: Your thinking about a question or an issue is sufficient when you've reasoned it out thoroughly enough for the purpose at hand, when it is adequate for what is needed, when you've taken account of all necessary factors.

Related terms: adequate, enough, complete, comprehensive, thorough.

Opposites: Your thinking is *insufficient* when you have left out crucial considerations or when you haven't reasoned the issue out enough to meet the needs of the situation.

Discussion

Sufficiency, Purpose, and Context.   A basic question is always "Have I reasoned this out enough?" A follow-up question is always "Enough for what?" A reasonable answer to the second question is "Enough to achieve the purpose." It is also reasonable to add "Enough to achieve it in this particular setting or context."

One crucial context is the **time factor**. I may have to make a decision about a patient whose life is in immediate danger. How much reasoning is sufficient under those circumstances depends heavily on the fact that it's an emergency. An administrator, reviewing the decision later, has much more time to evaluate what should have been done.

Sufficiency versus Proof.   It is always a temptation to say you need more information before deciding this issue, but it's unreasonable to require too much evidence before drawing a conclusion. Usually, important practical issues cannot be proved conclusively. No one can *prove* what is the best overall procedure for teaching math in an elementary education classroom because there are many reasonable alternatives. We usually cannot have complete evidence that an action will be environmentally safe; all we can have is strong evidence, and even that is often hard to come by. Scientists usually maintain that scientific laws are not *proven* by experiments—rather, they are confirmed by experiment, always allowing for the fact that some later experiments may disconfirm the law, especially in the light of a new scientific theory.

So requiring enough reasoning to prove a case conclusively is usually an unreasonably stringent standard.

A Courtroom Analogy.   How much reasoning is enough? In criminal cases, guilt has to be established beyond a reasonable doubt. That is a measure of how sufficient the evidence in the case has to be. The standard is set very high because a person's freedom depends on the outcome.

In civil cases like lawsuits, however, all that is required is a preponderance of evidence. The judge or jury merely has to decide which of the two sides has more evidence in its favor.

Sufficiency and Deductive Validity.   The term *validity*—often called *deductive validity*—is used in formal logic. Deductive validity is actually a more stringent concept than proof as used in a courtroom. For an argument to be deductively valid, the premises (if true) have to prove the conclusion not just beyond any reasonable doubt, but beyond any possible doubt as well. A familiar example is the syllogism:

> Socrates is human.
>
> All humans are mortal.
>
> Therefore, Socrates is mortal.

Deductive validity is an important concept for those dealing with formal logic.

Sufficiency and Success.   Suppose you reason out an important decision (like the one in the box), and you do so to the best of your ability under the circumstances. Suppose that, nevertheless, the decision turns out disastrously. Did you reason it out sufficiently? Well, if you did reason it out to the best of your ability under the circumstances, the answer is yes.

> After reasoning through the decision, parents let their sixteen-year-old son, a new driver, take the car out. There is an accident. The son is seriously hurt. The parents feel intense guilt. "If only we hadn't let him take the car out . . . . We should not have made that decision."

The success of a decision can never be the measure of whether you've reasoned something out enough. Success depends on many other factors besides good reasoning, and many of those factors are beyond your control and beyond your ability to anticipate. A successful decision depends, for example, on luck, the right (or the wrong) combination of events occurring at just the right moment in time.

Many times our feelings respond as if we had not done enough, as in the case of the parents letting the son drive. That's because grief often presents itself to us as guilt. Feelings like guilt and shame are not a good guide to whether we have reasoned decisions out sufficiently. It is more reasonable to let the grief come out purely as grief, mourning our loss but without self-recrimination.

Impediments: What's Difficult about Reasoning Through Something Sufficiently

- Jumping to conclusions
- A tendency to reason through unimportant issues too much and through important issues too little

- Sticking with preestablished views that seem sufficient because we have not examined alternatives
- Unreasonable standards (such as perfectionism) of what counts as enough
- Lack of relevant background knowledge
- Simply forgetting to ask, "Is this sufficient?" "Is it enough?"

In each item, a reason is given → then a conclusion is drawn. In each case explain why the reason is *not enough* to draw the conclusion. Do not *disagree* with the reason; focus instead on why it's not *sufficient*.

1. My 80-year-old grandfather smoked a pack of cigarettes a day his whole life. → Cigarettes are not harmful.

2. I've studied every night for a week. → I'll do well on the exam.

3. You have lied to me. → Now I can never trust you.

4. "I cried because I had no shoes, until I met a man who had no feet." → I shouldn't cry about my own suffering.

5. The Bible says "Thou shalt not kill." → Capital punishment is forbidden by the Bible.

How to Reason Things Out Sufficiently

Alone

- Ask yourself explicitly, "Has enough evidence been given? Has enough of the purpose been accomplished? Has the question been addressed sufficiently?" Such questions can be asked for each of the elements.
- Consciously seek out alternatives. Ask yourself, "What are the alternatives to the conclusion being drawn? How much reasoning is sufficient to decide between them?"
- Take more time to reason out important issues thoroughly.
- Acquire necessary background knowledge.

With Others

- Ask fellow students for alternatives they see and maybe you don't.
- Before you try to answer a critical-thinking question, discuss with others how much evidence is necessary to answer it.
- Get feedback from experts on whether your reasoning about an issue in the field is sufficient.

Depth and Breadth

- Has this been reasoned out deeply enough?
- Have I taken adequate account of underlying theories, explanations, and the complexities of the problem?
- Have I reasoned this out broadly enough?
- Have I taken adequate account of other related issues, other perspectives on the problem, other aspects of the context?

Definition: Your thinking about a question is deep enough when you (a) recognize that to accomplish your purpose, you must look below the surface of the question or issue (particularly at theories or explanations in the discipline); (b) identify the complexities that underlie it; and (c) take adequate account of those complexities and underlying issues in addressing the question.

Similarly, your thinking is broad enough when you (a) recognize the need to look at other aspects, other perspectives, other parallel problems, (b) identify them, and (c) take adequate account of them in reasoning through the question.

Related terms: complex, comprehensive, nuanced (sometimes), subtle (sometimes), probing, root questions.

Opposites: Your thinking is *too superficial* or *too narrow* when you oversimplify things; when you don't see that complex, multifaceted issues require complex, multifaceted responses; when you act as if large-scale, controversial issues are susceptible to easy answers and quick fixes.

Discussion

Differences between Depth and Breadth.   Depth and breadth are aspects of sufficiency: The question is always, "Is the person reasoning this out deeply enough (or broadly enough) to accomplish his or her purpose in a reasonable way?" The two standards are not always clearly distinguishable. The goal is to develop an intuitive feel for when it is important to delve more deeply into an issue and when it is important to look at it more broadly by taking account of other related issues.

The difference is one of emphasis, a difference of where to direct your reasoning. Imagine yourself on a path going toward a destination. Breadth says to look around you, at the forest, fields, mountains, other travelers, the impending weather. Depth asks you to look

---

STAIRCASING SEE-I: DEPTH

A good way to gain a deep understanding of a topic or an area is to "staircase" your SEE-I's. Concepts and vocabulary exist in an inter-related web, a logic, and to understand one concept deeply, I often have to understand others. It's a give-and-take process: as I deepen my understanding of one concept, I often see that I need to deepen my understanding of another as well, and that can make me then modify the first. To "staircase" these inter-related concepts, then, is to give an SEE-I for each of them, carefully seeing not only what each is in itself, but how they fit together.[2] Here is an example from philosophy (but staircasing works for any area): Aristotle, in his famous "doctrine of the mean," said (roughly) that "virtue" is the middle area ("the mean") between extremes. Courage, he says, is a mean between cowardice and rashness, and finding that mean requires judgment.

A way to understand Aristotle's ideas deeply, in their interconnectedness, begins with giving an SEE-I for "the doctrine of the mean" itself. But then I may see that I need to give an SEE-I for the concept of "courage" (and maybe "cowardice" and "rashness"), and another for what he means by "judgment." By the end, I will have acquired a rich, deep understanding of Aristotle's ethics.

---

deeper, at the solidity of the path itself, the strength of your desire to reach the destination, your knowledge of the human body's need for nutrition. One directs you to look around, to take a more comprehensive view of things; the other directs you to look below the surface, to see things in all their depth.

Suppose I'm a student and I'm dissatisfied with the grades I've been receiving. "I study—and still my grades are not as high as they should be." A good thing to do is to *broaden* my thinking: What are some other, more effective ways to study? Who can I consult about these? Are there other skills—reading skills, outlining skills, even shorthand skills—that will help me take better notes?

I can also look more *deeply* (this would be especially called for if I have tried other perspectives without improving the results): What underlies my difficulty in getting good grades even though I study a lot?

Psychological attitudes are a good place to look for depth. Depression, for example, often results in "shooting myself in the foot" right before exams. I may have unrealistic expectations of myself. Self-deception can also enter in: I think I'm studying a lot, but much of that time is spent *worrying* about studying, rather than studying. Maybe my concept of studying is off-base: I may be regurgitating information when the teacher expects me to understand it (or vice versa). Maybe I'm not really hearing what the teacher is saying.

Depth and Theory.   One fruitful way to gain depth in your thinking is to look at the theoretical underpinnings of the question you are considering. Often we operate by a rule of thumb: Take daily multi-vitamins, discipline your children without shaming them, set performance quotas as an important part of sales management. When these situations become problematic, though, a good place to look is at the theory that underlies them: nutrition theory, child development theory, and sales management theory. Theories answer, in far greater depth, the questions of *why* you should, or should not, follow the rule of thumb. One of the major payoffs of learning to think in a discipline is this ability to go deeper into the theory for greater understanding.

Here is an example of depth and theory that seems (to me) both simple and amazing.

We all know that hot air rises. That's accurate as far as it goes. But it's not *deep*. Physically, there is no *force* that makes light things rise. A deeper truth is that *cold* air *falls*. It's heavier, so gravity pulls it downward—the cold air then crowds the hot air out of the way. Hot air doesn't exactly "rise"—it is pushed upward.[3]

So, looked at deeply, what happens when wood *floats* on water?

Depth: Superficial versus Surface.   Richard Paul makes a nice distinction: My thinking is *superficial* when I take a question that requires in-depth treatment but my reasoning about it leaves out the important complexities. "Question: What can we do about the epidemic of obesity in the United States? Answer: More will power. Period." The answer is superficial.

Often, though, the problem we are addressing requires that we not go into depth but focus on the *surface logic*, those specific aspects needed to solve a specific problem. "Question: Where is the rest room?" The appropriate response addresses the surface of things: "Down the hall, on the left." The appropriate response is not "Why?"

Impediments: What's Difficult about Reasoning Deeply Enough and Broadly Enough

- It is difficult to live with ambiguity and uncertainty. We would like things to be simpler, more clear-cut. All-or-nothing answers give us a feeling of control over complex problems, even when another part of our minds tells us we have very little control over them. Even the illusion of control is sometimes comforting.
- Often you may not realize there are complexities to an issue. In fact, one of the things we learn directly from disciplines is the amount of complexity in seemingly simple issues.
- Recognizing that there are depths to a problem confronting us, that there are other related perspectives on it, forces us to refuse to accept a slogan as a guide to action, or to buy into an unquestioned commonsense viewpoint or background story.

How to Look Beneath the Surface of Things, How to Gain a Broader Perspective

Alone

- Ask, "Do other reasonable people have different perspectives on this?"
- Ask, "Is there a theoretical structure underlying this issue? How can I look at it from that theoretical perspective?"
- Work to understand theory, including fundamental and powerful concepts.
- Ask, "Are there other issues that underlie this?"
- Expect complexities and further problems to arise when you are making important decisions or thinking through important issues. Expect there to be depths to these questions. Don't go in with the expectation that the answers will be simple.

With Others

- Take account of the differing perspectives of others.
- Discuss what other factors or perspectives you need to consider. Take people's feedback seriously.
- Talk about the relation between theory and practice.

Precision

- Is the thinking precise?
- Is the reasoning detailed enough?

Definition: Your thinking is precise when you have been as specific and detailed as needed to reason through an issue.

Related terms: exact, specific, detailed, focused.

Opposites: Your thinking is imprecise when you are inexact, when you don't give enough details to pinpoint what you are saying, when you are satisfied speaking in generalities without getting down to specifics.

Discussion

Precision and Clearness.   Precision and clearness are related, but they capture different ideas. This can be seen more easily with examples. Saying an infant is running a temperature is clear. It means that the infant's temperature is somewhere above 98.6 degrees. Saying that the infant is running a temperature of 102 degrees is both clear and precise. E. M. Forster once illustrated the difference between a story and a plot by saying, "The king died, and then the queen died" is a story; "The king died, then the queen died of grief" is a plot. Both statements are clear, but the second is considerably more precise.

Precision and Purpose.   It is *not* precise to say that I am 5 feet, 11.735 inches tall. A person's height cannot be measured to that degree of precision. It is not that we lack sufficiently precise instruments, it's that such a degree of precision is meaningless when applied to a person. Our heights change during the day, and we are as much as an inch shorter at bedtime than in the morning; even subtly different ways of standing affect a measurement by tenths of an inch.

What is precise will always be relative both to the purpose of the reasoning and to the context.

Precision and Thinking in the Field.   It is difficult to think in a way that lets you see both the larger picture and also the details in that larger picture. Yet that is exactly what is involved in thinking in a discipline.

Knowing a field or discipline is not at all like memorizing long lists of details. It is also not the same as knowing a bunch of generalities. It's much more like an outline. You need to know the major general headings. But under those headings you need to be able to give well-chosen details and exactly formulated points to make your reasoning precise and to the point.

Impediments: What's Difficult about Being Precise

- We often overlook the need to be precise.
- It takes work to be precise. It means getting specific enough to spell things out exactly. It's easy to settle for generalities.
- It is difficult to see the forest for the trees, but it is also difficult to see the trees for the forest.

How to Become More Precise

Alone

- Anticipate where others will need details to follow your reasoning.
- When you report what other people say, or the results of an experiment, or an office procedure, try to say it exactly.
- Look up details in the text.
- When you take detailed notes, do so in outline form.
- Keep going from the general to the specific and from the specific to the general: What is a specific instance of this generality? How does this detail fit into the whole picture?

With Others

- Get feedback on where you need to be more specific, more exact.
- Ask fellow students where they need you to supply more detail.

Understanding and Internalizing Critical-Thinking Standards

The goal is not just to understand the standards in the abstract but to incorporate them into your thinking and your life. They don't work just separately but together as well. If you think of them as linked together to form a whole, that whole constitutes a major part of what critical thinking is. To internalize the idea of critical thinking is to understand deeply how critical thinking is different from thinking. The standards together, formed into a whole, constitute a good deal of the *critical* part.

Additional Critical-Thinking Standards

There are additional critical-thinking standards. Many of them overlap the standards already described, and some of them are critical-thinking standards in one context but not in another. Some of them are critical-thinking standards in a particular discipline. A list includes:

- reasonable
- logical, rational
- consistent
- falsifiable

- testable
- well-organized
- reliable
- effective

In addition, many terms are used to describe the opposite of critical thinking. Informal logicians often teach a set of logical fallacies—these are ways people characteristically go wrong in their thinking. Fallacies are ways of thinking that seem to be good thinking, but actually are not.

Non–Critical-Thinking Standards

A good way to increase your understanding of how the standards constitute critical thinking is to contrast them with non–critical-thinking standards. Here are a few:

- fun
- exciting
- feels good
- attention-getting
- popular

- chic
- spontaneous
- advantageous
- beneficial to me
- in fashion

There is nothing inherently wrong with such standards. They are *not opposed* to critical thinking. They are simply non–critical-thinking standards.

You can see the uphill battle you have ahead of you if you want to think critically—so many influences in the world tend to push these non–critical-thinking standards on us. Think of *popularity*, for example. It's not that popularity is opposed to critical thinking. Something can be popular and also an example of careful thinking. (For instance, a few years ago healthy, comfortable walking shoes became a fad.) The problem is that popularity is emphasized so much as a standard—it is often so very important to us to do what is popular—that it effectively pushes accuracy, clearness, and depth aside as less important.

Similarly with *fun*. Even in education, a great emphasis is put on making learning fun. Nothing is intrinsically wrong with that; it is beneficial in many ways. Authentic learning is often fun; certainly it is often deeply gratifying and fulfilling to take ownership of a fundamental and powerful concept in a discipline. Fun opposes critical thinking only when the assumption creeps in that learning *has to be* fun: that if it's not fun, we can't expect people to do it.

Catalog for yourself the number of influences in society that promote non–critical-thinking standards. Many of these non–critical-thinking standards are excellent if you incorporate critical thinking into them. Without critical thinking, however, even seemingly benign standards can be dangerous. Here is another list of non–critical-thinking standards, ones that go deeper than the previous list:

- evocative
- deeply felt, deeply moving
- moral, ethical
- held with deep conviction
- free
- religious, spiritual
- patriotic
- loving

Choose four of the non-critical-thinking standards listed, and describe how critical thinking is necessary to the application of each standard. As part of your answer, give a *contrasting* example: Describe how, without critical thinking, each of the non–critical-thinking standards is open to distortion and misguided application.

Can you think of examples from history (or from your background knowledge) where people had a deeply misguided sense of what it meant to be patriotic or religious or knowledgeable or free?

These standards are essential parts of life. In a way, they may be more important than critical thinking itself. The trouble with saying that, though, is that without critical-thinking standards incorporated into them, they can be demeaning, misplaced, hollow, and dangerous.

Naziism was extremely *evocative*. The Nuremberg Rally, according to nearly every observer, was *deeply moving*. Fanatics always hold their beliefs *with deep conviction*—that's why they are called fanatics. Among the things held *with deepest conviction* are prejudices. Without critical thinking, even *loving* can become caretaking and co-dependence.

Even a standard like "moral" exhibits this same two-edged quality. To be moral without focusing on accuracy, clarity, importance, without focusing on purpose, consequences, or assumptions, is virtually a contradiction. If you try to be moral without thinking critically, you become merely a rule follower, not using your critical-thinking skills even to assess whose rules you should follow. That is not really being moral at all.

Evaluating Around the Circle of Elements

To evaluate a piece of reasoning is to make judgments about its reasonableness; it is to assess how well it lives up to critical-thinking standards. Contrast **analysis** with **evaluation:**

- Going around the circle answers the question: *How* has this person thought this out? (That is *analysis*.)
- *Evaluating* around the circle answers the question: *How well* has this person thought this out?

The Basic Process of Evaluating a Piece of Reasoning

Even more than with the questions on *understanding* someone's reasoning, the following questions are *guides* only. You will have to be flexible and adapt the questions to fit the piece of reasoning you are trying to evaluate. (You may need to consult the list of standards frequently. When the guideline question uses a word like *adequate* or *better*, it often helps to use a more precise word from the list of standards: "Is it adequate?" can mean "Is it adequate with respect to a specific standard?" For example, "Is it deep enough?" "Is it broad enough?" "Is it complete enough, or does it omit something essential?") You also need to support the major judgments you make by giving *reasons* and *explanations*.

Evaluating Around the Circle

1. Does the person achieve his or her purpose in this piece of reasoning?
2. Does the person adequately answer the question at issue?
3. Look at the major pieces of information the person provides. Are they reasonable? Well-established? Are they relevant? Is more information needed to resolve the question at issue?
4. Do the person's conclusions follow from his or her reasoning? Is the person interpreting the issue accurately?
5. Are there other valid ways of understanding the central concepts, ways that would influence the outcome of the reasoning?

6. Are the person's major assumptions reasonable enough for you to agree with them?

7. Are the implications of the person's reasoning acceptable? Will the person's reasoning lead to other consequences, ones that would count for or against his or her reasoning?

8. Is the person aware of other reasonable points of view on this issue? Has he or she taken them adequately into account?

9. Does the person reason through the issue in a way that takes sufficient account of the context?

10. Are there better alternatives to the way the person has reasoned this out?

Writing an Evaluation   Your answers to these ten questions can form the evaluation itself. But, it is usually beneficial to pull the various answers together. To do this, think of your answers to these ten questions as the groundwork of your evaluation.

Now, write out (in normal paragraphs) an overall evaluation of the piece of reasoning as a whole.

a. This should be based on the most important threads from your answers to the ten questions.

b. It should identify both the strong and the weak points of the piece of reasoning.

c. It should incorporate a Standards Check. (See pages 158–159.)

d. Claims you make in your evaluation should be backed up with reasons.

Critical Reading

The foundation of critical reading is reasonable, reflective analysis and synthesis. In the deepest sense, reading is a critical-thinking process, and you can become an excellent critical reader by focusing on the elements and the standards as the heart of your reading. That means learning to go around the circle as you read, so you grasp the logic of the piece and check your reading with the standards. At first, of course, this may be slow going, and a lot of the analysis and synthesis will take place after you are "finished" with the reading. You will ask yourself, reflectively, about the writer's purpose, the question at issue being addressed, the information being given—on through all the elements.

As you become proficient at critical reading, you will find you are answering these questions *as you read*. This is critical reading in a highly integrated sense. You will be noting the author's main assumptions, conclusions, concepts, and point of view as you encounter them and as they develop, and you will be fitting them together. Even when you achieve that level of ability, though, the reflection afterward remains an important part of reading. Often reading in the fullest sense—reading with understanding and appreciation—gets completed only after you put the book down, sometimes long after. After you have read some of George Eliot, Stephen Jay Gould, or Friedrich Nietzsche, or a biography of Mohandas Gandhi, the meanings can still continue to connect inside of you.

In addition to analyzing and synthesizing, you will also be reading *evaluatively*. That is, you will apply the standards of critical thinking not just to your understanding of the writing, but to the writing itself. You will note where writers are, in your best judgment, accurate or inaccurate (or somewhere in between), where they are on target (the standard of *importance*), whether they present a *sufficient* case or go *deep* enough.

Reading and the Standard of Importance

As you read, you will be focusing on the elements in a continuous way, but you will be using the standard of *importance* as a kind of filter. That is, you will focus on the elements only as the answers are important. Thus there is little point to writing down all the assumptions or implications or pieces of information contained in your reading—you need to note only the ones that are important for the question at issue.

Reading for Information

You have to be wary of the idea of reading for information. As a critical thinker, always read for information *plus* concepts to organize that information *plus* the logical connections between those concepts.

Reading for Pleasure

There is no opposition between reading critically and reading for pleasure, though it often seems as if there is. Sometimes people love a poem or a piece of music. They are then assigned to analyze it, and that seems to eliminate the feeling response. Sometimes people say that, after analysis, they no longer like the piece.

That is a genuine experience many people have, but it seems to come more from the spirit in which you analyze things than from the analysis itself. By way of comparison, think about your friends. If you love your friends, you may want to understand them, maybe understand them deeply. That is not the same as dissecting their personalities. Instead, you think about what their goals, beliefs, and

STANDARDS CHECK[4]

Students: Photocopy these pages. Check (✓) each relevant box.

CLEAR

Is **my reasoning** clear?

❏ Do I understand this clearly?

❏ Do I know the implications?

    ❏ Can I *state* it in a clear sentence?

    ❏ Have I *elaborated* enough?

    ❏ Have I found good *examples*? Contrasting examples?

    ❏ Have I given an illuminating *illustration* (analogy, metaphor, simile . . . ?)

Is **my presentation** of my reasoning clear?

❏ Have I said clearly what I meant?

ACCURATE

❏ Is my reasoning accurate?

    Is this in accord with:

    ❏ the best knowledge I have?

    ❏ the findings of the discipline?

    ❏ reliable sources?

❏ Do I need to check this out?

Check: Could this be based on:

    ❏ wishful thinking?

    ❏ unexamined background stories?

    ❏ hearsay or questionable sources?

Does **my presentation** display accuracy?

Have I supported the accuracy of my claims

    ❏ With reasons?

    ❏ With *good* reasons?

IMPORTANT, RELEVANT

In **my reasoning**, have I focused on what is most important, given

❏ my purpose?

❏ the question at issue?

❏ the context?

❑ Do I have an overview?

❑ Can I *outline* my reasoning?

❑ Can I *summarize* it?

❑ Have I **presented** my reasoning in a way that displays what is important?

SUFFICIENT

❑ Have I **reasoned** this through enough, given:

   ❑ my purpose?

   ❑ the question at issue?

   ❑ the context?

❑ Have I left out crucial steps?

❑ Have I jumped to conclusions?

❑ Are there other essential issues to consider?

In **my presentation**

❑ Have I said enough to show my audience that it is reasonable to come to my conclusions?

DEEP AND BROAD

In **my reasoning**, have I looked beneath the surface?

   ❑ at underlying explanations, theories?

   ❑ at complexities of the issue?

   ❑ Have I taken account of other relevant perspectives?

In **my presentation**, have I presented my reasoning in a way that *displays* its ❑ depth and ❑ breadth?

PRECISE

Is **my reasoning** precise enough, specific enough?

   ❑ Do I need more details?

   ❑ Do I need more exactness?

❑ Have I **stated** the degree of exactness my audience needs?

REASONABLE OVERALL

❑ Is my reasoning reasonable overall?

❑ Have I presented a reasonable overall case?

life circumstances are. That is an analysis—specifically, it is looking at purpose, assumptions, context—and it is a natural part of caring for someone. If someone is not interested in these, it's hard to believe he or she really cares about you. "Analyzing" your friend can sound harsh, but it is really understanding that you are after. The same is true of studying a poem or a piece of music.

Reading and Listening

Virtually every remark about reading applies to *listening* as well. Critical listening is understanding what the speaker is saying in terms of the elements, understanding the logic of it (synthesis), and assessing your understanding of what the person is saying in terms of the standards. As with reading, much of listening-with-understanding can take place after the speaker is finished. You can continue to reflect on the speaker's purpose, the conclusions drawn, the main concepts, and so forth. As your critical skills develop around the elements, a lot more of your understanding will take place as you listen. As you practice critical listening in class, focusing on what is important and on *the logic of* what you are hearing, you will notice that your note-taking will change.

Some Outcomes

At the end of this chapter, you should be able to:

1. *Evaluate* your critical thinking by performing a Standards Check on your own work in the course (and in other courses as well), and to do so with a reasonable amount of expertise.
2. *Evaluate* the work of fellow students, using the standards and giving feedback in a clear, accurate, and relevant way; you should also be able to receive feedback on the standards and describe how you could remedy the flaws.
3. *Give an SEE-I* for main concepts in this chapter: "standard of critical thinking," "analysis versus evaluation," "evaluating around the circle," and "critical reading."
4. *Give an SEE-I* for each of the standards, including examples and contrasting examples for each.
5. *Identify instances* on your own of people who are using (and failing to use) the standards.
6. *Describe* how to revise and improve your work in the course, making it more in line with the standards. You will not always carry out the process adequately, but you will do so often, and you will know how to make good revisions.

7. *Integrate* critical-thinking standards with the outcomes of Chapters 1, 2, and 3 (pages 37, 76, and 123–124). You should be able to elaborate on and give good examples of how the standards mesh with critical thinking as a whole, the elements, and critical thinking in the discipline.

Ideas for Writing

(General guidelines for "Ideas for Writing" are on page 38.)

1. You can write on any of the standards: What it is; how you see it as important for good thinking; how adherence to that standard is important in people's lives; the negative consequences people experience when they are not careful about adhering to that standard; how it is important even in interests and activities that seem far removed from schoolwork (e.g., playing videogames, flirting, driving a car, etc.).

2. Critical-thinking concepts, such as the elements and the standards, are pre-eminently versatile. Thus you can write on any of the critical-thinking standards in relation to *any* topic or idea: To what extent is that standard adhered to (or violated) in advertising, in news reporting, in personal relationships, in classes you take, in celebrity magazines, and so forth? You can make up your own idea, research it if required, and write on it at an appropriate length. (For writing a paper critically, look on pages 190–195.)

3. How are the critical-thinking standards important in the discipline you are studying: both for a student in that discipline and for a professional in that field?

4. Contrast *explicit* versus *implicit* use of the standards. (People can, of course, be clear, accurate, relevant, and so forth, without using these terms *explicitly*. How is it helpful to have these terms explicitly rather than just in the background?)

5. A thesis of this book is that both *analysis* and *evaluation* are ordinary parts of what we all do every day (though almost certainly we would not use those words). Write about some of the "things" we standardly analyze and/or evaluate.

6. On pages 175–176 there is a brief description of some critical-thinking character traits. Though the description there is very brief, state, elaborate, exemplify, and illustrate how intellectual integrity and fair-mindedness are essential to internalizing the standards of critical thinking.

Tell Your Story

(The idea behind "Tell Your Story" and some suggestions about doing it are on page 39.)

1. What are some standards that are most important in your life? In this question, you can focus on either critical-thinking or non-critical-thinking standards (such as the ones on pages 153 or 154). For example, you might hold yourself to a standard of honesty, of ability in sports, of being a good sister or brother. How did you acquire those standards? How have they changed over the years?

2. In your day-to-day life, how do you go about telling what you should or should not believe among things you see or hear or read?

3. Analysis and evaluation. What are some things in your life that you standardly *analyze*? What are some things in your life that you standardly *evaluate*? (Remember, there is no assumption here that you use those words.)

4. Generate some of your own questions about how critical-thinking standards fit into your personal history.

CHAPTER 4 Exercises

4.1 Without looking back in the Chapter, write out an SEE-I for each of the standards. Use this as a way of finding out which you are clear about and which you are not.

4.2 In the Chapter 2 exercises 2.1–2.3, you went around the circle with respect to three different questions. Complete a Standards Check (see pages 158–159) for each of your responses, correcting and filling in aspects of your response where needed.

4.3 **Working in pairs on the standards.** Choose some piece of writing you have done in the course (at least two or three paragraphs, preferably involving critical thinking in the discipline). Duplicate it before you come to class, and exchange copies with your partner.

The exercise is to give your partner useful feedback on one of the standards. Begin with clearness: turn to the section "How to Become Clearer . . . with Others" (page 138). Using that list as a guide, give your partner feedback on the clearness of what he or she has written.

Repeat the exercise in seven different installments, one on each of the standards. It can be done over half a semester or over the whole semester, a little bit at a time. Choose different pieces of writing each time.

4.4 Here is a paragraph from a geography text:

> Culture, many argue, is the adhesive binding together of the world's diverse social fabric. A cursory read of the daily newspaper, however, raises questions as to whether the world is literally coming unglued since the frequency and the intensity of cultural conflict seems pervasive and ever-increasing. With the recent rise of global communication systems (satellite TV, movies, video, etc.) stereotypic Western culture is spreading at a rapid pace. While this is willingly accepted by many throughout the world, other groups and countries resist this new form of cultural imperialism through protests, censorship, and restrictions on film, TV, and music.[5]

Analyze the paragraph by identifying the elements of reasoning as they occur in it. Next, *evaluate* the paragraph using the standards of critical thinking.

4.5 As in Exercise 4.4, engage in the same kind of evaluative reflection with respect to important readings in your text in the discipline. Focus on key paragraphs, chapter summaries and reviews, case studies, entire books. Analyze them by identifying the elements as they occur in the readings. Next, evaluate the readings using the standards. (You evaluate, remember, not just for accuracy, but for how clear the reading is to you, whether it has been explained sufficiently for you to follow it, whether you can see its importance in the whole, etc.)

4.6 **Ask with a standard.** Sit in groups of four. At any point in the discussion, one person (A) will be answering questions, and three people (B, C, and D) will be asking questions regarding a standard:

B asks A a question. (For example, "Why are you taking this course?")

A answers. (For example, "It's a requirement for my major.")

From then on, B, C, and D ask A questions, each time in reference to a standard. (For example, "Can you make that clearer?" "Is that the most important reason?" "Do you have other important reasons?" "Can you take a broader perspective?")

A keeps answering. (The questions have to make sense given A's responses.)

Then switch roles, with everyone asking questions-with-a-standard of B, then C, then D.

4.7 As you read your text, pick out the five most important points in a chapter. Read about them the way you would normally. Then, close your book. Restate each of those points in your own words.

a. Evaluate your understanding of those main points on the basis of clearness. You've just *stated* them. Now *elaborate*, give *examples* and *illustrations*.

b. Evaluate your understanding of those main points on the basis of accuracy. How would you check? Do you have a background story there that may interfere?

c. Do the same for the other standards—always evaluating *your* understanding, not the points themselves.

4.8 People sometimes say that you can't teach someone to be a critical thinker? What do you think about that?

4.9 Referring back to the discussion in Chapter 2, evaluate Chris's reasoning about marriage by evaluating around the circle.

Next, notice that Chris does not directly address the issue of same-sex marriage. (When you read the example, which gender, if any, did you assume Chris and Sean each were?) Suppose Chris was strongly in favor of or strongly against same-sex marriage. How might you add to or change Chris's analysis to reflect this? As you do so, regardless of the side you are on, practice intellectual empathy in your changes.

4.10 Do at least a quick Standards Check for every piece of written work you do in this course. The next three questions are related to one another.

4.11 Take each important piece of reading you are required to do in the course and engage in critical reading by going around the circle (pages 155–156).

4.12 When you finish Exercise 4.11, do a Standards Check on your reasoning.

4.13 Still using the material from Exercise 4.11, evaluate the reasoning in the piece itself: How well has the writer reasoned out the issue? Do this by evaluating around the circle (pages 155–156).

4.14 **SEE-I.** Look back over the contents of Chapter 4:

- Find a clarifying *statement* (or definition) in the chapter.
- Find an *elaboration* of an idea in it.
- Find an *example*; a *contrasting example.*
- Find an *illustration.*

4.15 **Group work.** Separate into seven groups in the class. Each group will serve as the authority for one of the standards as it applies *within the discipline.* Prepare a presentation on the standard. Equitably decide who will perform each part of the presentation:

- Explain what the standard is.
- Give good examples of its use in the discipline.
- Give contrasting examples.
- Tell what the implications and consequences are when reasoning in the discipline does not meet the standard.

4.16 For X in the following questions, substitute the name of the discipline (or course) you are studying:

In what ways is it necessary to be clear in X?

What are the areas where people are most likely to be inaccurate in X?

What are the most important aspects of X to grasp?
What are the dangers of giving insufficient responses in X?
In what ways are depth and breadth central to X?
How precision important in X?

Give an example for each answer.

4.17 **Try the outcomes** (pages 160–161). Go through the list of outcomes to this chapter, and see how many of them you understand well with your book and notes closed.

4.18 Paleoanthropologists usually date fossils of *Australopithecus afarensis*, an ancestor of humans, to 3.6 million years ago. Do they mean "3.6 million years BCE (or BC)"? Or do they mean "3.6 million years before the present?"

DAILY PRACTICE
At incorporating critical thinking into your life and your learning

Before you start on Exercises 4.19 to 4.21, look back at the instructions on pages 44–45. Again, the key is to do the exercises as often as possible, daily if you can, in small repeated intervals, rather than doing them in a single big burst of effort.

4.19 **Spend a day on a standard.** Keep a log. Pick one of the standards. Let's say you've chosen clearness. Spend your day looking for instances of clearness and unclearness, writing down any of them you can find. Note if examples would have helped, if more elaboration was needed, if the speaker lost sight of the intended audience. Write down examples you find of things that were probably unclear in the person's mind. Also write down examples of things you believe may have been clear in the person's mind, but were not stated or written clearly. Find examples in your own statements and in those of other people, online, in conversations with friends, lectures in classes, anywhere. In your log, write down any questions that come up for you. Those may be questions you'll want to ask in class, of your teacher, or of a critical-thinking classmate.

Wait a few days. Then choose another standard to spend a day on. Go through all seven. By the time you have finished, you will find you both understand and can apply the standards significantly better than before.

4.20 Spend a day on a standard in your course. At the end of a class day, reflect back on the class and consciously apply one of the standards. Suppose you choose *depth* for that day. Look for examples of depth or the opposite that came up in class: complications that arose; cases where you longed for a nice, simple, all-or-nothing answer to a question, but none was forthcoming. Look for frustrations you felt: decide if they were the result of unsolved problems that couldn't reasonably be answered right then. Look for places where there wasn't much depth. Maybe just surface logic was at work: simple facts, straightforward, unproblematical procedures.

Engage with a different standard in your course after each class day.

4.21 Daily practice using the Standards Check as a questioning tool. Take a few of the questions from the Standards Check (pages 158–159) and turn them into questions you can ask others (by changing "I" to "you," for example). Then spend a day asking these questions of others. If a teacher in another course says, "Are there any questions?" you can ask, "Could you give me an example of X?" or "What sources is this based on?" If a friend says something, you can say, "I hear you. I just wonder if you left out any crucial steps in your thinking about this," or "Could you elaborate on that a little?" (You can practice being flexible, choosing questions that fit the situation and the person you are asking. And you may have to rephrase the questions so they don't sound too formal or confrontational.)

Observe people's reactions to your questions. Observe your own reactions as well. From your point of view, were they good questions?

Chapter 5
Putting It All Together: Answering Critical-Thinking Questions

I t would be natural at this point if you felt a large number of fragments swirling around in your head. First, there are the 8+ elements. Then, there are the standards, seven of them discussed in some detail. There are fundamental and powerful concepts, the central question, and the point of view of the discipline. There are also a number of impediments to critical thinking, and they may overlap significantly with ways you normally think things through. At this point, you probably have a mixed grasp of the elements, the standards, and critical thinking as a whole.

You are probably good at identifying some of the elements when you read a chapter or think through a problem on your own, and you are not nearly as good at identifying some of the other elements. You may be strong on identifying an author's purpose or the information an author is providing, but you may not be clear about the exact difference between conclusions and implications, and you may have trouble telling an assumption from a concept.

The same is probably true of your grasp of the standards. You may find that you are regularly giving examples to make your thinking clearer. Yet it may be difficult to tell when you have reasoned through a question sufficiently.

These all improve with practice and instruction—checking back with the book frequently, doing the exercises, or receiving feedback from your teacher. You may still be concerned that you don't see clearly how this all fits together. You may wonder, "Where am I in the process? How do I get an overview?" "I need some kind of a map, so I know which way to go, which critical-thinking move to make, and why." "I understand how to go around the circle and how to do a Standards Check, but how can I turn my critical thinking into an actual paper?" If you feel that way, it's based on a sound instinct. Part of understanding anything, critical thinking included, is seeing *the whole* and *the parts* in perspective: seeing how it all fits together. The purpose of this chapter is to give a sense of the whole, to provide a map.

The Core Process of Critical Thinking in a Discipline

So, what do critical thinkers do?

Core Process (QEDS)

- They address a question or problem (**Q**).
- They think it through using the elements of reasoning (**E**).
- When appropriate, they reason out all aspects of the issue through the lens of the discipline (**D**).
- As they do this, they monitor their reasoning using the critical-thinking standards (**S**).

That's the core process of critical thinking, the heart of it. Critical thinkers who have never taken a course in critical thinking engage in this core process. They may not consider all the elements or consciously name them as they think; they may not consciously realize that they are thinking in terms of a discipline they have internalized; and they may not be explicitly aware that they are using the standards, but if you

FIGURE 5.1   *The core process of critical thinking in a discipline.*

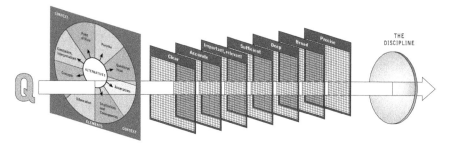

examine their reasoning, you will see that they are thinking about their purpose or their assumptions; they are using discipline-based concepts when it makes sense to do so; they are checking to be sure they are being accurate and that they have focused on the important parts of the problem.

Figure 5.1 offers a rough map of the core process **QEDS**, an annotated version of the one introduced in Chapter 1. Now you should be in a better position to know what it's a map of and what the parts are. Figure 5.1 is just a rough map, of course. Thinking is not as linear as this implies: when you think through something critically, you don't necessarily start with the question (Q), *then* go to the elements, *then* to the discipline, and *then* to the standards. You can think it out in that order if you wish, but the role of the standards is more of a persistent monitoring of your thinking. As you think through the question using the elements, you are striving to be clear, to stick to the important parts of the problem, to be accurate, to consider the problem sufficiently. You also use the standards at the end, to check on your reasoning and revise it to make it better. You ask yourself: "Okay, I tried to be accurate in what I was saying. Did I succeed? Do I need more evidence?" or: "I worked at being clear as I wrote my paper. But do I need to elaborate on what I said to make it clearer? Do I need another example, or maybe a contrasting example?"

If the question you are trying to address is one that's in a discipline, then you have to think it through using the fundamental and powerful concepts, relating it to the central question, and looking at it from the point of view of that discipline. Ask yourself, "How do people in this discipline address such questions? How do they go about answering such questions?" If it's a question in anthropology, you need to engage in thinking anthropologically. If it's a question in engineering, you have to think it through the way an engineer would. (See Chapter 3, pages 92–93.)

Even if it's a question outside the discipline, about your personal life, or about some decision you have to make, it is reasonable to think it out from the point of view of disciplines that are relevant to that question. A fundamental thesis of this book is that thinking things through in terms of disciplines gives people insight. So, if you have a decision to make about diet, exercise, or smoking, it will help to ask, "How can I think this out biologically? nutritionally? medically?" You may also gain insight by asking, "How can I think it out psychologically? (How does my psychological way of thinking influence the decisions I make about dieting, exercise, smoking?) How can I think it out historically? (How does my society's history with regard to dieting, exercise, and smoking affect me and guide my choices?)" Literature, math, sociology: each of these, and many others, can not only help you understand the issues in a deep way, they can also help you make better decisions.

Doing More Than the Core Process

Thinking in Terms of Critical-Thinking Processes

The core process, then, involves questions, elements, discipline-based thinking, and standards. For some questions, however, you may have to add to the core. A helpful way to conceptualize this for yourself is to think in terms of critical-thinking processes such as analysis, synthesis, evaluation, and a number of others.

You have already engaged in many of them. *Analysis* is a critical-thinking process of breaking something down into its component parts. You engaged in the process of analysis every time you broke something down into the elements of reasoning. At its root, analysis is going around the circle of elements. If you have gone around the circle with respect to a chapter in your text, you have analyzed the chapter in terms of its purpose, its main question at issue, its main assumptions, and so on.

You haven't merely broken the chapter down into its component parts, however. You have also gained an understanding of how those parts fit together as a coherent whole. In this book, we have been describing this whole as the logic of the question: after going around the circle, you have a good grasp of the logic of the chapter. This "bringing together into a whole" is often called the process of *synthesis*. So, in going around the circle, seeing each of the elements and grasping the logic of the question or topic, you have already been engaged in the critical-thinking processes of analyzing and synthesizing.

Depending on what is called for in the question, however, you still may have to do more than engage in the core process. You may have to engage in other processes besides analysis and synthesis. You may have to *compare and contrast* two different positions on euthanasia, for example. You may have to *evaluate* what a particular author says. You may need to *apply* a theory in the discipline to a new case. You may have to do some actual *decision-making* about a course of action. You may have to engage in some *action*—writing a paper, performing the part of Mercutio, or designing an experiment. Notice that *action*—doing something—is classified here as a critical-thinking process. As with any of the other processes, you want your actions to be infused with your best thinking. Even more broadly, you can rethink your life in an ongoing way using critical thinking. That is living in such a way that you are in touch with the elements (for instance, your goals and assumptions) and with the standards (for instance, paying attention to what is important and deep for you). Thus, according to this book, *living mindfully* is a critical-thinking process.

Each of these critical-thinking processes is built from the elements and standards. We can add these critical-thinking processes to the core process, as shown in Figure 5.2.

FIGURE 5.2 *Critical-thinking processes.*

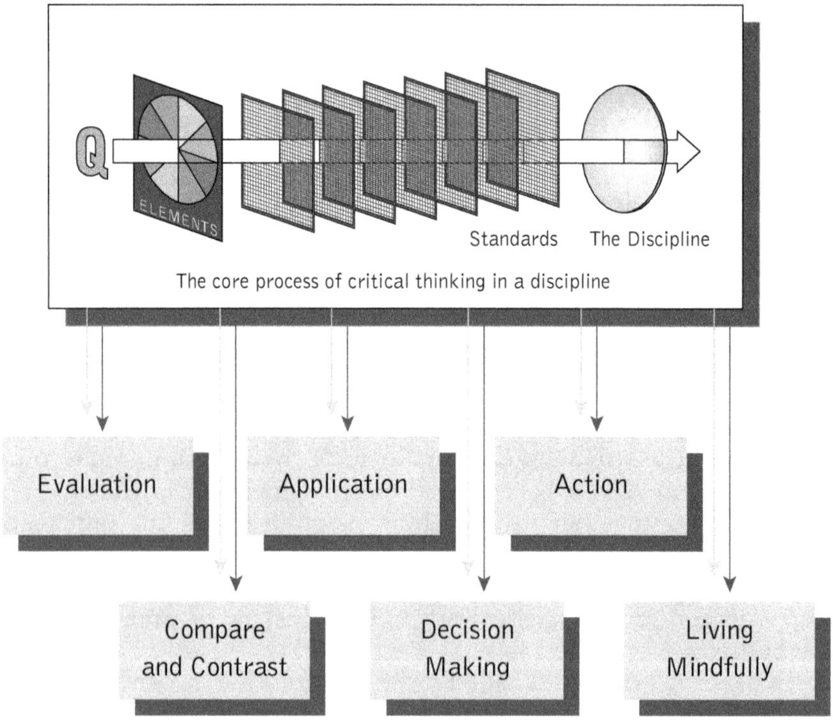

Doing Less Than the Core Process

The core process is the centerpiece of critical thinking. Many times you have to do more than this core process just to address the various complexities of an issue. You may have to add the lenses of the disciplines themselves, and you may have to add other critical-thinking processes.

On the other hand, you often have to do less than the core process. You may take an author's position on animal rights and simply identify a crucial assumption behind it. Sometimes, that will be all that's necessary. The act of simply identifying a single element can be a deep insight in your critical thinking. Moreover, getting into the habit of identifying that single element can be a vital step in the development of your ability to think well. It can be valuable to you all by itself, without even addressing the other elements.

Consider *consequences*. By simply focusing on anticipating the *consequences* of your decisions, you can make a crucial transformation in your life, especially if you do it in a regular way. To a certain degree, this benefit can be independent of how you handle the other elements. Of course, your thinking may be deeper if you also pay attention to the other elements. Nevertheless, the act of focusing on consequences all by itself can change your thinking and actions in a dramatic way.

That is true for the standards as well. Consider accuracy. In a classical Greek play, one character, Antigone, sees divine law and the ties of family as having more validity than the claims of human law; the opposing character, Creon, sees human law as taking precedence over religious injunctions and family ties. A crucial step in addressing the play mindfully is to do more than reporting on what the two characters see as valid. The crucial step is for *you* to evaluate that validity yourself. Reflecting on the accuracy or inaccuracy of each of those principles can open up many profound truths.

For any given problem, the elements and standards are not all equally important. The decisions about which of them to focus on, whether to go all the way around the circle, or whether to engage in one or more of the other critical-thinking processes—all of these are themselves critical-thinking decisions.

How Do *You* Fit into the Picture? Becoming a Critical Thinker

Critical thinking isn't done in a vacuum. It is always done by some particular person, someone who brings his or her own repertoire of skills and traits of mind, feelings, wants and needs, strengths and weaknesses. All of these influence how you do your critical thinking. Critical thinking can affect who you are and what you are able to accomplish. Similarly, who you are and what you are able to do affects the quality and direction of your critical thinking.

One trait that distinctly helps you become more of a critical thinker is if you *enjoy* it. Many people find that they do. If you enjoy thinking critically and figuring things out, or if you feel a sense of satisfaction or strength in being able to reason through issues well, it can have a major effect on the quality of your thinking and the quality of your life. But even if you don't enjoy it (or don't enjoy it *yet*), there are skills and traits you can work on to develop as a critical thinker. Some of these you may already possess, maybe to a considerable degree. With some, you may be really weak. Even accomplished critical thinkers have deficiencies in some of their skills and traits (that's part of being human), and even ones you are strong in may temporarily desert you in some circumstances. As your strengths increase, you may find that even if at first you didn't enjoy the process of thinking critically, you do now.

The traits listed below are *transformative*. As you become highly skilled at listening, for example, and as you practice your listening skills often, it starts a transformation in you: *you* start to become a good listener. It starts to become part of who you are.

So as you go through the list below, think of them not so much as skills but as character traits, habits, dispositions, attitudes, aspects of your personality.

A well-developed critical thinker is:

- A good listener
- Someone who speaks thoughtfully
- Someone who searches for explanations (who gets at the "why" of things)
- An observant person
- Someone who seeks out reliable information when making important decisions
- Someone who is centered: proactive rather than reactive
- Someone open to new ideas: not stubborn, not closed minded
- A truth-seeker
- A critical reader, a critical writer (someone who is reliably clear, accurate, and relevant in both areas)
- Someone who seeks to understand other people:
  → their reasons and motivations
  → their emotions
  → their points of view
- A self-aware person: aware of
  → strengths and weaknesses
  → abilities and disabilities
  → his or her own tendencies toward egocentrism

Critical-Thinking Character Traits[1]

Critical-thinking traits are parts of a person's character. Many of the traits are difficult to acquire to a full degree, or to act on in a consistent way. But we can improve in all of them. With commitment and practice, we develop them in ourselves over time. To a very real extent, you cannot think critically, in the discipline or in your life, unless you develop the traits in yourself. Critical thinkers:

- Have **confidence in reason**. They believe in trying to figure things out. They rely on thinking their way through questions and issues, to the best of their ability, rather than relying on the other influences that shape their thinking without their knowing it.
- Have **intellectual humility**. They recognize and own up to what they don't know, in all its fullness. As difficult as it is to admit sometimes, they realize that they make mistakes and are often less than perfect in their reasoning. They can accept criticism, and learn from it.
- Are **intellectually courageous**. They face up to challenges to their settled beliefs and habitual ways of thinking. They are willing to change their point of view—even a deeply held one—when that is the reasonable thing to do.
- Are **intellectually empathetic**. They willingly commit themselves to thinking through the logic of any point of view, without regard to whether they agree with it or not. They do that not just "in their heads": they are willing to *feel the force* of the logic inherent in that other point of view.
- Have **intellectual integrity**. They hold themselves to the same high intellectual standards they hold others to. They are "truth-seekers": in thinking through an issue, they are committed to giving the most reasonable account they can, even if the price of that is high.
- Are **fair-minded**. They do their best to be balanced and impartial when trying to understand, analyze, evaluate or apply any belief or point of view, no matter how different from their own.
- Are **intellectually engaged**. They are involved, on a deep and satisfying level, in wanting to understand things and think them through. They feel a strong desire to immerse themselves in an intellectual topic. They *like* thinking critically.
- Have **intellectual perseverance**. They are willing to stick with important intellectual tasks for as long as it takes to reach a reasonable conclusion.

■ Are **intellectually autonomous**. They think for themselves. They are committed to it. They habitually use the best reasoning they are capable of, including elements, standards, and the discipline, with awareness of the bigger picture.

For me, the best way to think of the traits is as something I'm on my way toward. I'm stronger in some, weaker in others, but I can work on them. Though they are often challenging for me, whenever I take even small steps toward exercising them, I start to feel like a fuller person.

Thinking Through Important Critical-Thinking Questions

Even with an overview, a series of maps, and a sketch of how you might fit in the picture, you may still be wondering what to do to think your way through a critical-thinking question in the discipline. How do you go about it? How do you start? How do you carry it through? How do you tell whether you have done it well? How do you improve? This section takes you through the basics of answering a critical-thinking question. It will also provide a more detailed exploration of putting it all together. Below, in outline form, is the core process of critical thinking. It is an overview of putting it all together, thinking through an important critical-thinking question.

THE CORE PROCESS:

QEDS

Look at the <u>q</u>uestion.   KEEP THE
Think it through using the <u>e</u>lements.   } STANDARDS
Think it through in terms of the <u>d</u>iscipline.   IN MIND

How to Start: Begin by Stepping Back

The most common ways to start thinking through a critical-thinking question are often not very effective. One typical way to start is just to start. I simply begin answering the question, relying on my mind to have sorted things out—or rather, hoping that my mind has sorted things out. Another common way to start is to look for information. I have to write a four-page paper about poverty in the United States. It has to have three references. So I scroll down the list of entries from my Internet search. I find three that look okay. I take a chunk of information from each and put it in my paper. I make sure it equals four pages.

A third common way to begin is not to have the slightest idea how to begin. I wait until time pressure drives me to answer the question at the last minute. By that time the situation is desperate, so I'll be satisfied with just having something to turn in—anything. I can't afford the luxury of spending time trying to think things out.

There are more fruitful ways to think through a question and try to answer it. These ways begin with a central critical-thinking move: reflection. Take a metacognitive step, a step back. The question is in front of you. The natural impulse is to answer it, but don't do that yet. Instead, take a step back from the question, detach yourself from it. Don't ask yourself, "What is the answer?" Instead, ask yourself, "What is the question asking? What does it call for? What would I have to do in order to answer it?" If you get the flavor of these stepping-back questions, you'll find that by thinking critically, you can construct a strategy for answering them.

Read the box on pages 171–181. Then pick out some questions from your text. Choose some from later in the book, ones that come after chapters you have not read yet. Outline briefly what you need to do in order to answer those questions.

Try the same thing with two or three questions from other courses you are taking.

Later, at the end of this chapter, try the same activity again. Assess how much your abilities have improved.

THINKING CRITICALLY ABOUT QUESTIONS

Here are a few questions from textbooks in different fields, and how I might step back from them to see what I need to do to think through them critically. (These are not the only ways to approach these questions, of course, but they are good ways to start.) Notice that each of the responses focuses on *how* to answer the question critically, not on actually answering it.

1. Here is a question from a geography text. The text gives a half-page labeled "Critical Thinking: Tombouctoo." There are two paragraphs telling about the city of Tombouctoo (Timbuktu), which was a fabulously

(continued)

THINKING CRITICALLY ABOUT QUESTIONS (*Continued*)

rich, important urban market city on an ancient caravan route across the Sahara. Then the trade routes changed and Tombouctoo was bypassed; it's now a poor, mostly deserted city that plays no important role in today's world. The book then asks:

> Compare Tombouctoo's location with that of Trabzon on the Black Sea in modern-day Turkey. Among which great empires was Trabzon once a major contact and trading point? How important is it today? Do you know of any other once-great cities that have declined as trade routes bypassed them?[2]

What do I need to do to answer the question critically?

a. Well, since the question calls for a comparison (a critical-thinking process), I will need to read about Trabzon. Even before reading, though, I can assume that Trabzon too was an urban trading center in a place where trade routes focused, and that it too was later bypassed. So, I will not simply be gathering information about Trabzon. I am thinking geographically: I am seeing that *"place"* (in this case, a city's position on a trade route) determines a great deal about that city—its prosperity, its origin, maybe its decline when bypassed. *Place* is a central concept in geography. So I am thinking in terms of a *system*, a *logic*. Figure 5.3 is a concept map of that system.

FIGURE 5.3 *A concept map of our critical thinking about Tombouctoo.*

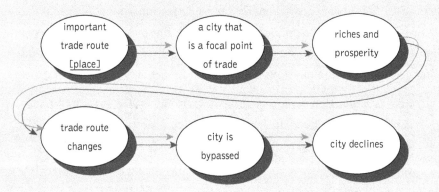

b. As I step back from the question, I also start thinking about another one of the elements, *purpose*: Are most cities located in a certain place for the purpose of cornering trade on some trade route? Is that how cities are founded?

c. The book then asks me to apply this geographical thinking to other once-great cities. For this, I can use my concept map. I begin at the beginning with once-important trade routes. Do I have any examples of that, either in my background knowledge or from other courses? (Some trade routes come to mind: there is the Oregon Trail; there is Route 66; there was the trade between Europe and America before the American Revolution.) I will then expect to find → cities that were a focal point of trade, that → achieved riches and prosperity, but → when trade routes changed, I should expect to find → cities that were bypassed and → then seriously declined. That is following the logic.

(There are implications of the critical thinking so far. I am surprised to find that a city's prosperity does not depend as heavily as I thought on the intelligence and individual business decisions of its inhabitants; those decisions, no matter how smart, may be overridden by the city's place on a bypassed trade route. It is even possible that I might later make a personal decision about where to live based partly on this geographical insight.)

2. Here is a question from a composition textbook. The question asks simply:

What is your definition of obscenity?[3]

Then you are directed to read a paragraph that quotes various Supreme Court justices saying that they can recognize obscenity even without an adequate definition. The paragraph also contains the current Supreme Court criteria for obscenity: "a work must be 'patently

(continued)

THINKING CRITICALLY ABOUT QUESTIONS (*Continued*)

offensive' and lack artistic, literary, political, or scientific value to be declared legally obscene." What many people would do at this point is just give their offhand opinion of obscenity. But as I step back from the question, I remind myself that I need to be clear and accurate, and take account of a wide range of possible obscenity cases. A good way to begin might be to write out a thoughtful SEE-I for the concept of *obscenity*. But I also know there are two major sides to this issue. On one side, I need to feel the pull of free speech and the need for free expression. There is a logic, a system, to that way of thinking. But I also feel the pull of those who are offended by obscenity, those who feel children and others can be harmed by it. There is a logic to that way of thinking also. Regardless of which side I am on, I need to write out the logic of both points of view. Doing so will make my written response much deeper and richer.

3. Here is a "Review Question" in a history text:

   How did slavery shape Southern society?[4]

   This question shows the difference between "learning history" passively versus thinking critically in history. I can answer the question by reading the relevant part of the chapter and writing down the six main ways the book says that slavery shaped Southern society. That's one way. A more meager way is to read the single paragraph of the chapter's "Conclusion." It gives a one-sentence answer to the question. Either way, it looks like a question requiring only recall on my part. If I happen to know some details from lectures or on my own, fine, but that's not expected. I will just find the place in the book where the topic is talked about, so that I can "review" it.

   There is not much opportunity here to think the way a historian does. Historians seldom simply repeat an account given by others. Instead, they re-think that account—they look for implications; they give interpretations; they try to make their understanding deeper, more comprehensive. The field of history is a lot more exciting and creative than simply regurgitating information.

I could do some historical thinking about the question:

- What in the American experience is illuminated by thinking about it in terms of the impact of slavery?
- How does this relate to slavery and questions of race in earlier chapters?
- How does the legacy of slavery still have an impact in the present?
- How can I gather evidence about these questions? What primary sources could I use?

4. Another "Review Question" from a different history text:

Discuss the 1928 election as a mirror of the divisions in American society.[5]

Since it asks me to "discuss," it looks like it might call for critical thinking. Really, though, it's merely asking me to repeat a "discussion" already given in the book. It is just a pseudo–critical-thinking question. If I'm going to think critically about the divisions in American society, I'll have to do it on my own.

Q: Looking at the Question

Systems Thinking

A major help in seeing how to answer a critical-thinking question comes when you think in terms of how many "systems" you need to use in order to answer it. Take a simple ethical dilemma as an example. You are a parent, and you wonder whether to tell your young child that there is no Santa Claus. You feel the pull of two systems. One system centers on the importance of honesty; the other centers on the importance of preserving the magic of childhood. This is not a battle simply between one principle and another. Rather, each principle is part of a system; each has a logic that you can think in terms of. What is your concept of honesty? Why is it important? What are its limits? The same questions apply to the importance of preserving the magic of childhood. To answer this question critically, then, you have to think it through using *both* systems.

Thinking through any complex issue requires that you feel the pull of the different systems involved in the question. Then, it requires you to weigh the importance of each and give each system an adequate voice. Maybe you can come to a definite conclusion about the issue, maybe not. But the heart of addressing it is thinking it through in terms of different systems.

Think of the question on page 179 about defining obscenity. To think through this issue critically, you must think in terms of at least two different systems, one centering on free speech and the other centering on people's desire to be protected from what is offensive to them. If you write an essay on obscenity and think it through using only one of these systems, it will be seriously flawed as a piece of critical thinking. You treated a complex question as if it required only one system to think it through. That would auto-matically diminish the quality of your response.

The word "system" is a good one because it is so flexible. Consider how it applies to a range of examples:

Question: In what major ways did Leonardo embody the spirit of the Renaissance?

Systems to think in terms of: System #1: how Leonardo thought, wrote, lived, and painted—the system that unifies these. I need to grasp the logic of this. I can't just begin writing or just collect information. Next I have to think of system #2, the Renaissance: its values, its tendencies, how it dif-fered from other periods. It is clear that this is a *system* because I could use this Renaissance way of thinking to address topics we have never consid-ered in class. With a solid grasp of that system, I could try to describe how a Renaissance person would think about almost anything—clothes, money, business, travel. Specifically, I could see how much of this system, the spirit of the Renaissance, fits in with the system I saw in Leonardo.

If this is a piece of writing I have to do about Leonardo and the Renaissance, or a presentation in class, thinking it out in terms of multiple *systems* provides a logical outline of how to go about my task effectively and practically. I'll have to do *research*—but I realize by now that research is not just gathering information. It is gathering information as it is linked together by a system or logic. In this case, it is both those systems described previously, plus a third—the way they fit together.

Question: How can I improve my test scores in my political science class?

Systems to think in terms of: You need to think this out in terms of the type of test the teacher gives in this course and the study strategy that fits that type of test. The way tests and strategies fit together is system #1. Thus, if the test is one that emphasizes sheer recall of individual facts, a good strategy might be to use the SEE-I process for important terms, to memorize them using flash cards, or (most effectively) to understand them in terms of the fundamental and powerful concepts of the discipline and the central question of the course. On the other hand, if the test requires overall understanding and reasoning in the discipline, memorizing won't work at all. A good strategy would be to engage in critical reading of the text and critical listening during class discussion, and to spend study time outlining in terms of fundamental and powerful concepts and the central question.

System #2 centers on *you*, what your study strengths and weaknesses are, the amount of time you're willing to invest in improving your test scores in this class, what is feasible to do in the amount of time you have.

Question: What is the atomic mass of hydrogen?

System to use? → You calculate it, using the formula.

Alternative system to use → you look it up on the periodic table.

Question: An exercise from a composition text: "Identify and correct any comma splices in the following paragraph."

System to use? → You look up "comma splice" in the index and apply the rule to the paragraph. Or, you have already internalized the rule: you check the system "in your head."

Question: How much water per day does a person need, on average, to stay healthy.

System to use? → You find the answer from a reliable source.

Almost any issue that is really important, in your life or in the discipline, will require you to think in terms of more than one system. On the other hand, some questions (for example, the last three above) require only a single system to answer them. (Many factual-type questions fall into this category.) Sometimes such questions are decribed as not requiring critical thinking. But that's misleading. It is true that they seldom require *deep* or *broad* critical thinking, but they do require us to be clear, accurate, relevant, precise and sufficient in our answers. Moreover, even if there is only "one system" to consult, we sometimes have a "wrong system" already in place in our minds. With commas, for example, a seriously misleading "system" that people often use is thinking that a comma represents a pause, and so whenever I would pause in a sentence, I should use a comma.

Even in a question as simple as the one about how much water per day a person needs, the source I consult has to be a *reputable* one, and that requires me to make a critical-thinking judgment. People sometimes answer such questions by simply using a Google search, clicking on a link, and reporting the result. Though there is nothing wrong with using Google, it is a tool, and it has to be used thoughtfully. Even for looking up a "fact," the links listed on the Google search page can be unreliable for any number of reasons (bias, poor research, vested financial interests, rumor-mongering, pushing an agenda, and so forth). For example, suppose I'm given the question: "How much water per day does a person need, on average to stay healthy?" So I do a Google search using the keywords "water per day health." In the first link listed, a reader asks how much water per day a person needs. Google then directs me to the next site which says, "The experts have always said, on average, that eight eight-ounce glasses per day will suffice. However, that might not be enough." If I settle for this answer, though, I'll be far from being accurate. The story about needing eight glasses of water per day turns out to be a myth: other more reputable websites (for example, the Mayo Clinic or *Scientific American*) say that there is no scientific basis for the claim and that (except in special circumstances) most of the water we need daily comes in the food we eat.[6]

> An effective "research path" for answering one-system questions is often to look them up in a reliable source. What are some of the main research paths (including reliable sources, if that is relevant) you would take to answer one-system questions in the discipline you are studying?

Thinking in terms of systems, using reasoned judgment to weigh the pull of one system against another, is the heart of answering important questions in disciplines. In each family of disciplines, we are required to do something similar: to think in terms of the various systems that are central to that discipline, how those systems interact, modify one another, and sometimes conflict. We also must think in terms of the systems in the world that the discipline investigates.

E: Thinking It Through Using the Elements

So, you start off with a question to answer. You interpret it. You identify the system or systems that you need to use to answer it. You apply these to the question. What do you need to do now?

You have to use the elements of reasoning; go around the circle (page 49).

Some Questions Need to Be Thought Through Fully; Some Don't

Suppose the question you are considering is important to you. Maybe it's a paper, a major assignment, a presentation in class, or your preparation for an essay exam. Maybe it's something that is important to you personally or professionally—a decision about how to budget your time between work, school, family, and recreation; or how to deal with a client, patient, student, or customer who does not fit the usual profile and requires special help.

You need to go around the whole circle.

Why? Because any one of the elements could turn out to be crucial for this problem. And, besides, this is an *important* question to you. You need to give it the time and attention it deserves in your thinking. With practice, thinking in terms of the elements can become as comfortable and natural as looking where you're going when you drive. Even if you spend only a minute or so on each element, make it a focused minute, with your attention riveted on that element as it applies to the question.

After going around the circle, step back once again. Do some synthesis and re-assemble the logic of the question and your answer to it as a whole.

On the other hand, maybe the question you're addressing is not such an important one; maybe it doesn't need to be treated as fully. Maybe, as you read it, one, two, or three of the elements jump out as the ones you should focus on. You don't always have to go around the full circle.

Here is an example (several others are given in the exercises). A political science text contains a short essay on the issue of gay and lesbian rights. It then asks:

> What is Your Opinion? Should churches and other religious institutions take positions on political issues and candidates?[7]

A critical-thinking response: the element *point of view* stands out from the question. To think this through, you have to give full weight both to those who favor such a thesis and to those who are against it. You have to give the strongest reasons on each side and state them fair-mindedly.

A second element is *implications and consequences*. What, in your most reasonable judgment, will result if churches and religious institutions *do* back political issues and candidates?

A third element stands out: *information*. You can give a thoughtful, balanced answer to this question or just shoot from the hip. You may have an impression about this question, but this is a political science course, not a place to trade unsupported opinions. You need to find information that is as accurate and up to date as possible.

S: Using the Standards

The standards are present in every single act of critical thinking. (If no critical-thinking standards are used, it's not critical thinking at all.) To think in terms of the standards you can:

- Use the standards check (pages 158–159)
- Evaluate around the circle (pages 155–156).

    You use the standards both:

- *While* you are answering a question.
- *Afterward*, when you are checking your work, and revising it to make it better.

Like the elements, the standards are something you need to internalize. That comes as you practice using them, especially as you consciously and explicitly practice using them. You will be better at some standards than others, and that can change from one topic to another.

Internalizing and incorporating even one standard into your way of thinking can substantially improve your thinking everywhere. Take *depth*. Looking for underlying complexities or underlying explanations can make your understanding of almost everything around you deeper. For example, often when people reason, they have a goal, and then they think out the means for achieving the goal. That's critical thinking, but it is probably not *deep* critical thinking. If I think about it more deeply, I'll ask myself what complexities will arise as a carry out those means, what problems will arise. I'll also ask myself, "What are some of the problems that will come about if I *do* achieve that goal?"

D: Thinking It Through in Terms of the Discipline

When you think critically about a question through the lens of a discipline, you use the whole QEDS core process (page 169). The elements and standards are essential in addressing any question. When we add the discipline, we can focus on four key approaches. Each of them is different, but all of them overlap to a considerable degree:

- systems
- fundamental and powerful concepts in the discipline
- the central question of the discipline
- the point of view of the discipline.

Systems

When you identify the discipline-based systems involved in the question, it gives you a key insight into how to go about answering it. It is a great benefit to think in terms of such systems. It means that you don't start off from zero, and you don't start off from unexamined background stories that may be misleading. Focusing on discipline-based systems gives you a framework for addressing a question in a way that is knowledgeable, centered, and often impressive.

In a straightforward way, thinking a question through in terms of the discipline means learning to think in terms of the main systems that are used in that discipline. Part of thinking in systems is knowing the preferred way that type of question is addressed in that discipline. There is a variety of systems, but here are some examples, together with some of the disciplines they might apply to:

- Use well-established theories and laws (natural sciences)
- Use respected points of view within the discipline (literary criticism, art theories)
- Use case studies and expert practice (business, health sciences)
- Use studies, experiments and their findings (social sciences)
- Use highly regarded opposing points of view (philosophy, political science).

All of these clearly involve thinking things through in terms of systems in the discipline.

Fundamental and Powerful Concepts, Central Question, Point of View of the Discipline

Recall that fundamental and powerful concepts are those basic concepts that lie at the heart of a discipline or course (see pages 101–104). (As a reminder, examples might be: homeostasis in biology, Romanticism in literature, supply and demand in economics.) The central question of the course is usually closely related: it is the most central question that the course is addressing (see pages 106–109). This book speaks of the central question as if there were only one, and that is the ideal case. There may in fact be several closely related central questions, but there cannot be many. (A biology example might be, "How do living things work?" Or, breaking that down only a little further, "How does the body work?" "How did organisms come to be the way they are [the origin of species]?" "How are life-forms in a community interdependent?") The point of view of a discipline is that distinctive way practitioners in the field look at things: it includes the domain (the objects or events the discipline focuses on), the way the items in that domain are categorized or classified (these form a system of concepts), and the connections someone in the discipline "sees." It is a major goal of the course that you incorporate those fundamental and powerful concepts, central questions, and point of view into your thinking patterns.

FIGURE 5.4   *Concept map for thinking about the influence of place.*

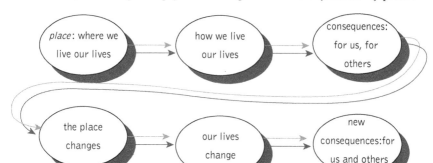

In an earlier example, we worked through a geography question about Tombouctoo and cities on trade routes. We worked it through using the system illustrated in Figure 5.3 on page 178. But we can think it through more deeply as shown in Figure 5.4.

Probably the most fundamental and powerful concept in geography is *place* or *the influence of place*. So, as you think the answer out in terms of this specific system, you are asking yourself, "How does the influence of place determine the fate of cities?"

You have already been addressing this question, but in a much more specific way, when you reasoned out how changing trade routes affect the prosperity of cities. But thinking it out explicitly in terms of *place* is much more conscious—and much more fundamental and powerful. Now, your answer to this question will relate to all the other topics you have learned to think out in terms of *place*. Instead of this being merely one specific system (amid hundreds of other specific systems), all the geographical systems you use are unified by the fundamental and powerful concept of *place*. Not only is the fate of cities influenced by their place on a trade route, but our lives in countless dimensions are also heavily influenced by *where* we live them.

The same is true for the central question. As you think through specific systems, or research some specific information, you relate it to the central question in the course. The central question and the fundamental and powerful concepts are usually closely linked. The central question in a geography course might be: How does the geography of *where* something happens influence *what* happens?

This is thinking geographically. It is thinking the way a geographer thinks. It allows us to see the world from the point of view of the discipline. Geographers can visit Tombouctoo or Washington, D.C., or Los Angeles, or the city or town you live in, and they'll see

Fundamental and powerful concepts sometimes sound unimportant when you write them down. "Place" may seem that way. Part of what makes concepts fundamental and powerful is that they are deep. So you have to make a conscious effort to see them as deep. "Place" can seem unimportant, but it can be incredibly deep: Without being a geographer, it's hard to comprehend just how fundamental and powerful it is, how much of people's lives—how they live, what they do for a living, whom they marry, when they die—is determined by *place*.

it in very different categories from those a non-geographer will see. As I write this paragraph, I am in a coffee shop in New Orleans. I see people (who look different from one another), old buildings (with balconies and high ceilings), streets (paved with shells rather than gravel), flat land; I smell gumbo in the air, feel the humidity (even in late September), and hear sounds of Cajun music. Looking with the eyes of a geographer, though, I see all of those plus a lot more: subtropical weather patterns, the ecosystems and topography of the alluvial lands of the Mississippi delta, cultural diffusion, the ongoing migration of populations. I automatically understand a great deal more about what I see.

When I wrote the lines above this, back in 2004, I did not anticipate Hurricane Katrina coming to destroy much of New Orleans and the Gulf Coast. Geographers did. By thinking in terms of *place*, they—virtually unanimously—knew a hurricane was coming, a devastating one, if not in that year then in another, but soon.

Why Use Fundamental and Powerful Concepts, Central Questions, and Point of View?

So why do this? Why add to your work in a course by thinking things through using fundamental and powerful concepts?

It's a misleading question. Though it is more work in the short run, it's not *much* more work. It just looks like more on paper, and because you're not used to it. It is really a shift in *emphasis*. Sometimes answering the question in terms of fundamental and powerful concepts comes in just a flash of realization, an Aha! After you get used to this way of thinking, it will make *all* the questions in the discipline much more answerable. In fact, it will cut down on the work you have to do. What *is* work is memorizing and retaining a hundred different pieces of information or thinking through a hundred unrelated specific systems. And then you're left with that sinking feeling as those memorized bits and pieces disappear without a trace—and it is as if you did it all for nothing, or just for a number on a transcript somewhere. Many of those pieces, though—maybe all of them—can be thought through far more efficiently (and even retained!) when you use fundamental and powerful concepts and central questions.

Critical Writing: Using the Core Process To Write a Paper

The heart of critical writing—as of critical anything—is reasoning through a question using both the elements and standards. What follows is a set of steps that can help turn your critical thinking into a piece of critical writing. These are general steps: they have to be adapted to fit the question, problem or topic you are writing on. Your teacher may have guidelines that will be more applicable than the general steps here.

Often when people write a paper, they just pick their main points "out of the air." Sometimes they don't even start with a thesis statement, but even if they do, their main points may still simply be ones that happen to come to mind. Critical writing is significantly different from that. It grows from the logic of a topic (pages 68–70), from analyzing the topic by going around the circle, so you see the interrelated parts of it and how they fit together in a coherent whole. In critical writing, then, both the thesis statement of your paper and all your main points come directly out of the logic of the topic. The *topic* of your paper is the question at issue you are addressing, and your paper is the way you answer that question. The content of your paper is therefore really the same as your analysis (or at least the most important parts of it), but written out and developed in paragraphs. The *thesis statement* is the important parts of your analysis crystalized into a single sentence. Thus everything grows from the logic, from going around the circle. As a result, the parts of your paper form a well-integrated whole.

There are six steps—three on pre-writing, two on the actual writing, and one on revision—so the process may look daunting at first glance. But you are already familiar with most of it. You are already used to writing an analysis by going around the circle, to doing a Standards Check, and to using SEE-I. What remains is to pick out the *main points* of your analysis, crystallize them into a *thesis statement*, and let the *logical outline* of your paper flow from them. You then have to *support the weak points* in your reasoning, and write the paper itself using SEE-I to develop your points. Of course, no set of steps will guarantee that the product you come up with will automatically be a finished piece of critical writing. There is a lot more to writing than can be listed. The steps described here may help substantially.

The whole process of critical writing can be compressed into three short sentences: **Reasoned analysis** of a topic generates the **structure** of the paper. The structure exposes the **weak points** and generates **writing the paper** itself using SEE-I. **Reflection and revision** lets you **complete** the paper as a piece of critical writing.

Step One: Reasoned Analysis.   Writing a paper begins with **going around the circle** of elements, analyzing and laying out the logic of the topic you are addressing: its purpose or goals, the main question at issue, the main information your paper will be presenting on the topic, the main assumptions you are making in the paper, and so forth. The analysis will include any research you have done that you plan to incorporate into your paper. It will also include the *multiple systems* (pages 181–184) you use to reason your way through the topic or question.

This is a pre-writing step. It will result in something like Chris's analysis of the logic of getting married (pages 71–75) or the analysis of the logic of earth sciences (pages 96–97) or perhaps like an analysis you have done by going around the circle (page 49). The result will be a bulleted list of well-thought-out responses to each of the 8+ elements and a sense of the logic of the topic as a whole. This is a solid foundation for writing.

You need to make a reasonable choice about how full your analysis needs to be. You may decide to include *more*—or *less*—than the core process. *More*: You can incorporate the discipline or other processes into your reasoning in a rich way. As you go around the circle, then, your analysis might well include fundamental and powerful concepts, the central question, the point of view of the discipline, and other insights from your course; it can involve evaluation, comparison and contrast, and so forth. *Less*: Or you may decide to focus on just a few of the elements, those you judge to be most crucial: there may be time pressure, for example (as in writing a timed essay exam), or you may have deeply ingrained paper-writing habits that are hard to break. There is a choice here you have to make.

You finish Step One by doing a **Standards Check** (pages 158–159). This is a reflection and revision step. The more important your piece of writing is for you, the more beneficial it is to confront the questions in the Standards Check in a conscientious and open way. If your writing project requires research, you have to check on whether the information you report is accurate, whether the sources you have used are reliable, and whether you have exercised intellectual integrity (page 175) by giving credit to your sources. And as you write the paper itself, you'll still be using the standards: checking for clarity, accuracy, relevance, and so forth. You'll be asking yourself if you should go deeper (exploring more of the complexities) or broader (looking at other points of view).

Going around the circle and then doing a Standards Check gives you a **reasoned analysis**, the foundation for critical writing.

Step Two: Structure.   The structure of your paper involves figuring out **the main points** you will be making, formulating a **thesis statement** in relation to them, and then constructing a **logical outline** of your paper. Again, everything flows from going around the circle.

Using your reasoned analysis of the topic from Step 1, you figure out the **main points** of your paper by focusing on those parts of the analysis that are most important for making your case in the paper you are writing. The most important points may be just a few of the elements, or they may include all or most of them. From these main points will emerge both your thesis statement and the logical outline of your paper.

You can then formulate the **thesis statement** of your paper directly from the main points. It is a sentence that crystallizes and unifies them, taken all together. It is a statement of the way you will be addressing the topic overall. The thesis statement will also be a touchstone to help you keep in mind how your main points fit together to make your paper a coherent whole. (There is an intimate connection between the main points of your paper and your thesis statement. Many writers formulate their thesis statement *first*, and then derive their main points from it; also, they often go back and forth between the two, adjusting each to get them to fit together well. The key thing is that both main points and thesis statement come from a reasoned analysis.)

The **logical outline** of your paper also comes directly from the main points, written in outline form. (Thus four main points will give the body of your paper four main sections.) In fact, if you write out the main points as sentences, they will often be usable directly as topic sentences in the body of the paper itself.

Step Three: Weakpoints.   If your paper says something substantive, there will almost certainly be weak points. The challenge is to **identify** them, to notice where the weaknesses lie, and then to **support** them with back-up.

Identifying weakpoints. Picture someone who strongly disagrees with what you are saying or at least is very skeptical. Ask yourself: Which of your main points would the person be most likely to take issue with? Those are weak points. Alternatively, the weakest points in your outline—the ones someone would object to—may be parts you have *not* stated. Maybe the objection would focus on unstated assumptions you are making or on a consequence you haven't noticed. If that happens, you need to state the weak point explicitly in your outline so you can support it. In critical writing, you don't hide the weak points of your paper. Rather, you put them out in front, you support them, and you let readers evaluate them for themselves.

Weak points are often difficult to see because as you write your paper you may become more and more attached to what you are saying. It can almost blind you to the objections someone else may raise. Here again the standards help. You can ask, from the point of view of someone who disagrees, "Is this relevant? Is the case being made sufficient? Is it accurate?"

→ A good rule of thumb is to take it as a *requirement* that you identify at least one important weakpoint in your outline.

Supporting the weak points. The weak points in your paper are ones that need to be supported—with reasons, with argument, with elaboration, with more information. You then need to incorporate that support into your outline.

Pause and reflect. At this point, you should have a fairly complete outline (although it can still be revised). You have the main points written out and organized. The weakest of your points are supported. You have a sense of the whole. You are clear about the purpose of your paper and the question at issue you are addressing.

Now is a good time for reflection, for contemplating the writing you are about to do, the logical structure it will rest on. This is a good time for making revisions to your thought process.

Step Four: Writing the Paper. The **introduction** can be just a paragraph or it can be a longer section. In it, you lay out for the reader the question at issue you'll be addressing in the paper, how you plan to answer it (your thesis statement), and your goals or purpose in writing the paper. You may also decide to summarize the main points you will be presenting in the body of the paper and the point of view you will be using to answer the question at issue.

Write **the body of the paper**. With the clear, logical outline you have constructed, writing the paper should be considerably more satisfying than if you just started writing from scratch, saying the first things that come into your mind and hoping it will work out.

A good way to write the body of your paper is to use SEE-I throughout (pages 30–33). Start off with just your first main point. *State* it clearly in a sentence or two. Then *elaborate* on it, explaining it more fully, in more detail. This may take several paragraphs. (You'll want to keep the audience in mind as you do, realizing that you will have to explain a lot more to the reader than you think you have to. After all, you've *done* the analysis; you've organized it coherently; you've seen how the parts fit together—*of course* it seems clear to you. But you have to put yourself in the place of someone who has not thought about this issue very much before. You have to elaborate enough so the reader understands you clearly.) Continuing the SEE-I, you next give a good *example*, maybe more than one, of that first main point. Maybe you can give a *contrasting example* so the reader can pinpoint what you are saying. Then, when appropriate, you give a good *illustration*. Again, the goal is to help the reader see exactly what you are saying, exactly what you mean.

Do this in turn for each of your main points, including the supporting ones. Your paper will grow organically. All the points you are making will be important ones. The sentences you write will not be filler. Rather, each of them will be directly relevant to the individual point you are making and to the overall development of your paper.

Step Five: Re-read, Reflect, and Revise.   You have written almost the whole paper now. Although it's OK to write the concluding section right away, this is a good time to reflect again and to revise what you have written. Read over the paper. Check for clear topic sentences, for breaks in the logical flow from one main point to the next, for weakpoints that need further back-up. Check for grammar and spelling too. It is often beneficial to take a break now, if you can, maybe to wait a day or two to get a fresh look at the paper you've written. It

FIGURE 5.5   *Critical writing.*

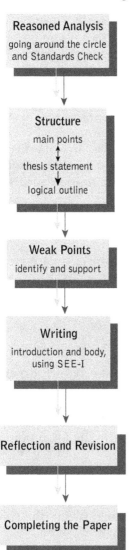

Reasoned Analysis
going around the circle and Standards Check

Structure
main points
↕
thesis statement
↓
logical outline

Weak Points
identify and support

Writing
introduction and body, using SEE-I

Reflection and Revision

Completing the Paper

often helps if do this before writing the concluding section. You need to guard against the feeling of finality, of being done with it. Your paper is still a work in progress.

This is also a good time to work with someone else. Have others read your paper. Get feedback. Ask them to make a mark every time they have to go back and read a sentence a second time. That is a good indication that you need to re-write that part.

Step Six: Completing the Paper. Write **the concluding section.** Again, this can be a single paragraph or it can be longer. In this section, you may want to recapitulate the question at issue you were addressing, your thesis statement, and your main purpose in writing the paper. You may also want to sum up how you have answered the question. Readers should feel they have been brought full circle now. They should have a clear sense of the logic of your paper.

The Work of Critical Thinking

Whether it is in writing or reading, in analysis or evaluation, in the discipline as well as in your life outside school, critical thinking creates value. It takes effort, especially before you get used to it. But it has clear practical benefits that far exceed the effort. It will produce better answers, better grades, in more courses, in more professions, with ultimately less work, than any alternative. More than that, it gives insight that can make your life richer, by bringing the elements, the standards, and the disciplines into learning to think things through.

Some Outcomes

As you finish this book . . .

1. You should be able to *state, elaborate, give examples* and *illustrations* (SEE-I) of the core process of critical thinking and how it applies in the discipline.
2. You should be able to *describe the path* you would take to think through a question, any question, and give examples of it as well.
3. Based on the way you've learned to think critically in this discipline, you should be able to *apply* the same processes to other courses you are taking. Taking this course, in this discipline should make many other courses and disciplines clearer for you. You should be able to give examples of this.
4. You should be able to *identify, describe,* and *give examples* of some of your main strengths and some of your main weaknesses as a critical thinker.

5. You should be able, at least in a preliminary way, to *identify*, *elaborate on*, and *give examples* and *illustrations* of some of the main critical-thinking character traits. You should also be able to *give examples* of when you or others have exemplified (or not exemplified) the trait.

6. You should be able to *identify* and *explain* the systems you would use to respond critically to questions.

7. You should be able to *engage in critical writing*: able to write a paper on a topic by going around the circle of elements, using the standards, constructing a logical outline, supporting weak-points, and using SEE-I for development.

8. You should feel a growing mastery of the outcomes in earlier chapters. You should be able to take any outcome from any chapter in this book and:
   ■ State, elaborate, exemplify and illustrate it
   ■ Relate it to critical thinking in the discipline you are studying
   ■ Describe how it fits into critical thinking as a whole.

As with some of the outcomes in the other chapters in this book, your accomplishments may not be as secure as the outcomes listed above might lead you to believe. Critical thinking takes time, practice, and commitment.

Ideas for Writing

(General guidelines for "Ideas for Writing" are on page 38.)

1. What are some standard activities that, in your best judgment, would work out better for all concerned if the people who engaged in them exercised more critical thinking? Explain.

2. Make the previous question more specific. What are some standard human activities that, in your judgment, would work out better for all concerned → if people reflected on their purpose more? → if people reflected more deeply on their assumptions? [continue, focusing on other elements]; → if people paid more attention to being clear? → to being accurate? [continue, focusing on other standards]; → if people reflected on what we can learn from biology, → from sociology [continue, focusing on the discipline in this course and on other disciplines you are studying]. Explain.

3. Explain the core process of critical thinking as if to someone who has never taken a class either in it or in the discipline you are studying. What are the overall benefits (within the course, in other courses, in life outside of school) of thinking critically from the point of view of the discipline? In your judgment are there significant disadvantages as well? Explain.

4. Look over the critical-thinking character traits again. To what extent can a person slowly build strengths in one or more of these traits in his or her life? What are some ways a person might go about doing that?

5. Think of writers. Many people are intellectually engaged in writing. They find it fulfilling; they take pride in doing it well; they develop themselves and their beliefs in their writing. Or think of Jane Goodall, going out to observe chimps in the wild. Or think of people who are deeply drawn to being in health-care, or science, or literature. Again, the name for that is intellectual engagement. What would it be like if you were intellectually engaged in a discipline (maybe the discipline in this course)? How would it affect the questions you ask, the answers you accept, the implications you search for . . . ?

6. Create your own ideas for writing in relation to this book, this discipline, this course.

Tell Your Story

(The idea behind "Tell Your Story" and some suggestions about doing it are on page 39.)

1. Look back at the "Tell Your Story" questions from Chapter 1. Your personal history has changed a little since then, in that you have read this book and reflected on critical thinking across the curriculum. Respond to some of those questions again, focusing on any changes that may have taken place in you since then. If possible, it is better to revisit them near the end of the semester. (Remember, that any changes will probably seem subtle or slight. Change takes time and practice.)

2. Choose one of the critical-thinking character traits to reflect on (for example, *intellectual courage*), and write it in the blank: Who in your life has shown significant _____?
Describe your experiences with that person. Give examples.

By contrast, who in your life has *seemed* to value_____, but in reality did not value it much? Describe your experiences here as well.

3. Have you ever found yourself taking a course "just for a grade?" Or giving answers that you think the teacher expects of you, without even wondering whether it made sense to you? By contrast, have you taken courses in areas you are intensely interested in? Or given answers that, after carefully thinking them through, seemed to you to be right? How were these experiences different for you? Do you see one as more positive than the other?

4. What is something in your life that *you* are intellectually engaged in? It will be a topic that you are intensely interested in, one you want to learn about, often not just for any practical good it will do you, but for its own sake. What disciplines or areas in school could you become intellectually engaged in? What about them appeals to you?

CHAPTER 5 Exercises

The exercises to Chapter 5 are geared to addressing questions in your specific discipline or disciplines. Those questions will be everywhere: asked in the text, asked by your instructor, by fellow students, by you. Some will be unasked but implicit in the readings and the class experience. You need to practice analyzing and answering these by using QEDS within the discipline, and you need to receive feedback from classmates and from instructors.

5.1 Go around the circle in the discipline; do a Standards Check.

a. Go around the circle with respect to the discipline as a whole. Make this a pre-test: keep your answer, but don't look at it during the semester. Repeat this analysis near the end of the course as a post-test; do a Standards Check; compare the two; assess how your understanding of the discipline has changed and deepened.

b. Go around the circle with respect to an important sub-discipline in your field (e.g., if your discipline is psychology, → analyze experimental psych, or social psych, etc.; business → marketing, accounting, etc.). Do a Standards Check.

c. Go around the circle with respect to the family of disciplines yours belongs to (e.g., social sciences, natural sciences, arts, humanities, business). Do a Standards Check.

d. Go around the circle with respect to this book on thinking critically. Do a Standards Check.

5.2 Here is an excerpt from a text on nutrition:

> In your lifetime, you are going to read thousands of newspaper and website headlines, as well as watch and listen to countless television and radio reports. Your critical thinking skill in evaluating the sources and information being presented will be your best friend when it comes to deciding which blurbs to believe. This skill may also save you considerable money by helping you avoid nutrition gimmicks. When it comes to assessing nutrition information in the media, it's worth your time and effort to find out where it came from and why (or if) you should care.[8]

For Exercises 5.3 through 5.7: Briefly describe the system or systems you would use to think it through to a reasonable answer. If it requires only one system to answer it, identify some questions you could ask to infuse it with more critical thinking.

5.3 A question from a biology text:

> If all organisms had not descended from a common ancestor, and did not possess many common genes and mechanisms of development, would we be able to perform valid medical research [for humans] using mice and in some cases, Drosophila? Why or why not?[9]

[Drosophila, I find out from the text, are fruit flies.]

5.4 A book on the history of the arts:

> SUMMARY. After reading this chapter you should be able to: Identify and explain the political and religious conditions that led to the Reformation, including the theological and dogmatic contentions of Erasmus, Luther, Zwingli, Calvin, and Montaigne.[10]

5.5 A question on a legal case from a business law text:

> Intoxication. Betty Galloway, an alcoholic, signed a settlement agreement upon her divorce from her husband, Henry Galloway. Henry, in Betty's absence in court, stated that she had lucid intervals from her alcoholism, had been sober for two months, and was lucid when she signed the settlement agreement on September 22, 1978. Betty only moved to vacate the settlement agreement on September 27, 1978, after she had retained present legal counsel. On January 23, 1979, Betty was declared incompetent to handle her person and affairs, and a guardian and conservator was appointed. Betty, through her guardian, sued to have the settlement agreement voided. Who wins? [*Galloway v. Galloway*, 281 N.W.2d 804 (N.D. 1979)][11]

5.6 One of 20 "Review Questions" in a chapter of a geology textbook:

> What is the cataclysmic event called in which an exploding star produces all of the elements heavier than iron?[12]

5.7 Someone asks you to give your reaction to the question of abortion.

5.8 Analyze the following passage in terms of the elements and standards. It is a paragraph from the Constitution of the Islamic Republic of Iran:

> The family unit is the foundation of society and the main institution for the growth and advancement of mankind . . . . It is the principal duty of the Islamic government to regard women as the unifying factor of the family unit and its position. They are a factor in bringing the family out of the service of propagating consumerism and exploitation and renewing the vital and valuable duty of motherhood in raising educated human beings . . . . As a result motherhood is accepted as a most profound responsibility in the Muslim viewpoint and will, therefore, be accorded the highest value and generosity.[13]

5.9 My geology text lists 28 "important terms" and 14 main points of "summary" for Chapter 2 alone. Chapter 2 is on minerals. Chapter 3 (on igneous rocks) lists 35 additional "important terms" and 15 main points of "summary." That's in 46 pages of the book, and there are over 600 pages all together. At this rate, by the end of the book I'll have to know almost 800 important terms and around 400 main points of summary. What can I do?

5.10 What elements would you focus on to answer the following question from a literature text? It follows a story by Ernest Hemingway, "The Short Happy Life of Francis Macomber," and it asks a question about the three main characters.

> What do Wilson, Francis, and Margot each think it means to be a real man? What would you guess Hemingway thinks?[14]

5.11 Why do many people (including you, maybe) spend so much money on their weddings? What is the best way to lose weight? Why is Chicago so much more prosperous than Buffalo, New York? Why are the Rockies so much higher than the Appalachians? Why do young people, on average, drive faster than older people? Why do people like watching sports so much?

5.12 Look again at the questions in Exercise 5.11. Notice that you may not know enough about the relevant disciplines to identify the systems you would use to answer them critically. Write out some ordinary, everyday questions that might be illuminated by the discipline in *this* course. What systems would you use to think it through?

5.13 **Writing thesis statements.** Look at any written examples of your course work in which you have analyzed something by going around the circle. For each one, do the following: pick out the main points from it as if you were going to write a paper. Then write out a thesis statement for the projected paper. Do this by crystalizing the main points into a single sentence.

5.14 **Critical writing.** In Exercise 5.1a, you gave an analysis of the discipline you are studying by going around the circle with respect to it. Now write a paper about the logic of that discipline: from your analysis, construct a logical outline, choose your main points, write out a thesis statement, support the weakest points, write the introduction, write the body of the paper using SEE-I, and (after a time to reflect and revise) write the concluding section.

5.15 Write a paper about getting married from your point of view. Use Chris's analysis of marriage (pages 71–75) as a model from which to construct your own. The analysis you give is the foundation of your paper. From it select the most important points (try to choose only three or four) and try to choose three or four and crystalize them into a well-written thesis statement. Pick out the weakest points—the ones that are most in need of support. Picture someone who disagrees with your analysis—maybe one of your friends or even someone you used to be involved with romantically. If possible, incorporate the discipline you are studying into your analysis and outline.

Alternatively, write a paper about getting married from Chris's point of view.

5.16 In your course, find an issue, a problem, or a critical-thinking question important enough to merit going around the full circle. Then, do the analysis and synthesis by going around the circle. Do a Standards Check.

5.17 Look carefully at some critical-thinking questions in your subject textbook. Identify the elements of reasoning that stand out and must be addressed in answering the questions.

5.18 Take some important paragraphs from readings in your course. Analyze them in terms of the elements and standards (as in Exercise 5.8).

5.19 SEE-I runs all the way through this book. That's because it is so widely usable. For example, suppose you are a student learning about X: without SEE-I, all you have is the *impression* that you understand X; with SEE-I, on the other hand, you have (a) a *test* of whether you actually do understand it; (b) a record of what you did understand; and (c) a study guide for the future.

Look back at three or four questions in this book, or some "Ideas for Writing," or questions from "Tell Your Story." Envision how much richer and clearer your response would be if you had included an SEE-I.

5.20 **Group work. Answer with critical thinking.** Sit in groups of four.

A asks a question in the discipline or related to it. The group gets two minutes for thinking.

B describes the systems that need to be thought through to answer the question.

C explains which elements need to be addressed to answer it.

D (having taken some notes) does a Standards Check on B's and C's responses.

Switch roles.

5.21 **Group work**. Discuss critically:

- How does Figure 5.1 work? How does it describe critical thinking?
- How much work will it take to engage in critical thinking in this course? To what extent will it save work?
- Will it transfer to other courses? to day-to-day life?

5.22 Look back at the outcomes for each of the chapters. Look only at the "Outcomes" section—don't look back at other parts of the text. See how many of the outcomes you can accomplish now. When you are finished, evaluate how clearly, accurately, and relevantly you did them.

DAILY PRACTICE

At incorporating critical thinking into your life and your learning

Look back at the instructions on pages 44–45. Remember that a major difficulty of engaging with critical thinking is bringing yourself to actually do it. The skills, though vitally important, are not enough.

5.23 **Engage with critical thinking.** Spend a period of time each day practicing your critical thinking as a whole. Listen. Observe. Read. Write. As you do, notice the elements. Notice the standards—their presence or absence. Apply the fundamental and powerful concepts. Question things using the central question. Observe and connect using the point of view of the discipline. Put it all together.

5.24 **Engage with the character traits of being a critical thinker.** Look on page 175–176 for a list of some character traits associated with being a critical thinker. Although these have not been explained in detail, spend some time each day exercising a trait, as you understand it. On one day, you might practice intellectual humility: admitting when you don't know things; explicitly taking back views you have when you realize you don't have the evidence to back them up; recognizing areas that matter to you where you don't really know very much; confronting the large number of beliefs that have simply been passed on to you (by peers, by entertainment, by popular culture) that you haven't really examined. The next day, do the same for another one of the traits on the list.

5.25 **Engage with critical writing.** You should have a host of questions now, about the discipline and about your life. Hold one of them in front of your mind and describe how you would go about writing a paper on it. Think of the elements it would involve most importantly and how you would turn it into a logical outline. Get a sense of the whole. Construct a thesis statement. Then, identify the weakest points and describe how you would support them. Think about how you would use SEE-I to develop your paper.

You don't have to do this all at once, and you don't have to actually write the paper. You can take notes, but the important thing is just to think it out, step by step. Try this with different questions.

Responses to Starred Exercises

Chapter 1

1.3 In almost any large group, the same answers occur: most people think that *others* are heavily influenced by advertising and conform a great deal, but that they themselves are influenced and conform only a little, maybe not at all. Most people think they are better-than-average drivers.

Clearly something is off-kilter about this. How might egocentrism be at work in the answers you gave?

1.4a From a critical-thinking point of view, essential questions to raise are ones (i) about *clearness*: "What does this mean? What are the implications of saying the U.S. is #1?" (ii) about *precision*: "Number one in what respect?" and (iii) about *importance*: "Why does it matter if the U.S. is number one in some respects?"

1.6 Here are three of my questions:

- Will the same film be there with all shampoos, even the store's?
- Is the film the result of the shampoo or of something else entirely?
- Is there anything negative about having that film on my hair that can only be seen with a microscope?

Note: You probably came up with these questions or with others just as good. That is a good critical-thinking response. But you were prompted by this book, and so it isn't an "authentic" problem—either for you or for me. Here's the real issue: Would you—or I—have actually asked questions like that if we were the ones getting the haircut? Would it have occurred to us to ask questions like these?

1.9 Here are some possible criteria you could have used:
I thought it through critically because I:

- Realistically assessed my need for something
- Gathered sufficient information to make the best decision
- Asked the important questions beforehand

I did not think it through critically because I:

- Engaged in wishful thinking
- Went along without asking the questions I needed to ask
- Put what I wanted at the moment over what was really important to me

Actually, the most common criterion people give is not a reasonable one at all. People often judge whether they reasoned something out *well* by whether it *turned out well*, and they conclude that they failed to reason something out well because it *turned out badly*.

But those are not reasonable criteria. A decision can turn out well or badly because of circumstances we have no way of knowing about. I may make a bad decision and it can happen to turn out well. If I make the most reasonable decision available under the circumstances, it is still the most reasonable decision even if it turns out badly.

Check your answers to see if you used this unreasonable criterion.

1.13 There could be many good hypotheses, and they can be different depending on where you live. (In New Orleans, one hypothesis would be that a festival is taking place in the French Quarter.) But this is intended as a question about egocentricity. Your list should contain the following hypothesis as a prominent possibility: *You* are the one who is driving erratically (and that makes it look as though everyone else is).

1.15 It is not "irrational" at all. Bodily processes usually result from biological factors. My "knowledge" is sometimes one such factor, but it is often vastly outweighed by the other factors at work. There is nothing irrational about that. It's just how things work.

What *would be* irrational is if I believed I should have complete mental control over my body. It would be like saying to a cut: "Don't bleed!" and expecting it to obey. (To a certain extent, emotions work that way too. Adrenalin rushes into my system and I feel angry. Saying "I have no good reason to be angry" seldom helps.)

Still, I do have a considerable amount of critical-thinking control over my body, but it works in a very different way. I can often avoid such food aversions (and the rush of adrenalin to my system) by using forethought (for example, by avoiding the occasions for getting sick or angry).

1.16 Here's an example:

Situation: I'm considering dropping this course because it looks too hard.

Question: What assumptions am I making about this situation?

Answer: I am assuming it will be too hard → I wonder if that's accurate?

Question: What conclusion should I draw about this situation?

Answer: My conclusion is to wait and see. I need more information.

Question: What are some other points of view that might help?

Answer: I could discuss it with the teacher. Maybe she can't help, but maybe she can. It won't hurt to try.

1.18 Maybe the person wrote down only vague, easy-going comments. This is a very common response. Some possible conclusions you might draw are that the person values being nice, the person wants to avoid hurting your feelings (whether your feelings would in fact be hurt or not), the person wants to avoid any possibility of conflict, and the person has not thought of any more focused comments to make. (What can you say to get the person to give you more helpful feedback?)

Chapter 2

2.4e An example might be sports that I engage in for fun (my purpose). I might become so fixated on winning that it interferes with the fun.

2.5b The question at issue: How can I learn to think through questions and problems in terms of the 8+ elements of reasoning?

2.5d Here are three that sound reasonable:

- What are the major ways *space* is depicted in art?
- What do they have in common and how are they different?
- How do three different modern schools of painting depict space in their art?
- I might note that *space*, at least on the basis of this chapter, is a fundamental and powerful concept for understanding art (see Chapter 3, pages 101–104).

2.6d Assumptions:

- That "needs" and "demand" are very different from one another.
- That all-or-nothing thinking is not very beneficial.
- That the concept *demand* does not encourage all-or-nothing thinking.

2.7c Here are two:

- Almost certainly, taking ginkgo will not improve memory in me or in others. → Further question: I wonder how to find out if something similar is true for other herbal remedies.
- The memory improvement my friends and I seem to experience after taking ginkgo is just a placebo effect.

Your answers may be different. Here are two points to use in evaluating your answers: *Are* they implications? Are they *important* implications?

- The book says ginkgo does not improve memory "in normal individuals": Is there an implication that ginkgo does improve memory in *non-normal people*?[7]

As an aside, the passage is also making an *assumption*: Controlled studies are the most trustworthy way to find out if a remedy works.

2.8e This is different from making a decision that turns out badly because of information you had no reasonable way of knowing.

2.9c Rats, mice, termites, cockroaches, scorpions, rattlesnakes; deer, pheasants, ducks, and geese (in season); calves (veal); and cattle during branding and castration.

2.10d What the drivers *did*—littering or not littering under the various conditions—is information. *Why* the drivers did not litter is interpretation by the experimenters.

2.11c A test of how fair-mindedly you've described Singer's point of view is if Singer would comment on your summary by saying, "Yes, that is exactly what I meant." If you disagree with Singer, a classmate should not be able to discover that by reading your summary. (Test it out.)

2.13c For example, if you were born just 200 years ago, you would not have played football, basketball, or baseball; listened to rock music; ridden on a train, car, or bike; lain on a beach for enjoyment; eaten any packaged food. You would never have heard of molecules, bipolar disorder, marketing, bacteria or viruses, genes, galaxies, psychology, plastic, sexism, toilet paper, or thousands of other things we take entirely for granted.

Chapter 3

3.2a Here is the way the authors reason: They start with a general point (a piece of information) about communicating effectively. Then they make their point clearer by defining a key concept: audience. Next, they become more precise, by specifying types of audiences. In paragraph 2 they focus on important questions at issue you need to raise. Finally, in the last sentence, they draw out an implication for how you can make better decisions about writing for an audience. In addition to the elements (*information, concept, question at issue, implications*), the question asks you to focus on standards of critical thinking to be discussed in Chapter 4: *clear, precise,* and *important.*

3.5 All you're buying is a little more time—you get nothing else to show for all that money. You are paying for the right to pay later.

3.6 This is a response only to the example part of the question. There are examples of actions that are legal but unethical: adultery is legal; lying is legal (except on contracts); breaking your promises is legal. There are also actions that are ethical but illegal (Rosa Parks's refusal to give up her seat on the bus).

So your explanation of the difference between ethical and legal thinking should fit examples like these.

3.7 Assess yourself. The instructions to 3.7 did not mention anything about SEE-I. As you read it (or actually started the log it suggests) did it occur to you that it would be a good idea to state, elaborate, exemplify, and illustrate the important vocabulary terms? To the extent it did occur to you, that is evidence you are starting to internalize some basic processes of critical thinking.

3.10 From the point of view of the discipline, the two questions are at least closely related (maybe even identical). It is an assumption of this book that if you answer the second question without even making reference in your mind to the first question, you have probably missed a major part of the impact of the discipline.

3.13 One such map is the one in Figure 1.3, at the end of Chapter 1.

3.14 The new paradigm highlights *plan, organize,* and *lead*—but to achieve *what*? That "what" is a fundamental and powerful concept that is missing. To think managerially, I have to think not just in terms of planning, organizing, and leading, but in terms of the *goals* these are intended to achieve. (Notice how actual managers can lose sight of this goal concept.)

3.16 The most usual answer is something like, "We're still here. Dinosaurs are long gone. So we are more fit!"

That's an irrational answer. You can't judge fitness by whether something is still around. By that logic, anyone who is alive now, no matter how feeble, is more fit than anyone in the past. ("Are you a better baseball player than Babe Ruth? Are you smarter than Marie Curie? Are you wiser than Socrates?" "Sure, they're dead.")

A good way to judge the fitness of dinosaurs versus humans is to see how long species of dinosaurs lasted in the world versus how long *Homo sapiens* will have to last to equal that time. Which is likely to be more fit by this way of measuring?

3.18 This kind of statement is a favorite of skeptics, in this case being applied to physics. There are many reputable versions of skepticism. Often, though, people think the sun's rising is doubtful because they reason that just because this event has always occurred in the past doesn't mean it will necessarily occur again tomorrow.

But there is a *logic* to our explanation for why the sun rises: the sun doesn't just happen to rise. The earth is spinning, and for the sun not to "rise" tomorrow, something horrendous would have to happen to the earth to stop it from spinning. It is hard to imagine what could possibly make the earth stop spinning without destroying it, and certainly it couldn't happen without our being well aware of it ahead of time. So if the sun wasn't going to rise tomorrow, we would know it today.

Chapter 4

4.4 (1) Culture, many argue, is the adhesive binding together the world's diverse social fabric. (2) A cursory read of the daily newspaper, however, raises questions as to whether the world is literally coming unglued because the frequency and the intensity of (3) cultural conflict seems pervasive and ever-increasing. (4) With the recent rise of global communication systems (satellite TV, movies, video, etc.) stereotypic Western culture is spreading at a rapid pace. While (5) this is willingly accepted by many throughout the world, (6) other groups and countries resist this (7) new form of cultural imperialism through protests, censorship, and restrictions on film, TV, and music.

Elements:

(1) The first sentence is an assumption.

(2) The second sentence identifies a question at issue.

(3) *Cultural conflict* is an important concept in the paragraph.

(4) This sentence is presenting information.

(5) & (6) Both halves of this sentence are presenting information.

(7) The phrase "new form of cultural imperialism" is interpretation; it is based on the concept of political imperialism.

Standards:

Clearness: It's not too clear exactly what the authors mean by "culture." Maybe they will clear that up later. They give some examples of Western culture spreading, and I know there are others. There is a KFC outlet in sight of the pyramids and Coca-Cola signs in Red Square.

Accuracy: As far as I can tell, everything is accurate—except for calling it cultural imperialism. To me, the concept of imperialism implies a takeover by force, against the will of the inhabitants. The protests and the rest could be by only a small percentage of the population. If nobody watched the movies, there would be no cultural imperialism. Moreover, *is* conflict increasing? Or does it just seem that way because it is all over the news?

Importance, relevance: The points made are certainly important because we value diversity among cultures. I don't see how the authors' point about cultural conflict is relevant to the spread of Western culture; they seem like opposites to me.

Sufficiency: The account so far is certainly not sufficient to convince me that the world is becoming "unglued." I will wait for the authors to give a more sufficient account as they proceed.

Breadth: I wonder just how broad the dissemination of Western culture is? Does it extend even into poor countries?

Depth: How deep does it go? Is it just *entertainment*, as in the examples? Or does it extend to language, social customs, economic systems?

I wonder what underlies this? Why aren't Americans avidly picking up foreign TV and movies?

Precision: Not many details are given: How many protests are there? How much censorship and restriction? Who imposed the censorship? What are the specifics of the "cultural imperialism"?

4.8 Though nothing in the question says so, you have to bring in *standards* to address this question. Partly, it is an issue of *clearness*. People might mean a lot of different things by saying this. For example, they might mean that you can't simply *make* someone learn to think critically—unless they are willing to learn. But sometimes people mean you can't *become* a critical thinker; you have to just *be* one. Now *accuracy* comes in: the statement is clearly false. It is probably the result of all-or-nothing thinking (which distorts accuracy)—the person is imagining someone with *no* critical thinking skills suddenly *acquiring* them. But of course critical thinking is not all-or-nothing. People can clearly be taught to think *more* critically.

4.8 This is a question about precision. (When people ask questions, they seldom mention a standard explicitly. A major part of becoming a critical thinker is learning to bring the standard to the question on your own.) Actually, neither answer is precisely right because the question itself is confused. Two thousand years is insignificantly small when dealing with such large numbers. (It is as if you asked "How distant are we from Mars?" and someone answered "It depends on whether you're talking about from your house or from my house.")

Chapter 5

5.2 There were no instructions about what to do with the quotation. Notice that once you are out of school, no one will any longer be giving you instructions about what to do with respect to what you read.

What is appropriate for you to do with this excerpt? (What would you have done with the excerpt if there were no instructions at all, not even these?) Is it appropriate to treat it in a very different way depending on whether you read it as part of a course you are taking?

5.3 I could address this question in many ways. The first element that jumps out is *information:* I need information to answer this question. But information about what?

Not about our common ancestors. Not about the common genes and mechanism of development of humans and *Drosophila*. Not about the medical research that has been done on mice or *Drosophila*. All of those would end up being unhelpful. I do need some good examples from these categories, but, despite how it looked at first, this isn't a question primarily about information.

So I need to *clarify* the *question at issue* for myself. It's a question about the relationship between having common genes and mechanisms (system #1) and an ability to do medical research on one species and transfer it to another (system #2). So it's an *assumption* I'm after: an assumption behind such medical research is that there are common mechanisms. So, as I see it, the question is asking me to evaluate that assumption.

5.4 This question is asking me to *regurgitate* information from the chapter. But I can easily infuse critical thinking into it and get a better grade. It is a question about *context*, the "conditions" that led up to these reformers. So I will answer it by finding and stating the main assumption each of these reformers made. (That will considerably narrow my search.) Then I'll relate each of these five men to one or two of "the political and religious conditions." That will be a description of the context. Finally, I'll tell what conclusions each reformer drew from that context.

5.5 This is a question looking for a *solution*, a *conclusion*: "Who wins?" *Information* will play a key role: dates, people, agreements, and circumstances. I need to find the relevant law (*information*: in the table of contents is a section on intoxicated persons), and I need to interpret it in relation to this case.

5.6 This is just a detail. All that's required is that I look it up in the chapter. The answer, supernova, appears word-for-word, a few pages earlier. When I look up "supernova" in the index, I see it only appears twice in this huge text; so that's more evidence it is not treated as an important term.

5.7 They asked for a reaction, but I'll give them a reasoned judgment. This is a question requiring multiple systems if there ever was one. I need to feel the pull of the different systems in the question. Clearly (1) I need to spell out the pull of a woman's right to her own body. That's a very strong point, and I need to describe it in such a way that I show its force. Next (2) there is the pull of the fetus's life and why it is important to preserve it. I need to describe the force of that too.

Assumptions are at stake here, and important consequences to any course of action. The judgment will hinge on accuracy (e.g., Does the fetus have a full right to life? Does a woman have the right to affect the living fetus inside of her?). It will also hinge on which aspect is most important for deciding this issue.

5.8 I read this as follows, using the elements and standards:

> (1) The (2) family unit is the foundation of society and the main institution for the growth and advancement of mankind . . . . (3) It is the principal duty of the Islamic government to regard (2) women as the unifying factor of the

family unit and its position. (4) They are a factor in bringing the family out of the service of propagating consumerism and exploitation and renewing the vital and valuable (5) duty of motherhood in raising educated human beings . . . . (6) As a result motherhood is accepted as a most profound responsibility in the Muslim viewpoint and will, therefore, (7) be accorded the highest value and generosity.

(1) The first sentence is an *assumption* they are making; the second half is doubtful (*accuracy*). (2) "Family unit" and "women" are central concepts: this is how they view the role of women. (3) is an *implication* of (1). (4) states the *purpose* of women, as they see it. That fills in the concept. (5) is an *assumption*: that motherhood is a duty. (6) is a *conclusion* being drawn (but it could also be described as a *consequence*). (7) is definitely a *conclusion*.

5.9 I desperately need fundamental and powerful concepts. I need to get hold of those fundamental and powerful concepts that will allow me to think through the logic of rocks: the general *ways they form*, their *structure*, and their *composition*. Once I get a good grasp of those three concepts, I can think through most of the terms and summary points in those two chapters.

5.10 This is a question that centers on *points of view*, four different ones, so it requires me to think in terms of different systems. In each case, answering it will rely on how I *interpret* each character, based on the information in the text. Then it centers on the *concept* of "real man," as understood by each character.

5.11 These all seem like ordinary, everyday questions you might wonder about. One way you might answer them is simply by just saying whatever you think. A thesis of this book is that, other things being equal, we are better off if we think through such questions from discipline-based points of view. So one thing I can do to infuse ordinary questions with critical thinking is to rephrase them as if they were being asked in a course. (Look back at the box on pages 120–121.) There is flexibility in the choice of which discipline to choose, but I could make a start by rephrasing the first question as "From an *anthropological* point of view, why do many people (including me, maybe) spend so much money on their weddings?" Similarly, I could approach the second question from the point of view of the *health sciences*, the third *geographically*, the fourth *geologically*, and so forth. If a relevant discipline does not even come into a person's mind when he or she wonders about ordinary, everyday questions, the benefit of critical thinking in a discipline is probably not carrying over into the person's life.

Notes

To the Instructor

1. Richard Paul and Linda Elder, *Critical Thinking: Tools for Taking Charge of Your Learning and Your Life*, 2nd ed. (Upper Saddle River, NJ: Pearson, 2006); and www.criticalthinking.org.

2. Richard Paul and Linda Elder, *Critical Thinking: Tools for Taking Charge of Your Professional and Personal Life* (Upper Saddle River, NJ: Pearson, 2002).

3. Jennifer Reed, "Abstract: Effect of a Model for Critical Thinking on Student Achievement in Document Analysis and Interpretation, Argumentative Reasoning, Critical Thinking Dispositions, and History Content in a Community College History Course," Doctoral Dissertation, University of South Florida, 1998. *Dissertation Abstracts International*, 59–11A (1998): 4039.

Chapter 1

1. "A Taxonomy of Critical Thinking Skills and Dispositions," in *Teaching Thinking Skills: Theory and Practice*, ed. Joan Boykoff Baron and Robert J. Sternberg (New York: Freeman, 1987), 9–26. I especially like Ennis's definition, not only because it is the classic one (I believe his first formulation of it came in 1964), but because Bob told me, years later, that it was because of my arguments at the Second International Conference on Critical Thinking at Sonoma State (back in 1982) that he added the "or do" to the end of his definition. I hold deeply that critical thinking needs to be infused in our doings (anything from recycling waste to riding my bike) as much as in our believings.

2. Matthew Lipman, *Thinking in Education* (Cambridge: Cambridge University Press, 1995).

3. The answer is that they stay in prison until they die. Actually, in Louisiana a person can be sentenced to life in prison for many crimes, including drug offenses and armed robbery. For these people too, "life" means life.

4. Michael Scriven, *Reasoning* (Point Reyes, CA: Edgepress, 1976), 26.

5. Frederick H. Martini, *Fundamentals of Anatomy & Physiology*, 7th ed. (San Francisco: Pearson, 2006), 23.

6. Teresa Audeskirk, Gerald Audeskirk, and Bruce E. Byers, *Biology: Life on Earth*, 8th ed. (Upper Saddle River, NJ: Pearson, 2008), 202.

7. Penelope J. E. Davies, et al., *Janson's Basic History of Western Art*, 8th ed. (Upper Saddle River, NJ: Pearson, 2009), 17.

8. Brian M. Fagan, *People of the Earth: An Introduction to World Prehistory*, 13th ed. (Boston: Prentice Hall, 2010), 87.

9. Rachel Herz, *The Scent of Desire: Discovering Our Enigmatic Sense of Smell* (New York: William Morrow, 2007), 51.

Chapter 2

1. Adapted from Richard Paul © The Foundation for Critical Thinking, www.criticalthinking.org; cct@criticalthinking.org. Reprinted with permission.

2. Richard T. Wright, *Environmental Science: Toward a Sustainable Future*, 10th ed. (Upper Saddle River, NJ: Pearson, 2008), 644.

3. *Courage to Change* (New York: Al-Anon, 1992), 115.

4. John Adkins Richardson, *Art: The Way It Is* (Englewood Cliffs, NJ: Prentice Hall, 1973), 6.

5. Paul Heyne, *The Economic Way of Thinking*, 7th ed. (New York: Macmillan, 1994), 22.

6. Scott O. Lilienfeld, et al., *Psychology: A Framework for Everyday Thinking* (Boston: Pearson, 2010), 201.

7. No. The passage implies only that ginkgo does not work for normal people. It leaves open the question of whether it works for non-normal people.

8. Elliot Aronson, *The Social Animal* (New York: Worth, 2008), 30.

9. Thomas A. Mappes and Jane S. Zembaty, *Social Ethics: Morality and Social Policy* (Boston: McGraw-Hill, 2007), 482.

Chapter 3

1. Richard Feynman, *What Do You Care What Other People Think?* (New York: Norton, 1988), 16.

2. Jennifer Reed, conversation with author.

3. *Tampa Tribune*, September 17, 1996.

4. Actually they do have a bit of a logic: the keyboard was originally designed to slow down your typing. That's why the keys are in an "illogical" arrangement that makes you use your weakest fingers to strike the most frequent letters.

5. This question comes from Anisa Al-Khatab, conversation with author.

6. Sarah Blaffer Hrdy, *Mother Nature: A History of Mothers, Infants, and Natural Selection,* (New York: Pantheon, 1999), xi.

7. Adapted from Kurt Reusser, "Problem Solving Beyond the Logic of Things," cited in A. H. Schoenfeld, "On Mathematics and Sense Making: An Informal Attack on the Unfortunate Divorce of Formal and Informal Mathematics," in J. Voss, D. Perkins, and J. Segal (eds.), *Informal Reasoning and Education* (Hillsdale, NJ: Erlbaum, 1990), 311–343.

8. They are not exactly the same question. (I have, for example, omitted virtue ethics). The point is that to answer the ordinary everyday question we have to explicitly consider the two ethical theories.

9. Lynn Quitman Troyka and Jerold Nudelman, *Steps in Composition,* 7th ed. (Upper Saddle River, NJ: Prentice Hall, 1999), 31.

10. Stephen P. Robbins, *Managing Today,* 2nd ed. (Upper Saddle River, NJ: Prentice Hall, 2000), xiii.

Chapter 4

1. Gerald Nosich, *Reasons and Arguments* (Belmont, CA: Wadsworth, 1982), 53.

2. My thanks to John Draeger for the idea of staircasing SEE-I's, as well as for his ideas about using SEE-I's as study guides (see p. 202). Conversation with the author.

3. Actually, as Randall Curran pointed out to me, the explanation in the text is not an example of thinking like a physicist. It isn't really deep because it isn't sufficiently grounded in physics: Cold air isn't really "heavier": it is less energetic than hot air, and therefore it is more dense, so it has more mass per volume. That's why it "falls." As Calvin Kordela said after he read this: "So wood doesn't really *float.* Instead, water *sinks.*"

4. Adapted and expanded from *Critical Thinking: Basic Theory and Instructional Structures* (Rohnert Park, CA: Foundation for Critical Thinking, 1998), 3–32.

5. Les Rowntree et al., *Diversity Amid Globalization* (Upper Saddle River, NJ: Prentice Hall, 2000), 19.

Chapter 5

1. A fuller description of the traits of mind can be found in Paul and Elder, *Critical Thinking,* (2006), 2–19.

2. Edward F. Bergman and Tom L. McKnight, *Introduction to Geography* (Upper Saddle River, NJ: Prentice Hall, 1993), 148.

3. Troyka and Nudelman, 128, 161.

4. Jennifer D. Keene, Saul Cornell, and Edward T. O'Donnell, *Visions of America: A History of the United States*, vol. 1 (Boston: Prentice Hall, 2010), 280.

5. John Mack Faragher et al., *Out of Many: A History of the American People*, vol. 2, brief 2nd ed. (Upper Saddle River, NJ: Prentice Hall, 1999), 444.

6. The first site is http://www.answers.google.com/answers. This site then directs us to "The Importance of Water and Human Health" (n.d.), http://www.freedrinkingwater.com/water-education/water-get-enough.htm. Contrast: Mayo Clinic Staff, "Water: How Much Should You Drink Every Day?" (17 April, 2010), http://www.mayoclinic.com/health/water/NU00283, or Karen Bellenir, "Fact or Fiction? You Must Drink 8 Glasses of Water Daily" (4 June 2009), http://www.scientificamerican.com/article.cfm?id=eight-glasses-water-per-day. Sources accessed 7 March 2010.

7. Neal Tannahill, *American Government: Policy and Politics*, 10th ed. (Boston: Longman, 2010), 87.

8. Joan Salge Blake, Kathy D. Munoz, and Stella Volpe, *Nutrition: From Science to You*, (San Francisco: Benjamin Cummings, 2010), 17.

9. David Krogh, *Biology: A Guide to the Natural World*, 2nd ed. (Upper Saddle River, NJ: Prentice Hall, 2000), 325.

10. Dennis J.Sporre, *The Creative Impulse: An Introduction to the Arts*, 5th ed. (Upper Saddle River, NJ: Prentice Hall, 2000), 383.

11. Henry R. Cheeseman, *Contemporary Business Law*, 3rd ed. (Upper Saddle River, NJ: Prentice Hall, 2000), 242.

12. Edward J. Tarbuck and Frederick K. Lutgens, *Earth: An Introduction to Physical Geology*, 9th ed. (Upper Saddle River, NJ: Pearson, 2008), 624.

13. Quoted in Margaret L. King, *Western Civilization: A Social and Cultural History*, vol. 2 (Upper Saddle River, NJ: Prentice Hall, 2000), 928.

14. Pamela J. Annas and Robert C. Rosen, *Literature and Society* (Upper Saddle River, NJ: Prentice Hall, 2000), 279.

Index